Energy Cultures

Technology, Justice, and Geopolitics in Eastern Europe

Michael Carnegie LaBelle

Associate Professor, Department of Environmental Sciences and Policy, and Department of Economics and Business, Central European University, Hungary

Edward Elgar
PUBLISHING

Cheltenham, UK • Northampton, MA, USA

Published by
Edward Elgar Publishing Limited
The Lypiatts
15 Lansdown Road
Cheltenham
Glos GL50 2JA
UK

Edward Elgar Publishing, Inc.
William Pratt House
9 Dewey Court
Northampton
Massachusetts 01060
USA

A catalogue record for this book
is available from the British Library

Library of Congress Control Number: 2020944599

This book is available electronically in the **Elgar**online
Social and Political Science subject collection
http://dx.doi.org/10.4337/9781788975766

Printed on elemental chlorine free (ECF)
recycled paper containing 30% Post-Consumer Waste

ISBN 978 1 78897 575 9 (cased)
ISBN 978 1 78897 576 6 (eBook)

Printed and bound in the USA

Contents

Preface

The impetus for this book stems from my time spent in Hungary since my first trip in 1994. Observing the 2004 eastward expansion of the European Union highlighted the dramatic social and political readjustments countries make. The 2009 Russia–Ukraine gas crisis brought to the fore the different perspectives held by leaders in the 'old' and 'new' EU Member States. Before then, the electricity and gas system were treated like other networked industries, with a political impetus for privatization and elimination of market barriers. Suddenly, the security of gas supplies and Russia's associated political leverage over the former Communist countries became apparent to leaders across the EU. The subsequent prioritization of security of supply and the building up of the Agency for Cooperation of Energy Regulators (ACER) demonstrated the seriousness of the Single Energy Market project within the EU. However, subsequent actions by national governments show support for cross-border projects, but domestic energy markets remain the domain of national politicians.

This book provides an analysis of three countries' political-economic transition from Communism to a system marked by market competition, and, for two out of the three countries, the presence of a weakened democratic system. The use of culture to frame the energy transition, and the power struggles around it, come from my experience in the region. Culture emerged as the most appropriate term to describe the differences between countries and the social practices and policies within the energy systems.

My professional background in the region began when I moved to Budapest, Hungary, in 2006. I started work at the Regional Center for Energy Policy Research (REKK) at Corvinus University and later moved to Central European University (CEU). Now CEU is forced to move from Hungary by the Orban government. Despite this, I plan to remain on this side of what is again a political divide. Through this vantage point, one can observe the political events since the 2009 financial crisis (and now the 2020 Covid-19 crisis), challenge the idea that the freedom to exercise political rights is a natural progression for the region. What I hope to convey in parts of this book is the lack of recognition for society's demands undermines the ability to build a just energy transition in the EU. If the EU wants a just energy transition, then democratic norms also must be respected in the energy system.

This book provides an assessment of how Hungary, Lithuania, and Poland changed their energy systems since their EU membership and their likely trajectory towards implementing a just energy transition. I use a critical tone to question the geopolitical and equitable decisions made in each country. As the case studies show, there is an almost inevitability of the economics and geopolitics that shape the region and constrain the choices for political leaders. But it is in the choices and actions of the political actors that expose the power relations interconnecting society, the EU, and Russia. A just transition requires the state to act in the interests of society by recognizing a broad spectrum of rights.

The central task of the book is to raise awareness of these three countries and the challenges faced by governments and citizens to build an equitable energy system. As the book points out, policies from the European Union come up short in addressing the financial and security aspects of the energy system in these new EU Member States. This book provides an in-depth account of the power struggles within each country and the two super-powers of Russia and the EU, forcing each state to decide the orientation of their energy system.

The conceptual framing of 'energy cultures' stems from the observable, but hard-to-describe differences between each country. Culture is describable but not definable. This book advances two theories, energy justice and a culture of geopolitics, to set up and expose power relations within the energy system. These power relations, and the struggle to gain power and influence the types of resources and technologies in use, lead to the production of energy cultures. There are demarcations and choices in each country's use of energy resources and technologies. Common social, political, and economic histories in the three case studies provide the context to explore the different geographical context and tension within the exertion of geopolitical power. The framework of energy cultures provides a means to understand the strong power relations within the energy system.

The European Union built a system of governance, endowing national energy regulators with a specific job of balancing the political, business, and social demands. These efforts came out of the Lisbon Treaty that reformed the Union to enable an expanded EU to function. There are now calls to implement a just energy transition in the EU. This transformation would require a scheme that would rival the process of comitology and institutional building in the East. The energy system is central to the political and economic control of a country. Changes to the energy system require broader systemic changes in state and social relations. For the EU and governments to be successful in building an equitable energy transition, then the people of Eastern Europe need to be heard. As this book describes, those who control the energy culture also choose the resources and technologies of the energy system. A just transition requires recognition of all members of society while providing them with access to affordable and sustainable energy.

Michael Carnegie LaBelle
Budapest, Hungary

Acknowledgments

This book reflects the generosity and aptitude of people who volunteered their time and expertise. Many go unnamed, but each page represents the input, cooperation, and coordination of a wide range of friends and colleagues from Europe and North America. Special thanks go to those most immediate in helping me compile, check, and organize the data and arrangements with the manuscript. Ana Stojilovska was an excellent research assistant and administrator, helping not only with this book but with related project work. Neringa Stropute made the interviews, travel, and site visits possible in Lithuania. The generous funding from Central European University (CEU) and funding from the European Union Jean Monnet Activities made the travel and research assistance possible. I like to think the concepts in this book align with the efforts of Jean Monnet and his work to unify Europe.

In addition, my colleagues at CEU were kind enough to give me the time and space to write this book – whether they knew it or not. Being given the freedom to hide can be an effective way to get work done. Long-term intellectual support from Alex Antypas, Aleh Cherp, Larry Knopp, Gabor Szorenyi, even editors and reviewers at Energy Research and Social Science prompted me to think more clearly. Additionally, thanks go to those who reviewed and contributed thoughts on draft versions or were encouraging on the energy cultures concept: Steffen Bettin, John Szabo, Tekla Szep, TRACC5 consortium. Also, to Isna Pujiastuti for mapping skills. Additionally, the assistance of Rachel Downie and the persistence of Alex Pettifer at Edward Elgar Publishing helped me realize my ideas into a book. Finally, I express my appreciation to research participants, particularly those in Hungary, Lithuania, and Poland. Despite the tremendous assistance in writing the book, it reflects my work, so I take full responsibility for the content inside.

Grant support:

Financial support for research was provided by Central European University's Intellectual Theme Initiative, and through the Jean Monnet Chair, known as the European Union, Education, Audiovisual and Culture Executive Agency under the Jean Monnet Activities within the ERASMUS+PROGRAMME, project number 587860-EPP-1-2017-1-HU-EPPJMO-CHAIR and the Central European University Intellectual Theme Initiative.

Abbreviations

ACER	Agency for Cooperation of Energy Regulators
CEU	Central European University
COMECON	Council for Mutual Economic Assistance
ERRA	Energy Regulators Regional Association
EBRD	European Bank for Reconstruction and Development
ECSC	European Coal and Steel Community
FERC	Federal Energy Regulatory Commission
FSRU	Floating Storage Regasification Unit
IEM	Internal Energy Market
LNG	Liquified Natural Gas
NRA	National Regulatory Agencies
NPP	Nuclear Power Plants
SEM	Single Energy Market
USAID	United States Agency for International Development

1. Introduction: energy culture in an age of transformation

1.1 INTRODUCTION: THE PRODUCTION OF ENERGY CULTURE

Energy creates material well-being for society. Energy is hot food on the table, a warm home, and a job. Modern societies require the state to deliver a functional, efficient, and sustainable energy system. There is an inherent tension with the state pushing to meet social demands and guide industry to deliver economic growth. Eastern Europe provides a good example of when social demands align with political and economic change. After 1989, the collapse of the USSR and later membership in the European Union, changed social policies and how citizens were able to put food on their tables. For the low-carbon energy transition, it is important to understand this previous round of state-social change. The reason for this is that the energy system in the region exposes ongoing political, economic, and social pressures to build a more just and sustainable way of life.

Current European Union effort for net-zero carbon emissions by 2050 is ambitious for including society, industry, and governments in the ongoing energy transition. Likewise, specific policies like a 'just energy transitions' supported by the EU (European Commission 2020) demonstrate the political importance of building an equitable energy system. Fostering the technical transition away from fossil fuels to renewable energy technologies involves energy policies rooted in social engagement. The task of this book is to understand how energy transitions occur at different scales and deliver a just energy transition for society in three Eastern European countries: Hungary, Lithuania, and Poland. Developed here is an 'energy cultures' framework showing how cultural struggles create power relations with the winners choosing the energy resources and technologies of the future. This contribution provides an effective lens to understand whether Europe is rolling out a just transition or simply extending current political and economic arrangements.

At the turn of the twentieth century, scholars also sought to make sense of their rapidly changing energy system and the social implications. The study of 'energetics' sought to explain the rapid industrialization of countries and the role of society in the technological transformation (Stewart 2014). This view relied on a positivist socio-cultural perspective, which highlighted efficiencies created through rational choices. An 'efficiency culture' was viewed as essential to increase savings in the energy system and thereby benefitting society. Likewise, efforts to mitigate climate change revolve around changing the efficiency of society and technologies in the energy system.

Identifying who is responsible for improving technologies and practices is essential to affect systemic change. In 1908, physicist and Nobel laureate turned sociologist, Wilhelm Ostwald outlined how it was only humans that could use fire to transform inorganic matter into material well-being (Ostwald 1907, in Stewart 2014). Ostwald identified a broader social responsibility when he wrote that, "The general task of culture as a whole consists in ensuring the most favorable transformation" of energy (Stewart 2014, 344). Through this view of culture and efficiencies, mechanical engineers to diplomats hold a responsibility to lower the cost of energy for the "working classes" at all stages of the energy system (Stewart 2014, 344). While this may be interpreted as a bourgeoisie perspective, it underscores the importance of society and individuals working together to lower costs and increase efficiency along with reducing waste. The study of energy cultures identifies social and individual actions as contributing towards a more efficient and socially just energy system.

Culture provides a means to understand how society utilizes the energy system for its material well-being. Digging deeper into cultural connections in the energy system, Ostwald did not develop this concept in isolation. Geographer Friedrich Ratzel and others at the Leipzig School of Cultural Sciences also influenced Ostwald's theoretical development; with Ostwald giving an inaugural address in 1887 on 'Energy and its Transformations' (Stewart 2014, 334). While sociologist Max Weber criticized the attempt of a physicist to inform those in the "sciences of culture" (Weber, Mikkelsen, and Schwartz 1984, 51), Ostwald, nonetheless, abstracts the production of energy into the 'production of culture' by framing access to the energy system as a reflection of individual and social actions creating material well-being. In contrast, the failure to develop material well-being reflects the failure of society and individuals to operate in an equitable energy culture. The study of 'energy cultures' exposes the relational struggles of individuals and society producing a socially just energy system.

This perspective of cultural struggles fosters an understanding that culture emerges by contestation. Culture created from contestation enables the expression of differences within and between different groups (Mitchell 2000). Despite 'difference' highlighting what culture is, defining culture remains difficult. Cultural Geographer, Donald Mitchell identifies five ways to describe 'culture', from patterns of people to a looped 'culture-making-culture' and ending with "culture is everything" (Mitchell 1995, 104–5). An anthropological perspective sees culture as a scaffolding providing structure to meanings people experience (Geertz 1973, 312). A sociology perspective asserts social practice creating cultures (Giddens 1982). In short, culture is a description of social interactions, but lacking a 'definable definition'.

If culture cannot be defined, then what is culture? Clearly, culture is also not benign. Culture is an active political and economic tool that can control and influence the material well-being of society. Mitchell explores how culture represents the expression of power, rather than just how people live. Through this lens, it is the relationship between social groupings that produces culture (Mitchell 2000, 73).

> My argument is that it is in the interaction – the struggle – between the production of 'culture' and its use that 'culture' is produced, not as a thing, but as a relationship. So when I ask who produced culture, I always turn to the study of relationships; when I ask why it is produced, I turn to questions of power. (Mitchell 2000, xviii)

Culture is politics, culture is power, and culture is relationships. Social practices, perceived through cultural representations, such as cars or cooking fires, also represent power relationships of resource access or affordability. These relationships emerge through relational struggles at a range of scales, whether in the international or local community. Power relations influence the material well-being of society and access to energy.

The importance of Ostwald's energetics perspective is in the conversion of resources through interactions, such as social, technical, and physical. Rather than defining energy culture, we can describe it as: *Energy cultures are the social and physical interactions forming relations in the energy system, extending from resource extraction through technologies of conversion, combustion, and networks, providing for society's material and physical well-being.* Understanding interactive relationships around the point of 'combustion' is essential in the modern energy system because it underlies our modern efforts to address climate change.

The point of combustion turns out to be the central point to examine the Anthropocene. As Dalby points out, the examination of "combustion and fire ... bridges the divides between human and physical sciences, and as such offers a way for linking traditional social science discussions of geopolitics with the forcing mechanisms that are driving biosphere change," of the Anthropocene (Dalby 2018, 720). One hundred years ago, Ostwald grasped the point of conversion as linking these broader social and physical systems. A physicist turned sociologist, he was able to grasp the *conversion point* of resources and social interaction in an economic order that also applies to our present environmental and energy challenges. Energy cultures provide a means to understand the power relations meeting at the point of combustion within the broader energy system. The conversion from resources to material and emotional well-being is where energy cultures expose embedded power relations.

This chapter quickly engages in the question of how to define energy cultures and expose the power relations. This is done in the next section by developing a set of axioms to explain, rather than define culture. Section 1.3 reviews existing energy culture literature and identifies the inability to more explicitly understand power relations within culture and how these shape energy practices. Section 1.4 extends this literature review to outline the importance of cultural relations as essential components to the energy system. The task in section 1.5 is to deconstruct the energy system into a physical and social energy system which is proposed as a means to differentiate between more explicit uses of energy in the form of artifacts or seen on the landscape, contrasting with a more implicit understanding of deep power structures shaping the way society interacts with the energy system. Section 1.6 provides further framing of the role of energy justice and geopolitics to conceptualize and understand how culture is created through relational struggles at both the domestic and international scales. Likewise, section 1.7 outlines the ontological framings and epistemological perspectives on the energy system which provide the necessary tools to deconstruct and construct a cultural representation of culture. Application of the theoretical construct of energy cultures is introduced to the case studies in section 1.8 while section 1.9 provides the outline of the book and the perception of how energy cultures construct the energy system.

1.2 ENERGY RELATIONS: AXIOMS OF ENERGY CULTURES

Since culture cannot be defined, then a set of axioms provides the means to explore what is energy culture. Three axioms serve as a guide to energy cultures jostling around the conversion point. These axioms provide a means to structure the analysis and understand how energy cultures, and the embedded power relations, work to convert resources into material well-being for society. Their development is based on a set of four criteria developed by Heinberg, originally in relation to refining the concept of 'sustainability' into a set of "self-evident truths" (Heinberg 2010):

a. To qualify as an axiom, a statement must be capable of being tested using the methodology of science.
b. Collectively, a set of axioms intended to define sustainability must be minimal (with no redundancies).
c. At the same time, the axioms must be sufficient, leaving no glaring loopholes.
d. The axioms should be worded in terms a layperson can understand. (Heinberg 2010, 15)

In a similar spirit of guidance, in the area of energy and climate change, Sovacool and Brown develop six maxims to structure effective energy analysis (Sovacool and Brown 2015). These are more value laden and meant to guide decisions that are "ethical or at least informed" (Sovacool and Brown 2015, 41). But they are meant to spur improvement in the daily actions of researchers and policy makers. From this viewpoint of axioms and maxims, it is useful to introduce into energy cultures a set of axioms that assist in identifying both the representation of culture and the methods of cultural (re)production, thereby avoiding an epistemological trap of defining what culture is. Rather, three axioms describe through a set of "self-evident truths" (Heinberg 2010), what energy cultures are and how they are produced:

1. Energy cultures are *spatial* expressions of the social milieu around energy systems and perceived through physical expressions of artifacts, imaginaries, and inequality of material and environmental differences.
2. Energy cultures play out at different *scales* and are both *socially and economically transformative* and reliant on *power relations* between scales.
3. Energy cultures are *relationally transformative* in energy systems, including mechanical and thermal, social, political and economic.

Framing the axioms is the role of the state. The state is essential in the creation of energy cultures. The interlinkage between state and society is connected through industrialization within national boundaries. For the energy sector, the built energy system is reliant on the government regulation of the utility sector, which supplies services to industry and households. An historical perspective frames both Ostwald's observation on the modern energy system delivering material benefits to society (Stewart 2014, 344), and the rise of the sovereign state assisted by industrialization (Knutsen 1992, 128–9). The state, society, and industry interlink to create unique national energy cultures based on a social pact.

The growth of utilities, and their economic and social importance, became central in the daily life of society and industry. The dramatic impact of the Great Depression, initially triggered by utilities' financial accounting tricks, required government intervention to either take over ownership or to administer regulatory oversight of activities (Hirsh 1999). In an energy system with government regulation, there emerges an informal 'regulatory compact,' which allows utilities to operate *for* the public good. Society and industry benefit from a coordinated utility sector with shared infrastructure and long-term technological renewal. Energy companies may be privately or publicly owned, but the global rise of National Regulatory Agencies (NRAs) since the 1990s corresponds with the liberalization of electricity and gas markets across the globe. The universal regulatory compact cements government oversight of the utility sector.

The concept of the regulatory compact extends back to English Common law in the sixteenth century. At this time, franchises were issued for 'common calling,' monopolies granted in exchange for providing goods and services at reasonable rates, such as ferry boats, highway operators, and wharves (Hirsh 1999, 15–18). In 1903, the US Supreme Court used the term 'public utilities' to describe monopolies operating in the public good (Hirsh 1999, 15–18). The right of the state to regulate public utilities is seen through an 'institutionalist' perspective utilizing "regulation as an instrument of social control" (Hirsh 1999, 18). That is, industry – or the energy sector – is regulated for the social good. In a 'regulatory compact' form of governance, society gives the state the right to regulate utilities. This means there is coordination in the energy system to ensure the use of a single network and consumers benefit by lower costs due to greater coordination or minimalizing competition in specific areas.

The regulatory compact focused on state-industrial relations, likewise, state and society were bound in a social contract. The sovereign state held power given to it by society. From an Enlightenment viewpoint Vatn outlines how individuals and the state develop a *social contract*, which through a Hobbesian perspective, "give away some of their freedom to the sovereign whose assignment is to secure order" (Vatn 2005, 26). That is, people entrust their freedom to the state to more efficiently provide protection. This understanding stems from how people exist in a 'state of nature,' which is characterized "by universal values of freedom and equality. People are, according to [John] Locke, 'born' with a sense of equality and freedom, and the state is foremost an articulation of these human values or human rights" (Vatn 2005, 28). The authority of the state, and society's expectation, rests on this transfer of freedom to the state and in turn the provision of equality and freedom. Therefore, there is a social contract between individuals of and the state to build and maintain utilities for the public good.

Over time, an equitable and secure energy system is built to serve society and industry. State institutions, therefore, are essential managers of energy services and resources. From a functional standpoint, the social contract is translated into political activity, where politicians are responsible for ensuring energy services meet the needs of the people. Universal access to energy is a modern fulfillment of the social compact between the state and society. "Alleviation [of energy poverty] is a fundamental political duty rather than simply an optional act of benevolence" (cf. de Vita 2007; Bouzarovski and Simcock 2017, 645). Thus, the social pact is fulfilled by political action mobilizing state institutions to deliver (and ensure) delivery of energy services. The public service of politicians requires them to ensure the protection of "universal values of freedom and equality" (Vatn 2005, 28), reflecting obligations of the modern state under both the ancient social contract and the modern regulatory compact. The state is authorized, by society, to act both internationally and domestically to secure a modern energy system to ensure universal access to energy services and resources.

The state holds the ultimate responsibility to organize the energy system, but there remain fundamental political, social, and philosophical trade-offs that ensure perpetual tension and injustices within the system. Delivery, affordability, and accessibility to energy services require a balancing of rights. Negligence in one area may be a product of action in another area:

> Energy systems can be reconceived as a political, deliberative challenge involving the satisfaction of competing preferences; a social dilemma pitting, at times, the climatic and development goals of energy security or improved resilience against the pressing needs of marginalized and vulnerable populations; and a moral quandary revolving around how energy burdens and benefits are fairly, or unfairly, disseminated. (Sovacool et al. 2017, 689)

The investigation of tensions within the social compact and how governments organize the energy systems requires a broader picture of policy and security choices, along with moral quandaries. Utilizing 'culture' as a conceptual framing of relational struggles around justice and security within the energy system provides a means to understand power relations enabling or preventing access to energy resources and services. More specifically, an energy cultures approach utilizes the academic framing of energy justice to provide a whole systems approach at different scales of the energy system. "At each stage of the energy system – resource mining or energy production, for example – energy justice can engage with local, regional and national justice questions" (Jenkins 2018, 119). Energy justice goes beyond cost-benefit analysis and engineering projects; energy systems "are about political power, social cohesion, and even ethical and moral concerns over equity, due process and justice" (Sovacool et al. 2016, 5). Energy justice provides a geographic perspective on 'bounding out' scales of activities around justice occurring within the energy system, such as identifying local, regional, and national processes (Jenkins 2018, 120).

Geography and politics are bound up in the energy system. Therefore, understanding international political economy is essential for understanding how the state ensures the delivery of resources and the continued operation of its domestic energy system. Geopolitics is essential to understand how international political actions influence and are influenced by domestic energy cultures. "A culturally informed political geography is about identifying and showing the mutually constitutive effects of cultural signs and symbols, on the one hand, and political acts, on the other" (Toal and Agnew 2002, 456). This reading, influenced by societal norms, values, and the physical barriers surrounding a state, produces *new critical geopolitics of culture* (O Tuathail and Agnew 1992). Rather than geopolitics describing a clash of nationalistic imperialist interests, geopolitics reflects cultural struggles influencing each nation-state's social and political practices.

The conceptual framing by geopolitics and justice provides a multi-paradigm approach (Burrell and Morgan 1979; Gioia and Pitre 1990; Sovacool and Hess 2017) to energy cultures. This paradigm approach contributes both a subjective and objective perspective: geopolitics of cultures (subjective) and an energy justice (objective) bridge ontological divisions within an energy culture concept. Geopolitics and justice contain the tools to expose and assess a continuum of international and domestic power structures within the energy system. Energy cultures, as a conceptual framing, provide the means to bridge the local/international dichotomy and the supply/demand sides of the energy system. The global security apparatus of the state serves to secure resources to meet the cultural energy practices of industry and households. Political leaders exert their power by delivering on the social contract and regulatory pact of the modern state. Energy cultures are diverse; discussed next is how the energy cultures literature spans both domestic and international contexts, which account for both the supply and demand sides of the energy system.

1.3 ENERGY CULTURE LITERATURE

The term 'energy culture' already benefits from a diverse set of research identifying the role of culture in the energy system. Current efforts explain alterations and orientations of energy systems and use culture as a broad explanatory device that reflects a cohesion and division within society over material and social practices within the energy system (Stephenson et al. 2010; Sheller 2014; Sovacool 2016; Rosicki 2017). Their strength is exposing social unity or difference; however, their weakness is providing a critical examination of how culture is created and how power relations influence and orientate the trajectory of energy systems. The existing terminology of 'energy culture' focuses on the interactive consumer behaviors of "cognitive norms, material culture, and energy practices" (Stephenson et al. 2010, 6125) or broadly applied to the socio-economic change in the second industrial revolution (Sheller 2014). The literature provides a means to both understand explicit cultural representations, such as signs and symbols, or implicit socio-political and economic interactions.

This review of energy cultures literature will use an 'explicit' and an 'implicit' categorization of approaches. This enables a more precise means to capture the powerful role culture holds in societal values and norms within the energy system. Energy culture is more than a descriptive device of social interactions; it is a powerful expression and tool of authority, affecting public access to resources and technologies. Culture is both seen and hidden. *Implicit energy culture* is the expression of power relations within an energy system, such as rules, regulations, values, and access. *Explicit energy culture* is the expression of materiality seen on the landscape through forms such as infrastructure and poverty. Culture emerges as the expression of social and economic value (Mitchell 2000), while within the state-controlled energy system, political authority influences the structure of economic and social activities. This political influence includes the *cultural orientation of the energy system* towards different types of configurations, reflecting implicit social values, explicit built and natural environmental factors, and historical geopolitical alignments. The political system emerges as a central component to direct both the explicit and implicit orientation of the energy system. The term 'energy system' therefore refers to the politically influenced physical and social components that comprise the material and social practices around the combustion of energy resources.

1.3.1 Explicit energy culture: assembling practices of culture

Explicit energy culture focuses on material practices of society embedded in the physical energy system. The reconfiguration of an energy system and the resulting cultural transition is outlined by Ruotsalainen et al. They assess a 'peer-to-peer' future where "self-organizing citizens" are empowered by "automation, ubiquitous digital communications" and declining costs of energy, living, and production (Ruotsalainen et al. 2017, 237). Despite using the term 'energy culture,' the authors avoid explaining what energy culture is. This article is representative of other articles discussed. There is an implicit assumption that the reader accepts there is an energy culture formed through the interaction of technology and social relations; however, there is no explanation as to what creates an energy culture.

In a similar explicit exploration of energy culture, but with more exceptional care of context, cultural barriers to energy efficiency stymie the uptake of clean energy solutions in the US (Sovacool 2009). The abundance of resources led Americans to celebrate "sheer abundance and limitless consumption" (Sovacool 2009, 370). Culture for Sovacool is rooted in the industrial and resource history, including the engagement of people with the land, which

Implicit Energy Culture

- Rules enforcing adherence to institutional or social structures
- Regulations influencing systemic development in a politically chosen technological or socially acceptable direction
- Values and norms of society expressed through different means such as economic and environmental expectations and transactions

Explicit Energy Culture

- Visually expressed as part of the landscape through environmental conditions and infrastructure
- Physical access to energy resources and services
- Social practices seen in energy use such as transportation, heating, cooling and cooking

Cultural Orientation of Energy System (ethical/justice and geopolitical orientation)

- Alignment of an energy system to:
  - Economic models encompassing rules, regulations and market strutures
  - Social support models
  - Environmental protection
  - Technological choices

Source: Author.

Figure 1.1 *Systemic expressions of energy culture*

ultimately results in the celebration of abundance and high energy consumption. However, here as well, energy culture is described without fully setting up what culture is or how it is created. It is representative of energy culture existing in energy transitions, without a critical engagement with interactions that shape culture.

Extending this explicit label of energy culture is the literature using the previously developed Energy Cultures Framework, containing three core elements of (1) material culture; (2) practices; and (3) norms. The framing assists in understanding practices around fuel poverty, buying habits, and generational energy choices (Stephenson et al. 2010; Stephenson 2018). A description of the application of energy culture demonstrates institutional processes fostering a particular energy culture, which resists change to using energy-saving LEDs (Dew, Aten, and Ferrer 2017).

> The study identified how shipboard technologies, practices and norms came together to form a naval energy culture that was impervious to change, and reinforced by external influences such as congressional appropriation processes, qualified supplier bases and executive actions of the federal government. (Stephenson 2018, 244)

The energy cultures framework draws from Actor-Network Theory (ANT), which explains scientific or technical artifacts' integration into social relations. "technological change is the product of complex relations of alliance and conflict among divergent actors and their interests" (Sovacool and Hess 2017, 720). The Energy Cultures Framework considers the broader energy system with individual behavior at the center. It explores outward aspects of the system which strongly influence behavior, then finds what interventions can change behavior (Stephenson et al. 2010, 6121). This framework serves as a conceptual way to understand influences on consumer actions to prompt change to lower consumption practices or technologies. The concept has been extended to include practice theories application to a sustainability cultures concept (Stephenson 2018). The limitation (which is also its strength) lies with the focus on behavior and networks within specific systems of alliances of actors; by design it neglects larger state power relations, geography, and supply-side political actions – essential elements to understanding historical epochs of energy transitions impact on socio-political (cultural) perspectives.

A final noticeable use of explicit 'energy culture' is a socio-technological perspective provided by Sheller. Energy culture draws on the "circulation of energy" to describe "how built forms and material assemblage" develop ways of life around energy consumption practices, while also perpetuating "particular energy use patterns" (Sheller 2014, 128–9). The interaction between material and life practices perpetuates particular energy regimes (similar to Sovacool's framing). Using this approach, the energy culture around the global aluminum industry is examined, exposing subjective and socio-ecological experiences wrapped in energy transitions. The explicit use of the term 'energy culture' provides a means to frame material practices in society. This approach fits well with a neo-Marxist perspective that will be described below to understand the use-value between relations in energy systems. First, as the next section describes, it is essential to understand how narratives and stories are created around energy relations.

1.3.2 Implicit energy culture: expressing relations through narratives and stories

The implicit existence of energy culture as a social construct emerges through a descriptive approach of energy relations. A critical reading of energy transitions can expose energy cultures in a range of formats. The book, *Total Transition: The Human Side of the Renewable Energy Revolution* (Pai and Carr-Wilson 2018) is a narrative travelogue of two students researching energy transitions by comparing locations in Canada and India. Extraction of coal in India is contrasted with the extraction of tar sands in Canada. The result is a surprising parallel of experiences and yearning for clean energy transitions from both Indians and Canadians, with individuals literally sickened by fossil fuels.

As described from an excerpt on living with coal in India:

> Sandeeep asked Suresh how his house flooded and where he lives now. Suresh explained as he continued to brush water from the house. "The underground fires burnt the coal lying below my house, the land subsided, and the level of my house went below the level of the pond." Since Suresh's house had no doors, water from the pond had an easy ride into the house. (Pai and Carr-Wilson 2018, Loc. 996)

As described from an excerpt on living with the oil sands in Canada:

> We had smelled a strong chemical odor when driving into town, and asked them to tell us about the air. "You've got to be tough to live here!" Harvey exclaimed. "The air will kill you in no time. We're right in the middle of the oil sands." (Pai and Carr-Wilson 2018, Loc. 1354)

By writing the book in a travelogue format, cultures are explored along with the impact of corporations and government decisions on the environment and human life. The authors themselves (students of this author), were steeped in energy transitions literature during their university education. Therefore, it is interesting that these scholars used narrative to describe their own and others' lived experiences of energy transitions. The power of stories to communicate energy transitions provides perspectives missed by more formal framing of energy transitions.

> Stories are used to communicate with, influence, and engage audiences; they serve as artefacts to be investigated in terms of content, actors, relationships, power, and structure; they can be used to gather information, provide insight, and reframe evidence in ways that more science-ordered formats miss. But they are not benign or neutral … . (Moezzi, Janda, and Rotmann 2017, 1)

Creating a "purposeful cultural turn" on climate change and uncovering cultural influences draws in cultural interpretation in the arts and humanities (Smith et al. 2017, 287), demonstrating how people's lives and their landscapes influence perceptions of energy transitions. Assessing these perceptions requires both a top-down and bottom-up methodological approach. The top-down perspective given by the energy trilemma politically constructs notions of energy poverty (Cloke, Mohr, and Brown 2017). The description emerges that socio-technical imaginaries influence development of energy policies and systems, thereby affecting the interpretation of what energy poverty is. By shaping energy discourses, energy transitions are given a direction which is driven by the top (or elites) (Cloke, Mohr, and Brown 2017, 264), negating more social influences on how an energy transition should occur that accounts for those living in energy poverty. The example above provided by Pai and Carr-Wilson of a bottom-up perspective gives context to the socio-cultural lived experiences enabling an effective method accounting for the economic and technical barriers to energy transitions (Cloke, Mohr, and Brown 2017, 263–4).

Reading about 'energy cultures' on the landscape or through stories exposes energy lifestyles that more rigid theoretical literature misses. Symbolic actions expose social practices between people and between communities and the landscape. At the material level, then, "It is about seeing pipelines as cultural objects" (Macdonald 2017, 39). The literature around 'petrocultures' deploys this humanistic method to understanding relations within a petroleum energy system (Wilson, Carlson, and Szeman 2017). These methods expose the "oil-reliant capitalism seeking to extend and perpetuate supply while downplaying the ongoing, exploitative shame of extraction" (Macdonald 2017, 39). 'Reading' energy requires both implicit and explicit examination of cultural interactions within the energy system.

Explicit and implicit uses of energy culture demonstrate both the diversity and variety of examples involving culture in energy transitions. From the geopolitical and security perspective to stories of the everyday lives of people living with pollution or in energy poverty. The above descriptive analysis captures a range of approaches to describe a culture in energy transitions.

However, the diversity of approaches to energy culture neglects a more critical reading that deconstructs culture in terms of power relations and who is creating culture. The next section provides a means to deconstruct and identify different paradigms of culture within the energy system and within the energy transitions literature.

1.4 LITERATURE REVIEW: CURRENT WEAKNESSES OF ENERGY TRANSITIONS LITERATURE

The energy culture literature is broadly placed within an energy transitions framing. There are descriptions of how people interact with each other or with the built environment. However, to make a conceptual framing of energy cultures requires going deeper to understand how culture is created and who creates culture. Therefore, a more in-depth understanding of the paradigms of theories is necessary. By identifying who creates culture, my purpose is to empower researchers with a conceptual tool to expose power relations in order to foster change. Conceptually, exposing power relations can lead to a more equitable and just energy system. However, 'justice for whom?' is also questioned (see Sovacool et al. 2019, 214). In an era with the slogan 'just energy transition' being adopted by the EU (European Commission 2020) and others (McCauley and Heffron 2018), questioning what justice is and who decides is even more relevant.

Energy transitions literature creates boundaries of ordered frames of perceptions (Geels 2010). These break down energy transitions into ordered frames of politics, technology, society, and a range of other processes – thereby fracturing the ability to understand power relations within the whole energy system. A cultural approach to energy, in contrast, provides a holistic approach to understanding power relations within the energy system. This matches the call by energy justice scholars for a more holistic perspective of the energy system (Jenkins 2018; McCauley and Heffron 2018; Sovacool et al. 2016; Goldthau and Sovacool 2012).

The development of nested frameworks to conceptualize the energy system by Cherp et al. provides the context to understand the divisions within current theoretical approaches. This approach encompasses a multitude of frames into a meta-theoretical perspective: interlinking the puzzle pieces of an energy system into a dynamic transition process becomes daunting. "One diffculty in explaining energy transitions is the disciplinary diversity of required scholarly approaches. Existing reviews of the vast transition literature identify relevant knowledge from economics, sociology of technology, political science, geography, history and other disciplines" (Cherp et al. 2018, 175). The task in this section is to establish the limits and boundaries of existing frameworks and paradigms, thereby enabling bridges between the conceptual fissures of the energy system.

1.4.1 Missing culture

The conditions for energy technologies to grow or decline are dependent on the socio-political relationship. Innovation is critical, as the above theories identify; it is also wrapped up in cultural influences. However, within energy transition literature, culture is marginal, and instead the focus resides with structural forces, such as controlling 'regimes' (Turnheim and Geels 2013), 'carbon lock-in' perpetuated by institutional complexes (Unruh 2000), or perceptions and interactions of actors through imaginaries of the nation or society (Kuchler and Bridge 2018), or actions of entrepreneurship and innovation (Seyfang and Smith 2007; Kivimaa and Kern 2016). Transition literature places the control of technology within structured frames of regimes and imagined perceptions that fail to engage with the source of either *who creates the structure* or *who controls the perceptions of the structures*.

In a review of energy transitions literature, Sovacool and Hess provide a wide-ranging assessment of theoretical approaches. They identify 96 theories and approaches to describe energy transitions (Sovacool and Hess 2017). Despite the diversity, the limitations of some of the most popular result in the inability to explain socio-political action inhibiting the choice of technology. Instead, the approaches emphasize the driving inertia of technology to force social and political change. Within this book, culture is perceived to be the vehicle driving or preventing technological change. The role of culture in energy transitions is clear. For example, Kuchler and Bridge provide an apt observation of the outcome of culture. "During this time the slogan 'Poland stands on coal' derived its shared meaning and *cultural power* by mobilising several of coal's distinctive material properties" (Kuchler and Bridge 2018, 144, emphasis added). The result of cultural mobilization is displayed. But to understand how culture reflects power relations, then a more in-depth examination needs to pay attention to *what culture is*, or *who is* controlling or influencing culture.

Culture slips through the energy transitions literature, despite its undeniable presence. The term 'culture' is 'downgraded' to a fuzzy "topical focus" (Sovacool and Hess 2017, 735), which demonstrates both the unwieldy broad nature, but also the importance to understand why it appears so unbounded by modern conceptual framings. Table 1.1 reflects the centrality of culture across theoretical approaches of energy transitions, but also the recent inability in the literature to properly label culture as a source of power within the energy system. Within the four paradigms, 'culture' resides in these four ideal types of theoretical paradigms by means of description or name, which are drawn from Gioia and Pitre (1990): functionalist, interpretivist, humanist, and structuralist (conflict). The categories also align with the descriptions of 'implicit and explicit' energy cultures (second half of Figure 1.1). The four paradigms provide a means to understand the energy transitions literature and how culture operates within the energy system.

Table 1.1 *Paradigms of knowledge aligned with implicit and explicit energy cultures*

	Functionalist-Institutionalist	Interpretivist	(Radical) Humanist	Conflict/(Radical) Structuralist
Topical focus: Sovacool and Hess (2017, 735)	Norms, values, and institutions	Discourse, practice, and culture	Historical change and cultural difference	Societal conflict
Geels and Verhees (2011, 912)	Culture shaping, "action by defining what people want ... Because people are socialized into existing values, there is little space for agency, freedom and creativity."	Developing agency and creating agency, "culture thus becomes a 'toolkit': actors draw upon deep cognitive structures or 'repertoires' and actively use symbols and categories for sensemaking."	"Meanings that have been produced do not go away, but provide background material for the next round" of social construction.	Culture as a deep cognitive structure that forms perceptions of reality and provides people with frames of meaning prompting action; however, this holds elements of cultural determinism and neglects agency.
Type of energy culture: Implicit or Explicit (see Figure 1.1)	*Explicit energy structure*: Socialized into existing energy practices. Loss/lack of agency to foster change due to institutional structures. Labels provide meaning to actions, including the built environment and landscape.	*Explicit energy structure*: Perceptions shape and are shaped by symbols and physical practices. Physical and social access to energy resources shape social practices within the energy system.	*Implicit energy structure*: Active engagement for placemaking. Historical re-narratives possible, thereby influencing both structural forms and societally contested norms.	*Implicit energy structure*: A cosmopolitan view of justice drives change to conform with perceptions of reality aligning with cultural interpretations of equitable relations.

Source: Categories from Sovacool and Hess (2017, 735); Geels and Verhees (2011, 912); Gioia and Pitre (1990).

Perceptions of energy cultures influence how energy transitions occur. Each category in Table 1.1 holds different 'paradigms of knowledge' that reflect the fundamental beliefs of the social construction of 'reality.' An example of how these different paradigms can be used is provided by Geels and Verhees (2011), who draw on these framings to understand technological change through the innovation of the Dutch nuclear energy sector. For them, 'cultural legitimacy' is essential to know where innovations may have social acceptance or rejection. Thereby cultural framings not only shape how the world (or the energy system) is viewed but what technologies are allowed into the world – thus expressing a source of authoritative power from an energy culture.

More specifically, energy transition literature holds weaknesses unable to exploit the elements of culture to humanize technological trajectories. For example, in the theory of 'Sociotechnical Imaginaries' which fits within both the Interpretivist and Critical Humanist categories; this approach examines the "imagined forms of social life and social order reflected in the design and fulfillment of nation-specific scientific and/or technological projects" (Sovacool and Hess 2017, 719). That is, technological projects driven by an (innovative) scientific perspective drive forward technological change, which is 'forced upon' society. The problem with this approach is it negates the power of society to choose its technology, with elites or regimes at the center of technological change (see Unruh 2002). It is unfit to explain political and social activities and conflicts stemming from societal choices and the interaction with elites, including history and localized perspectives.

Another widely used concept is the Multilevel Perspective (MLP). This theory sits within the Functionalists-Institutionalist category and is centered on how the innovation of new technologies eventually disrupts a socio-technological regime (Geels 2002, 2010). Regimes guide innovation and diffusion of technologies resulting in a gradual or sudden change in both technology and society. The limitation of this approach is heavily on the social side because it removes agency and human need from the evolution and deployment of energy technologies (Sovacool and Hess 2017, 710–11). Socio-techno systems utilize technologies, services, and other components of the energy system to fulfill society's energy needs through a 'deep structure' or 'grammar' that organizes actions (Vinichenko 2018, 28). Despite the 'deep structure,' technology (and its innovation) remains a primary organizing mechanism. The theory cannot explain political decisions and where authority and power reside, which influence technology deployment. As will be described further below, current uses of the energy justice framework also fit into this category because of the normative and positivist labeling of perceived injustices.

Aligning with the final category of social 'Conflict' is Social Practice Theory, which focuses on behaviors "driven by beliefs, values, lifestyles, and tastes that express personal choice" but excludes explicit mention of culture

(Sovacool and Hess 2017, 711–12). It is important not to lose culture in trying to be too precise. Culture is essential and influences and reflects both performance and interactions with technologies and material choices made by society. Thus, cultural interactions are meaningful and influence the types of technologies in use. The limitation of this approach lies with how broader systemic change and social practices are void of a strong authority taking action (Sovacool and Hess 2017, 713). In other words, Social Practice Theory accounts for culture, but is unable to account for drivers of change.

Figure 1.2 provides an overview of the paradigm axis and position of theories associated with the different quadrants. The diagram provides a description of the division between theories working closer to a radical orientation and those working closer to a social regulation framing. The theoretical framings are updated from Burrell and Morgan to account for changes identified by Gioia and Pitre (1990) and renaming by Sovacool and Hess (2017, 735). The axis is framed on the bottom and top by two different perspectives. The bottom is the 'sociology of regulation' which provides "explanations of society in terms which emphasise its underlying unity and cohesiveness" (Burrell and Morgan 1979, 17). The top is the 'sociology of radical change' which explains "deep-seated structural conflict, modes of domination and structural contradiction … [which are concerned with] emancipation from the structures which limit and stunt this potential for development" with a focus on material and psychic deprivation (Burrell and Morgan 1979, 17). Here, society and politicians interact to create a socially based energy system. This system aligns with the subjective social construction of reality (left). At the same time, a more positivist objective view of events and a realist interpretation characterizes the physical energy system (right) (discussed next).

The strengths of these individual theories within their quadrants are an acknowledgment of the diversity of assumptions underpinning how people perceive order or conflict in the world – and perceptions of the energy system. There is a structure that organizes perceptions of the energy system. There is a radical perspective that perceives conflict fostering change, and the other is social cohesion, which regulates transitions. Both influence technology development in different ways. The socio-techno imaginaries and MLP assume levels of social cohesion in the energy system. In contrast, the literature on social practice theory and geopolitics of cultures assumes higher levels of conflict values and diverging interests fomenting change in the energy system. More specifically, there is graduated scale of perspectives on the energy system. Each framework can lie closer or further from a sociology-of-regulation or a sociology-of-radical change. These frames help understand, through frameworks, how systemic change and cultural influence transform the energy system.

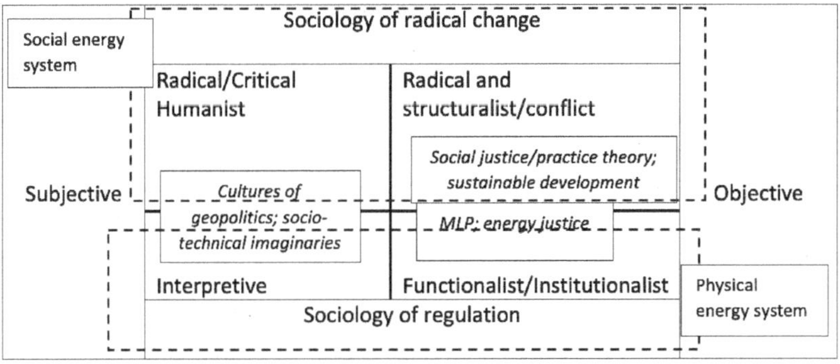

Source: Modified from Burrell and Morgan (1979, 23).

Figure 1.2 Paradigms of social theory analysis within the energy transitions literature

1.5 PHYSICAL AND SOCIAL ENERGY SYSTEMS

Describing the energy system needs to advance beyond a simple 'subjective' and 'objective' view. This is complicated by the multi-paradigm concept of 'culture,' which spans each of the paradigms. Therefore, a new conceptual alignment that views the lines of a 'sociology of regulation' or 'radical interpretation' enables established theories to apply to a 'physical' or 'social' energy system. This differentiation of perspectives of the energy system results in highlighting the unique qualities in each paradigm. The bottom-half of Figure 1.2 outlines the shared assumption of social cohesion and social regulation (sociology of regulation); this is observable in the *physical form of the energy system.* The cohesion provides the glue to organize through social or state institutions, thereby creating an energy system with established social practices observable through norms, values, regulations, or legislation. In contrast, the top half of the diagram highlights the *social construct of the energy system* (sociology of radical change), which assumes socio-political relations create conflict within the energy system. These two energy systems are explained next.

The physical energy system (representing a functionalist/institutionalist objective perspective, see Figure 1.2), is composed of the observable physical components, such as power plants, pipelines or automobiles. In contrast, for the interpretivist paradigm, the physical construction is interpreted for what it means or represents. The physical system impacts the reality of the everyday experience, with the assumption that society is "cohesive, ordered and integrated" (Burrell and Morgan 1979, 17, 31), with society experiencing life through subjective experiences. The physical energy system is based on social cohesion and the ability to observe energy use in the landscape or infrastructure.

The social energy system assumes that the structure of the energy system creates relational conflicts. This approach is best explained by contrasting the definition of 'institution' and contrasting what are institutions through the two paradigms of Sociology of Regulation and that of Radical Change. First, through the regulation perspective (bottom half of Figure 1.2) institutions simply exist as objects in the natural world. They are viewed as independent of societal conflict because they are created and organized by the state. This view is "concerned with providing an explanation of the status quo, social order, consensus, social integration" of stability within institutions (Burrell and Morgan 1979, 27). It is a favorable view of the state. Second, in a more flexible radical interpretation (top half of Figure 1.2) the energy system is a social construct with institutions representing structured (historical) social practices recognized – and respected – by the majority of society (Giddens 1982, 9–10) thereby enabling their continual existence. More specifically, the 'system' is "reproduced relations between actors or collectivities, organized as regular social practices" (Giddens 1982, 35), with structured social practices forming institutions. In this critical interpretation of how institutions work, the socially constructed institutions hold deep power relations. The danger here is that the relations translate into dominant and subjugated relations (often mediated by socio-political and economic relations). For example, the *sociology of radical* change seeks to explain, "deep-seated structural conflict, modes of domination and structural contradiction" (Burrell and Morgan 1979, 17). The social energy system requires a critical approach to unpack contested power relations.

The social and physical energy systems are explored through the frameworks of energy justice and a geopolitics of cultures. Figure 1.3 provides a visual representation of the interlinkage of the main paradigms around energy cultures. The framing demonstrates the subjective and objective views of the energy system. Energy justice and geopolitics sit opposite each other, the latter representing an 'objective' view of justice (Heffron, McCauley, and Sovacool 2015), while the former represents a subjective world view of diplomacy (Toal and Agnew 2002, 456). Each provides an effective means to formulate international and domestic events through a cultural prism. The cultural landscape of a country affects relations between countries. The question must be asked, to understand state relations: "How does the *geopolitical culture* of a state spatialize world politics and fill it with certain defining dramas and dangers, friends and enemies?" (Toal and Agnew 2002, 457). The study of geopolitics involving the energy sector exposes deeper power relations within an energy system and embedded cultural practices.

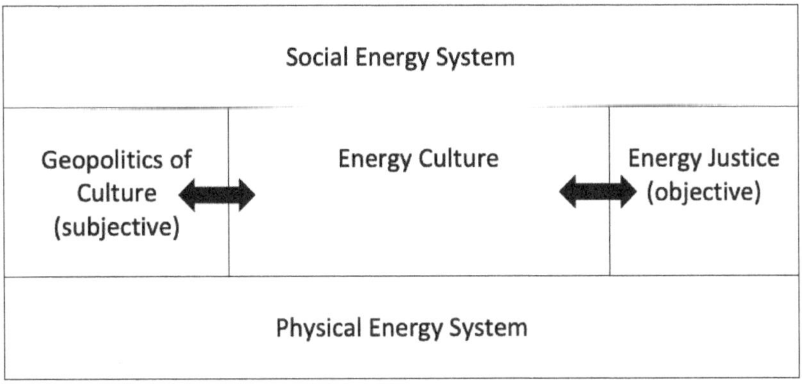

Source: Author.

Figure 1.3 *Conceptual components of energy cultures*

1.6 ENERGY JUSTICE AND GEOPOLITICS

Geopolitics and energy justice work through the state by operationalizing and institutionalizing relations within the energy system, thereby creating an energy culture. Therefore, it is important to understand *who* is creating culture and their motives. *The culture of a society informs how the political-economic system organizes the energy system to meet social, political, or economic objectives.* This means culture, with the power to influence and interpret a just energy system, along with the policy environment, contains both economic and political value. Thereby, controlling or influencing an energy culture delivers social, economic, and political benefits to those shaping an energy culture.

Just as Mitchell asks, "who produces culture and why," Jenkins et al. ask the question of "justice for whom" and "justice by whom" (Jenkins, McCauley, and Warren 2017, 837), thereby seeking out who is responsible for creating a culture *and* delivering equity and fairness in the energy system. This is an objective perspective of a geopolitics of culture. In contrast, 'soft power' is a subjective view, which reflects internal cultures. This domestic culture can appeal to other nation-states prompting cultural alignment of states (J. S. Nye Jr. 2004; Toal and Agnew 2002). Together, energy justice and a geopolitics of culture represent tools to assess the contiguous cultural alignment of states from domestic energy systems to international energy systems. Comparing and contrasting state cultural alignment, in energy systems, fosters a deeper understanding of cultural perceptions of justice and security. The next two sections delve deeper into how each of these conceptual framings informs a deeper understanding of energy culture.

1.6.1 Energy justice

Energy justice is framed by core notions of the 'three As,' which is the *availability* of specific forms of energy, *access* to energy services and the *affordability* of energy. These 'As' also include distribution of environmental risks and fair treatment in accessing the benefits of energy services and resources (Jenkins, Sovacool, and McCauley 2018, 67). The state in developed countries is important for organizing the marketplace, and creating institutions to monitor and shape the rules and regulations to provide an equitable energy system. Nonetheless, there are challenges in delivering a just energy system.

Explaining efforts by the state to meet social commitments draws on the strength of energy justice (Hiteva and Sovacool 2017, 632). The diversity of a country's society requires the state to steer energy transitions while also accounting for social diversity, norms, values, and ensuring long-term system stability. "Failure to adequately engage with questions of justice throughout the transition process is dangerous. It may lead to aggravated poverty, entrenched gender bias, and non-participation as outcomes or by-products of 'blinkered' decision-making" (Jenkins, Sovacool, and McCauley 2018, 67). Energy justice, through the three 'As,' provides a top-down perspective to explain and explore normative cultural understandings within an energy system. In contrast, a bottom-up perspective is provided by recognition and restorative justice, these 'two Rs' acknowledge local perceptions of justice. Space and scale emerge as lenses to perceive types of injustices within the energy system and highlighting inherent tensions between a universal and particular application of justice.

The spatial interpretation of energy justice rests on the placement of the framework in the spatial justice literature (Harvey 1996; Massey 1973; Gibson-Graham 1996). Scale provides the framing; for example, it brings in cosmopolitan justice that perceives a universal human right to access energy resources and services. This spatial and scale approach embraces consideration by Harvey of spatial injustices (Harvey 1996) and highly localized interpretations of justice that differ when juxtaposed against a universal cosmopolitan framing of justice (Sovacool and Dworkin 2014). Energy justice, as a conceptual tool, enables a multi-scalar perspective that focuses on different sections of the energy system – used as units of analysis (see Jenkins 2018, 119) – to account for both local and global processes that lead to engagement with the energy sector by a range of actors. Two defining camps of justice emerge, these are 'universal' and 'particular' energy justice (see LaBelle 2017c) with the following attributes:

1. *Universal energy justice* holds to values reliant on historical judicial and philosophical groundings that are based in (a) procedural justice, (b) distributional justice, and (c) cosmopolitan justice (for a discussion of these forms see Heffron et al. (2015), Jenkins et al. (2016), Sovacool and Dworkin (2015)) (cited from LaBelle 2017c).

2. *Particular energy justice* is a nuanced accounting of localized issues and interpretations of social, political, and economic actions affecting access to energy resources and services. Recognition justice, which provides cultural and political representation of groups with distinguishing features such as social, ethnic, and gender differences; freedom from distortion, devaluation, degradation, and physical threats by other groups (Heffron and McCauley 2014, p. 436) (cited from LaBelle 2017c).

Bridging universal notions of justice, such as the basic right to energy services along with localized (particular) interpretations of justice stems from situatedness and positionality of individuals in society (Harvey 1996, 342). The historical and geographical representation of the state is expressed through national cultures and state institutions (Harvey 1996, 351). These are localized interpretations and are particular to a location and informed by scalar relations. Building a sense of a 'just energy system' constitutes a range of cultural, institutional, and historical experiences and structures which are designed to deliver energy services to match social expectations within a nation-state (particular) and through global connections and awareness (universal).

The universal notion is demonstrated by Sovacool et al., who develop a "transboundary nature of injustice" (Sovacool, Sidortsov, and Jones 2013a, 29); this emphasizes universal burden-sharing by a global citizenry. Universal energy justice provides "global energy system that fairly disseminates both the benefits and costs of energy services and one that has representative and impartial energy decision-making" (Sovacool and Dworkin 2015, 436). Access to energy services is a universal human right of all citizens (United Nations General Assembly 1948). The justification for this is that access to energy services enables access to other services such as health care, education, and employment (Sovacool, Sidortsov, and Jones 2013a, 25–6). Therefore, the state is central in ensuring access to energy services (for further explanation, see LaBelle 2017c). There are three universal justices: procedural, distributional, and cosmopolitan. Each of these is reliant on institutions to assist implementation (see, Table 1.2 for definition). Additionally, the second perspective, the 'particular energy justice,' stems from how energy services are perceived and delivered locally.

> The particular approach is defined as a nuanced accounting of localized issues and interpretations of social, political and economic actions affecting access to energy resources and services. It gives voice to grievances even within seemingly universally just energy systems. (LaBelle 2017d, 616)

Cultural and political representation are heavily present in the concept of energy justice and rest within the institutions of the state. Cultural features such as gender and ethnic divisions are highlighted within the provision of energy services enabling local stories to highlight differences in access to energy services (Schlosberg 2004, 534–5; Fuller and McCauley 2016, 2). Recognition and restorative justice lie within the particular energy justice grouping; however, for restorative justice to occur, there first must be a recognition of both groups and the injustices, therefore the discussion going forward is largely on recognition justice. Table 1.2 outlines the different types of energy justice. Splitting of types of justices enables a more nuanced accounting of how societies create perceptions of justice.

There is tension within the definitions of energy justice. For example, particular energy justice does not exclude universal notions of a working legal system but envisions a particularized application to the legal norms. "Decisions and actions will be evaluated less according to whether they are right or just than according to their legal validity, that is, whether they are consistent with the rules and follow the appropriate procedures" (Young 1990, 77). This objective view of the legal system, therefore, also must conform to long-established legal norms to ensure fair representation and freedom from political interference. There is an inherent tension between a global (universal) interpretation and local (particular) interpretation of delivering a just energy transition. Fairness applies in both a universal and a local justice interpretation, meaning alignment between the two approaches is a necessary attempt to ensure a fair process. Nonetheless, there is failure to provide a just energy system. Justice is always in the process of becoming as cultures shift. The *processes of pursuing* a universal form of justice differ from any final *form* of universal justice: "Utopianism of process looks radically different from a Utopianism of form" (Harvey 1996, 333, cited by LaBelle 2017c). That is, there is no end-state. Just as culture continues to evolve, so does the definition of justice within the broad parameters of energy justice.

Type of justice	**Definition** (extracted from LaBelle 2017)	References
	Universal Energy Justice	
Procedural justice	The delivery and protection of energy services through administrative or judicial means including the right to appeal.	(Sovacool, Sidortsov, and Jones 2013a, 439; Bouzarovski and Simcock 2017)
Distributional justice	Facilitates other human rights like education and health, including access to energy services.	(Heffron and McCauley 2014, 435–36; Walker and Day 2012, 69–70; Sovacool et al. 2017).
Cosmopolitan justice	Defined as a collective approach to creating "meaningful global change specifically in energy behaviors and attitudes" (Heffron, McCauley, and Sovacool 2015, 170). This extends our perspective to future generations and beyond short-term economic thinking	(Heffron, McCauley, and Sovacool 2015, 170)
	Particular Energy Justice	
Recognition justice	Provides a cultural and political representation of groups with distinguishing features such as social, ethnic and gender differences; freedom from distortion, devaluation, degradation and physical threats by other groups. Activists' perspectives and actions that mobilize and interpret events "in ways that are intended to mobilize potential adherents and constituents" (Fuller and McCauley 2016, 2).	(Heffron and McCauley 2014, 436; McCauley and Heffron 2018)
Restorative justice	Repair the harm done to people, society, nature rather than focus on punishment for the offender. Also utilize for prevention of injustices	(Heffron and McCauley 2017)

Source: Adapted from LaBelle (2017).

Table 1.2 Types of energy justice

1.6.2 Geopolitics of culture and soft power

The extension of justice, reflecting both domestic cultural practices and universal concepts, parallels a geopolitical approach which incorporates domestic cultural reflections into international action. The discussion centers on 'a geopolitics of culture' which observes cultural traditions in nation-states and interprets international actions through a cultural reflection (Toal and Agnew 2002). This approach moves beyond 'discursive geopolitics,' which draws on a traditional geographic perception of "socio-cultural resources" (O Tuathail and Agnew 1992, 193) describing power ideologies of imperialism on the landscape and through state (military) actions (Mackinder 2004; Bassin 1987). Rather, through this revised framing, the identity of nation-states is understood to help expose power alignments through cultural practices on the landscape and implementing policy goals. This geographic gaze produces a conceptual 'power continuum' extending from soft to hard power. Geopolitics of culture describes domestic cultural interactions in the international geopolitical arena.

Within a broader alignment of culture and geopolitics, an example is provided by Hadfield who utilizes a 'strategic culture' lens, which identifies culture as governing EU-Russia relations through "national cultures or regional requirements, in which cardinal beliefs are perceived to be at odds with other viewpoints, prevent cooperation and prompting belligerence, even aggression" (Hadfield 2016, 781). The essential point is culture influences international relations, it formulates perspectives on areas of cooperation or disagreement, thereby providing the context of actions with other international actors. From this point, the question can be proposed: How does culture influence spatial relations and provide labels of friends or enemies? (Toal and Agnew 2002, 457). The study of geopolitical cultures seeks to understand domestic discourse and debates about nation-state identity and international relations drawing from a territorial position (Toal and Agnew 2002, 457). The geographic gaze shifts from looking at the Imperial Powers fight over territory, and instead looks at the clash of cultures and the expression of power relations occurring both domestically and internationally.

Culture has an important role expressing soft power in geopolitics. According to Nye (2011), soft power relies on three basic resources: culture and how attractive it is to others; expression and practice of political values; and foreign policy perceived as legitimate and holding moral authority (the last two categories also connect with perceptions of justice). Making or breaking the possession of soft power is behavior around attraction of a state and whether it can wield this power to influence outcomes. Socially constructed, soft power is hard to use and can be lost (Nye 2011, 83–4). Therefore, tension exists between those wielding softer and harder approaches to geopolitical power relations. This tension underscores the considerable gray area between hard and soft, which can include using military and economic resources to exert power (Goldthau and Sitter 2015).

The study of geopolitical cultures benefits from this soft/hard power continuum and power of (cultural) attraction. Soft power shapes nation-states' identities and international alignment within a less militaristic state alignment. The diversity of culture flourishes in another gray area and is exemplified by understanding culture as attractive for its knowledge and values, which motivates participating in a culture.

> Culture can be an important power resource. "Culture" is the pattern of social behaviors by which groups transmit knowledge and values, and it exists at multiple levels. Some aspects of human culture are universal, some are national, and others are particular to social classes or small groups. Culture is never static, and different cultures interact in different ways. (Nye 2011, 84)

Rather than viewing culture as only soft power, Goldthau and Sitter propose the existence of 'soft power with a hard edge,' to describe the governance and stability of the EU's Single Energy Market (SEM) (Goldthau and Sitter 2015). The authors describe the attractiveness of the EU's energy market as a means to influence third-party states to conform to the market and moral conditions inherent in the EU's energy system. The EU's internal rules are accepted by external actors (such as Gazprom) for the chance to 'come and play' in the EU's Single Energy Market (SEM). In this scenario of soft power, the EU exerts power by having attractive values, institutions, and (liberal) market ideology operating in an attractive market environment (Goldthau and Sitter 2015, 8).

Geopolitics of culture provides a means to understand that the internal culture of a nation-state holds international ramifications in alignment with friends and enemies. This geopolitical culture is not devoid of values and norms; rather it reflects these while asserting the power of the state into the international arena of states and organizations. Geopolitics of culture, therefore, enables both an alignment of states and assertion of power stemming from traditions and historical relations. Moral authority and social practices are bound up in soft-powers, serving to attract rather than force a spatial alignment of allies. This embeddedness of justice aligns with the normative framing of energy justice, reflecting structured values and norms of nation-states and the provision of energy resources and services.

1.7 ENERGY CULTURES: FROM EMPIRICAL TO THEORETICAL

The right to access energy resources and services as a universal human right, combined with the fundamental transformation of the fossil fuel-based energy system, requires re-engaging with the concept of energy culture. The confluence of the energy transition reminiscent of the second industrial revolution experienced by Ostwald and his contemporaries was a time of rapid social and technological transformation, including the development of academic disciplines, like geography and sociology. They attempted to capture and explain both the lived cultural experiences and transformations of the landscape. The site of combustion in the Anthropocene (Dalby 2018) is also the site of power relations. These relationships flow through the physical infrastructure and are visible on the landscape and in the environment. The development of energy culture matches the call by Nye, who states, "More research needs to be done on the connection between culture and power behavior" (2011, 84). The concept of energy culture re-emerges in this transformative period to capture the power relations in culture, its use and interpretations of justice to inhibit or speed up the energy transition.

An energy cultures framework provides a conceptual means to interpret and explain how and why each country orientates and changes its energy system. This chapter set out to review and reframe the production of energy culture, including a critical critique to operationalize it through cultural geography, geopolitics, and energy justice. This chapter briefly captures these overlaps and enables a structured paradigm formulation exposing cultural processes influencing national energy systems. The following three chapters represent case studies that highlight different types of energy cultures and efforts to produce just energy systems while also expressing geopolitical cultures.

The strength of the energy cultures framework is in erasing the binaries of demand/supply and domestic/international. This also results in limitations. For example, it does not replace the reviewed conceptual framings used either in current energy cultures literature or energy transitions theories. The state, in this framing of energy cultures, is the central organizing structure. Therefore, decentralized and citizen-led initiatives may reflect the failure of the state, but the organizing structure will rely more on a social informal structure to shape and build an energy culture. Power relations will occur at the community level, in the absence of a powerful state. A critical approach to energy cultures seeks to uncover these hidden power relations; in this effort, insufficient attention will be given to the broader impact of a culture on the landscape or in the field of technology. Finally, more granular interpretations of culture and social conformity or contestation may be missed due to the joint demand/supply side focus.

Empirical	Scale organization	Spatial organization	Ontological framing	Epistemological framing	Energy culture
Case study framing	Shallow Structure Level of struggle Shallow Structure	Landscape and materiality	Expressed social reality in discourse and narratives	Norms, laws expressed through institutions and actions	What is the representation of injustice?
Level 1, Identify: Manifestation of energy culture in artifacts or practice	Explicit representation (surface level)	Social practices and materiality Intermediate Structure	Intermediate Structure Paradigms: Interpretivist framing	Scale: Particular (local) social justice framing	How does culture represent injustice and power?
Cultural Milieu	Internal/domestic ethics	Equity in access and services	ENERGY JUSTICE	Ethical/injustice	What are the power relations?
	External & international power relations	Use of networks, technologies and resources	GEOPOLITICS	Spatial justice	How are relations socially transformative?
Level 2, Constructions: Social; physical; individual; gender; economic; political	Implicit representation (deep structure)	Socio-economic and political-economic	Paradigms: Radical Subjective framing	Scale: Universal social justice framing Deep Structure	**How do relations create energy culture?**

Source: Author's own conceptualization.

Figure 1.4 *Levels of abstraction to operationalization of radical energy culture*

Figure 1.4 provides a stepped perspective of how energy culture is theoretically and geographically constructed. The categories in the first column build the empirical framing at both the surface level, in terms of how energy cultures are expressed in the everyday or in landscapes (level 1: artifacts and practices), while level 2 is representative of deeper processes and relations intertwined with political-economic and social constructions. The 'cultural milieu' is descriptive of the area of interaction of social relations where culture is created and influenced by both the operation and construction of institutions and infrastructure. The columns listing 'space' and 'scale' structure the organization of specific levels and spaces of noticeable representation of energy culture. The use of ontological and epistemological framing influences the perceptions and scale of analysis of framing of social processes (epistemological) which are explained through the theories and paradigms (ontological). This leads to the exposure of the relations that create radical energy culture, in the last column. The process is framed at different levels through the exposure of the structures that build into the question, 'How do relations create energy cultures?'

There are different levels of analysis that frame the energy system in different ways. It is necessary to work through these to understand both the representation of culture and how it is created. There are three levels to the energy cultures framework. The first, the 'shallow structure' draws from the everyday, while the second, the 'intermediate structure' provides an explanatory value of observations of both deep and shallow structures. The third level, the 'deep structure,' arrives at an answer of how relations create energy culture. Energy cultures rely on the spatial-scale and the ontological-epistemological scaffolding to expose relations and social processes within an energy system.

1.8 CASE STUDIES OF ENERGY CULTURES

One of the vestiges of the Communist period dominated by the USSR is the built energy infrastructure in Eastern Europe. Oil and gas pipelines, along with nuclear power plants and large concrete panel houses are the most prominent symbols of the energy resources, production, and consumption which continue to function today. The geographic routes and supply lines along with technical expertise unified the Eastern Bloc countries to Moscow's scientific and technical expertise. Each of these sources of power delivered low-cost energy to households and factories. The fall of the Berlin Wall in 1989 was a symbol of deep changes in all the Soviet Union's satellites in Eastern Europe. Gaining membership into the European Union on May 1, 2004, for many of these countries, represents even deeper changes. The base of this economic change was an energy system that was forced to straddle two economic and political systems. As the chapters explore, each former Communist country developed a unique approach to assert its own domestic energy culture with the new geopolitical alignment. Three case studies of Lithuania, Hungary, and Poland describe in detail how different energy cultures express different geopolitical and energy justice approaches.

The geopolitics of energy are displayed in the vast sums for infrastructure development. The European Union is dedicating 100 billion EUR in the 2021–7 funding cycle to Member States to create a 'Just Transition Mechanism,' while Russia completes its North Stream Two pipeline through the Baltic Sea and its Turk Stream in Europe's southern gas corridor for about half this amount. Two competing projects, one focused on 'green' energy solutions and the other sending a fossil fuel, demonstrate the underlining values and strategic infrastructure projects within a clash of energy cultures. The geopolitical alignment of Eastern European countries is wrapped up in their use of resources and technologies, with the cost borne by social justice issues and geopolitical conditions. Infrastructure projects and the conversion technologies along with the built electricity and gas networks represent the international alignment of states along with the consumption habits of citizens. The energy cultures of

Eastern Europe are tied to the geopolitical power centers to the east and west. Chapter 2 describes these in more detail.

The clash of culture emerges even within the international orientation chosen by a country. In Hungary, the expression of a 'Christian green policy' is compared to a Brussels bureaucratic approach (Varga 2020); in Poland, the defense of Polish coal is a defense for Polish technology (Sitarski 2019); while Lithuania's EU membership meant shutting down Lithuania's Soviet nuclear power plant, thereby "killing the golden goose" (personal communication, Straupaite 2018). EU membership transformed Eastern Europe's energy system and created a clash of energy cultures, because technologies and resources reflect deeper social, economic, and political relations. The push by EU institutions to go 'greener' pushes up against Eastern Europe's Communist energy system of inefficient consumption. It is important to consider that energy systems hold explicit and implicit socio-political relations. The reason for the clash between East and West perspectives are the authoritative power relations within energy cultures, such as the EU 'forcing' Member States to change their technologies and resources. The transformation in turn affects the relationship between society and politicians.

Relations within the energy system are contested at a range of scales. There is also contestation over what creates a just energy system. Is it only a sustainable and green energy system? Or is it one with low prices where consumers can afford to heat their homes? Energy justice becomes a contested phrase depending on the local (particular) interpretation. At the heart of the EU's 'green and just' project is the assumption there is a definable 'just energy transition' (European Commission 2020). As will be discussed in the next chapter, the cost of the transition is a serious concern for Eastern Europeans. Understanding the injustices within the current energy systems highlights domestic political social relations and policy choices shaping national energy cultures. Lithuania, as Chapter 3 discusses, chose to diversify away from the Soviet-era energy system and embrace EU competition rules. The price of energy for households is a fundamental problem in both Hungary and Poland. For example, in Hungary, as Chapter 4 describes, each year around 200 people die of hypothermia, half in unheated homes (personal communication, Simo 2018). This underscores the cost of energy as an essential social and political issue. Poland, described in Chapter 5, also grapples with high rates of energy poverty and uses cheap coal to ensure adequate heating, but with a trade-off of dangerous levels of air pollution. Polish cities and villages have some of the most dangerous levels of air pollution emanating from coal furnaces and power plants; with 36 Polish cities in the top 50 most polluted cities in Europe (Radio Poland 2018). The case studies provide the chance to understand both geopolitical orientations of the energy system as well as society's request for a just, affordable, and clean energy system.

1.9 CONCLUSION: THE CLASH OF ENERGY CULTURES

Culture is not a benign representation of a nation or social practices (Mitchell 2000), but rather culture actively transforms the energy systems through (power) relations. Energy culture, as a concept, exposes the reasons and relations within the transformation. The production of energy culture is expressed in the *explicit* in the physical form seen in resource extraction, combustion technologies, and networks. The *implicit* relations in energy cultures are perceptible in social and power relations within the energy system. The production of geographic inequality and flows taps into the bounding out of energy justice (Jenkins 2018, 120) at different scales of the energy system. These arrangements are reflective of "underlying structural mechanisms that produce spatial inequality" (Bouzarovski and Simcock 2017, 645). The explicit demonstration of energy culture on the landscape provides a visual representation of inequity and unjust systemic constructions of the political economy.

Finding the value in energy cultures requires a stepped theoretical approach, which moves from the surface-level representation of culture to expressions of culture that structure power relations and the political economy of society within an energy system. Chapter 6 provides a more in-depth understanding of energy cultures as a theoretical contribution which provides a radical interpretation of spatial justice that emphasizes the geographic "dimensions of inequality and inequity" (Bouzarovski and Simcock 2017, 640). Applying the term, 'culture' enables a multidimensional approach to assist understanding the diverse perspectives that influence the operation of the energy system.

Chapter 7 builds the interconnection between energy justice and geopolitics within the energy system. The cultural significance for geopolitics rests with the boundaries of the nation-state and how internal social processes influence external relationships. Domestic cultural interpretations of actions influence interactions between states. Access to resources and energy services also differ within and between countries. This inequality is raising moral and ethical questions of how state institutions and society ensure fair and equal access; access to energy resources and services has been an established universal human right since 1948 (United Nations General Assembly 1948). Just as nation-states have sovereign rights in the international realm, citizens have the basic right to energy services. This reinforces other "basic goods to which human beings are entitled, like welfare, security, health care, education, and the right to employment" (Sovacool, Sidortsov, and Jones 2013b, 25–6), thereby underscoring the importance of the state in the provision of energy resources and services and creating tension between a universal notion of access and local interpretations of sufficient access.

The state is the container of a government mediated energy system. Geopolitics and energy justice work through the state by operationalizing and institutionalizing relations that also create a culture of energy. Therefore, it is essential to understand who is shaping culture and their motives. *The culture of a society informs how the political-economic system organizes the energy system to meet social, political, and economic objectives.* Culture has the power to influence and develop a just energy system. Controlling or changing an energy culture delivers social, economic, and political benefits. The question is, 'Who benefits from an energy culture?'

Just as Mitchell asks, 'who produces culture and why', Jenkins et al. raise the issue of "justice for whom" and "justice by whom" (Jenkins, McCauley, and Warren 2017, 837), thereby seeking who is responsible for creating culture *and* delivering equity and fairness in the energy system. Extending energy cultures into a global framework is the geopolitics of culture, which expresses soft power. The expression of domestic cultures works by appealing to other nation-states, prompting a cultural alignment of states (Nye Jr. 2004; Toal and Agnew 2002). This expresses a subjective arrangement of states. Energy justice and a geopolitics of culture represent tools to assess the alignment of states. Chapter 6 compares and contrasts these alignments of cultures in energy systems, enabling an understanding of states based on perceptions of justice and security.

Finally, Chapter 8 provides a broader view on the "sciences of culture" (Weber, Mikkelsen, and Schwartz 1984, 51) which have shifted over the last century. The chapter explores the importance of the energy system, and relations within it, which have grown more substantial to meet social and economic needs in the period of transition away from fossil fuels. There is a need for a fundamental reorientation of both the social, political, and economic systems to build a sustainable energy transition. At the center of this transformation are cultural practices within the energy system. It is these practices and the relations that create energy cultures that this book addresses. Chapter 8 concludes this book with a summary of how the concept of energy cultures can meet the challenges in this transition. Exposing the power relations, and both the explicit and implicit expressions of energy cultures, identifies where injustice prevents the development of a just energy system. Politicians hold a moral and political responsibility to honor both the social contract and regulatory compact in modern developed energy systems. The basis of the modern democratic state with a centralized energy system requires politicians to pursue a just energy transition.

2. Combustion of energy cultures in Eastern Europe

2.1 INTRODUCTION: INFLUENCES IN EASTERN EUROPE'S ENERGY SYSTEM

There are two fronts in this book. The Eastern front is Eastern European energy security and how it diminishes or retains Russian resource and technology. The Western front is about EU market integration into a competitive market underpinned by an American system of regulatory governance. This chapter addresses the social, economic, and political orientation of energy systems and how there is a balance between pursing the lowest cost energy with the most secure energy system for economic growth. The 'home front' is the domestic political and economic environment where society and elites have a say in orientation of energy policies. Hungary, Lithuania, and Poland provide a perspective on choices revolving around energy resources and technologies. Both their geopolitical position, endowment (Poland), or lack of natural resources (Hungary and Lithuania) influence choices around energy imports of technologies and resources. This ability to choose creates tension between the EU's governance system and Russia's political sphere of influence.

Reflecting on the East-West division that dominated Europe during the Cold War is important to understand the diverging social and economic spheres. In the 1980s, the General Secretary of the Soviet Union, Mikhail Gorbachev and President Ronald Reagan pursued a strong bridging strategy. That is, Reagan played the stern bargainer, while Gorbachev sought to loosen the cultural and centralized economic chains constraining economic growth in the Soviet Union and the Eastern COMECON countries. COMECON was set up in 1949, as an economic counterweight to the military and political alignment within NATO. It served as a driving force in the building of gas and nuclear energy infrastructure, cementing economic and political relations between the Soviet Union and other COMECON countries throughout the Eastern Bloc. Thus, the energy infrastructure influencing today's political landscape in Eastern Europe is an artifact of this Cold War division.

The high energy intensity of the Eastern Bloc countries also meant a huge amount of financial resources were expended to support unsustainable energy development. The entire Communist sphere was ripe for modern Western technologies, management skills, and individual liberties to allow citizens to pursue their own economic paths. In the 1981–5 period, the Soviet Union planned to allocate 85% of all new investment money to energy projects, drilling new oil and gas fields and building pipelines westward (Gustafson 1989, 36). Subsidized gas pipelines and nuclear power plants in Eastern Europe all necessitated these energy and economic ties to the Soviet Union. Gorbachev attempted to manage a social and economic opening. The rapid failure of the political-economic system underscored the social tension with the imposed political system. After the political and economic collapse of Communism Eastern Europe opened to the West to try market capitalism, resulting in an inflow of FDI along with industry experts and financial institutions (Larner and Laurie 2010). Figure 2.1 shows a map of the former COMECON countries that joined the EU.

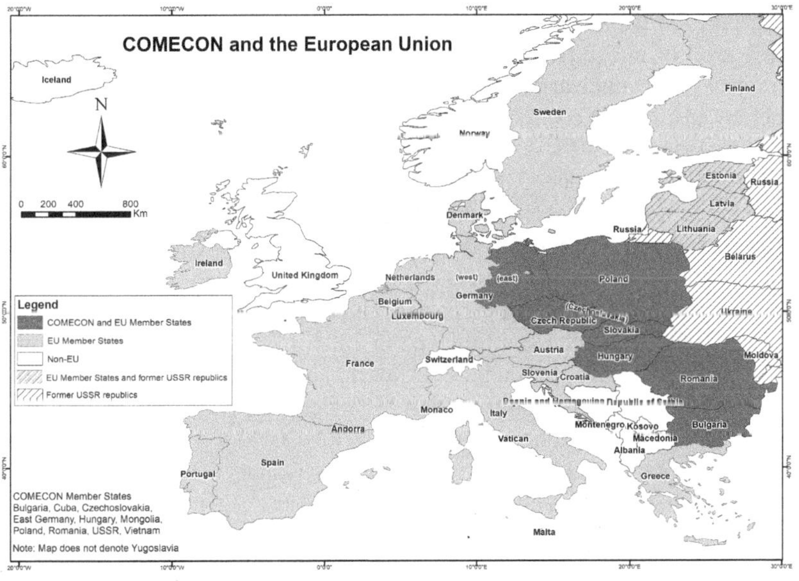

Source: Pujiastuti (2020).

Figure 2.1 *Map of COMECON countries and EU Member States*

The Soviet satellites of the COMECON countries developed significant levels of interconnections for electricity between countries. The gas infrastructure was likewise robust, with the gas network piped directly from the core of the

Soviet Union and containing little interconnection between Eastern European countries. This transmission infrastructure is not just a geopolitical tool, but also an engineering feat that represents the massive effort to build an integrated Soviet energy system across the Eurasian landmass. Geopolitical tension would only later develop with an independent Ukraine and fights over money to pay the Russian gas debts, with the tension culminating in the 'reclamation' of Crimea by Russia (Grigas 2017). Integration of cross-border infrastructure was engineered in the East for security of supply and later was perceived as a geopolitical weapon. EU membership heightened this geopolitical tension as the new Member States pushed to break the Russian/Soviet alliance and integrate into the EU.

Nonetheless, despite integration efforts of EU Members States, Western European national markets remained largely protected with electricity generation operating to satisfy national demand. This stands in contrast to the Communist system in Eastern Europe which integrated both pipelines and electricity systems along with the diffusion of nuclear power technology and transport infrastructure for oil, gas and coal throughout the Soviet landscape. This level of integration was not without its detractors. This enabled Poland to reject Soviet nuclear power and enabled it to retain its own coal technology thereby ensuring an economically sustainable and largely independent national energy system.

Eastern Europe's energy security issues are interlinked with the activities of the United States' general attempt to assist the region's diversification away from Russian energy sources and technologies. Security concerns are the main pillar of this relationship. NATO expansion occurred between 1999 and 2009 to the former Warsaw Pact countries. Hungary and Poland were the first to join in 1999, and Lithuania followed in 2004. In terms of direct engagement in energy security, the US imposed export bans on US oil and gas technology necessary to power the pump stations of Soviet gas to Germany and Austria in 1975 (United States Congress 1975; Högselius 2013).

After 1989, the US Federal Energy Regulatory Commission (FERC) was instrumental in working with United States Agency for International Development (USAID) to train energy regulators along the lines of the American system of energy regulated as a public good (LaBelle 2011). The Energy Regulators Regional Association (ERRA) was first established by USAID in Budapest in 2001. Later, ERRA would assist implementing EU requirements for independent energy regulators. Further ties revolved around US nuclear technology sold to Eastern Member States in the 1990s and early 2000s. Later, US interests were expressed in terms of LNG deliveries to diversify the region away from Russia. After 2012, when the US shale gas revolution took off with hydraulic fracturing technology, and American shale LNG deliveries, both would become important diplomatic and commercial ties, directly linking American technologies and resources to Eastern Europe's diversification away from the security threat of Russian gas. In 2019, President Trump signed a law imposing economic sanctions against companies assisting Gazprom in completing the Nord Stream 2 pipeline between Russia and Germany (BBC 2019). Overall, US energy activities in Eastern Europe were strongest in educating and helping to build a system of regulatory governance (before EU expansion), while more recent efforts focus on excluding Russian gas which can result in higher US LNG imports in Europe.

The splintering of Europe during the Cold War led to a different alignment of energy resources and technologies. NATO and COMECON countries developed different technologies as well as international interlinkages based on geopolitical security and resource requirements. The end of the Cold War brought about a shift towards integration between the two halves in Europe and an attempt to foster a unified energy market. Before the expansion of the EU, the US held a strong influence in developing the institutional capacity in Eastern Europe. Once the former COMECON countries joined the EU, the US left it to the EU to continue the roll-out of regulatory governance. Subsequently, as will be described in the next section, an attempt was made to dampen down national political interests in the energy sector. As strains appeared in the fractured EU energy market, including its physical infrastructure, compounded with the political pursuit of national interests, the EU's Single Energy Market received renewed political backing.

2.2 THE ENERGY UNION: ENERGY GOVERNANCE

The basis of today's European Union is a descendant of the 1951 Treaty of Paris that established the European Coal and Steel Community (ECSC). Regional integration was viewed as preventing further wars with a common market serving two purposes: First, linking coal and steel production to increase production efficiencies would create dependency between countries, while also developing social support schemes for workers, such as work mobility. Second, a buying pool was created to avoid buying lower-cost US steel. European peace was secured with the integration of energy and industry (Mathieu 1970). This founding logic can be seen in the expansion of the EU in 2004 and afterwards European security and economic prosperity is accomplished through an integrated energy market. Figure 2.2 demonstrates the evolution of EU energy policy over the past decades. The SEM reflects a continual process of market integration extending back to the early 1990s.

The first large expansion of the EU in 2004 brought in Poland, Slovakia, Slovenia, Cyprus, the Czech Republic, Hungary, Latvia, Lithuania, Estonia, and Malta, with further expansions in subsequent years. Preceding each country's accession was a realignment of legislation and regulations fulfilling

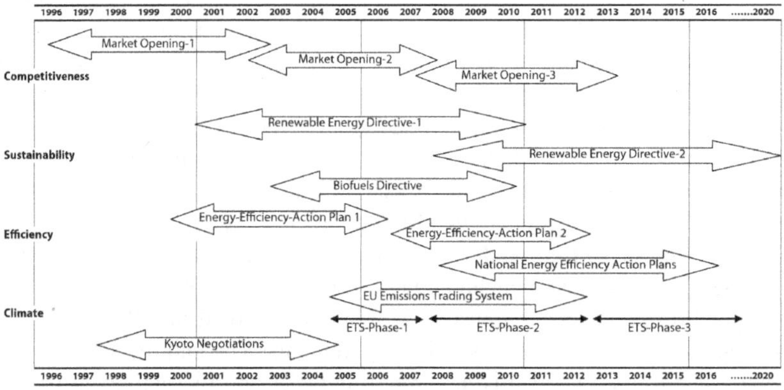

Source: Eurostat, European Commission (2009, 3).

Figure 2.2 Timeline of development of EU energy policies and directives

different 'chapters' on social, environmental, and other key issues areas. In the energy sector there was a wave of privatizations and unbundling of gas and electricity companies. Vertical integration and the price of energy was shifted from the economics or energy ministry to an independent energy regulator. As Eastern European countries floundered and readjusted to a market economy, industrial subsidies were removed under the watchful eyes of international organizations (e.g. the European Bank for Reconstruction and Development (EBRD) and the World Bank). National politicians accepted the new economic reality of foreign investors working to stabilize and improve the energy sector. Largely American and European energy companies, supported by international consulting firms and banks, moved in to acquire and modernize the decaying state firms. Russian firms also played a role, largely to retain a role in the gas sector.

Building on the external threat to the EU's energy system, the European Commission pushed further with market integration as a protective measure against external security and supply threats – just as the founders of the ECSC did. Investments into infrastructure increased after 2009 and market integration – to assist during a security of supply crisis – became a driving motive for energy developments. In 2014, Donald Tusk, the Prime Minister of Poland (2007–14) proposed a joint sharing of gas resources through storage and bargaining under the auspices of an Energy Union (as a protective measure against Russia) (EurActiv.com 2014). This concept of collective action would emerge in the Energy Union Package issued by the European Commission in the winter of 2015; this attempts to build an Internal Energy Market (IEM) by boosting energy security through market integration. "The key drivers of energy security are the completion of the internal energy market and more efficient energy consumption" (European Commission 2015b, 4). To accomplish the task, the Commission laid out the regulatory governance mechanism that will put an end to 28 national regulatory frameworks (European Commission 2015b, 3). The central actor in driving the IEM forward and eroding market separations is the Agency for Cooperation of Energy Regulators (ACER). "The Energy Union also needs an integrated governance and monitoring process, to make sure that energy-related actions at European, regional, national and local level all contribute to the Energy Union's objectives" (European Commission 2015b, 17).

The regulatory approach, represented by ACER and National Regulatory Agencies (NRAs), holds significant potential for implementing key agenda points for the Energy Union. Unification with common standards is the pursuit. To accomplish the task, the Commission lays out how ACER will achieve coherency across the 28 Member States and differing regulatory environments by building the IEM. The IEM also serves to boost energy security (European Commission 2015b, 3). Nonetheless, market and regulatory failures are cited as leading to a situation where "an unacceptably high percentage of European households cannot afford to pay their energy bills" (European Commission 2015b, 3). The Energy Union pursues a coherent IEM to improve both energy security and reduce inefficient costs and consumption of energy.

In 2016, the European Commission launched an energy security package that for the first-time linked energy efficiency to energy security. Consolidating more authority in ACER and to overseeing a technological transformation in the EU's heating and cooling systems are top priorities fitting within the concept of the Energy Union. The connections between the heating and cooling sector are linked to the level of gas consumption, "59% of total EU gas consumption (direct use only) which equates to 68% of all gas imports" (European Commission 2016a). This is particularly relevant for Eastern European countries which import large quantities of gas for residential heating. In the view of the Commission, financial outlays for energy services for households can drop from 1,500–2,000 EUR to 300–500 EUR, based on switching to heat pumps and solar water heaters (European Commission 2016a). The explicit policy connection between energy efficiency and energy security is a first by the Commission and may create a confrontation between eastern Member States who are not investing in energy efficiency (a supply-side focus is discussed in later chapters).

Increasing transparency in the gas sector is also a central element for the energy security package, which heavily involves ACER. In the view of the Commission, "Energy policy is often used as a foreign policy tool" (European Commission 2015b, 6); the Commission holds the power of *ex-ante* review of intergovernmental agreements (The European Parliament and the Council of the European Union 2017a, 684); this specifically targets Russia and mainly Eastern Member States. NRAs also hold greater authority to review private gas transactions impacting the regional security of supply (Portfollio.hu 2016; European Commission 2016a), thus boosting the role of energy regulators. In regard to moving towards the IEM, European energy security regions were created with each country agreeing to assist the other in a state of energy crisis (The European Parliament and the Council of the European Union 2017b). In the short term, this would expand risks within a region, with one country forced to assist, (possibly) at higher costs, another Member State. In the long term, this would also prompt countries to work together to build infrastructure to mitigate risks and build a stronger IEM, thereby fulfilling key IEM criteria. Market integration is the primary goal of the European Commission to create coherency across countries. This is done through regulatory mechanisms implemented and overseen by ACER.

2.3 ENERGY PROFILE OF EASTERN EUROPE: RESOURCE AND TECHNOLOGY DEPENDENCY

The socio-economic disparity in Eastern Europe provides a picture of the legacy of Communism and the disparity between income levels and cost of energy. The previous economic system was tightly integrated into the Soviet model of technology and resources, the shift in Eastern Europe relates to rebalancing in a market economy. The common experience of moving to a market economy and an age of 'wild capitalism' is slowly shifting towards transparent and mature markets providing goods and services in a transparent form (personal communication, Janeliunas 2018). Eastern Europe is divided into four distinct parts: (1) the Baltic states (Estonia, Latvia, and Lithuania); (2) non-EU and former Soviet states (Belarus, Ukraine, Moldova, and the eastern portions of Russia); (3) Central Eastern Europe (CEE), (Czech Republic, Slovakia, and Hungary); and (4) Southeast Europe (Romania, Bulgaria, Slovenia, Croatia Serbia, Bosnia and Herzegovina, Montenegro, Albania, Kosovo, and Macedonia). The region is ringed on the west by the Scandinavian countries, and the central European countries of Germany and Austria, to southern Europe with Italy and Greece.

The social and economic profiles of Eastern Europe (Estonia, Lithuania, Latvia, Croatia, Hungary, Poland, Slovakia, Slovenia, Bulgaria, Romania, and Czech Republic) reflect diversity in income levels and political orientation. The region is composed of over 105 million citizens (Eurostat 2020b), with average monthly earnings in 2014 ranging from 404 EUR to 1,508 EUR (Eurostat 2020a) (see Figure 2.3). Energy services, such as heating and electricity, comprise a high share of a monthly salary. In 2010, from 6.9% of households in Hungary up to 21.4% of households in Lithuania had a share of energy expenditure in income higher than twice the national median share (EU Energy Poverty Observatory 2020). Figure 2.4 (the percentage of income for first income quintile devoted to household energy expenses in 2015) shows the percentage of salary outlays for energy expenses. In 2015, Lithuania has the lowest with 10%, while Czech Republic has more than 17% of monthly income going to cover energy costs. However, this income ratio does not explain the full story of energy poverty. Figure 2.5 shows the inability of homeowners to keep their homes adequately warm. The difference between countries and the number of homes represents a higher percentage of the population affected by energy poverty. Thirty-one percent of Lithuanians are unable to keep their homes warm in the winter months. Bulgaria returns the highest result (over 40%), while Hungary and Poland give a moderate 10% of households experiencing difficulties.

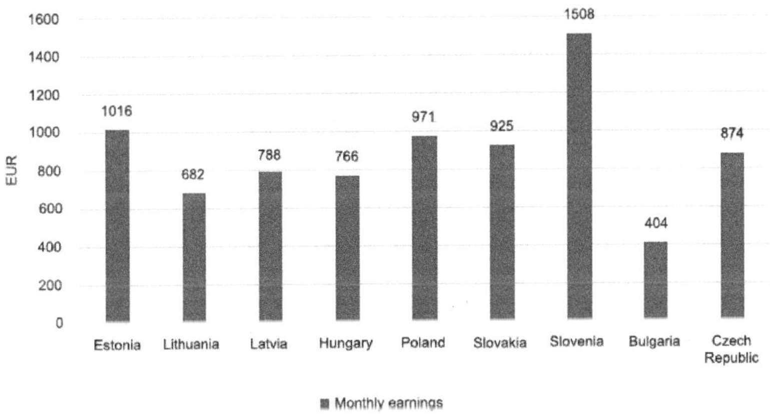

Source: Eurostat (2020a).

Figure 2.3 Income levels of selected East European countries

More recent political moves have seen a rise of right-wing populist movements in Hungary and Poland, and incorporated into the political mix of other countries. Nationalism and anti-Semitism are acceptable forms of public discourse and provide a basis for transformation of state institutions aligned more towards a political and anti-democratic system than to EU democratic norms, thereby prompting investigations by EU institutions on the rule of law. Other regional countries grapple with a range of political parties and ori-

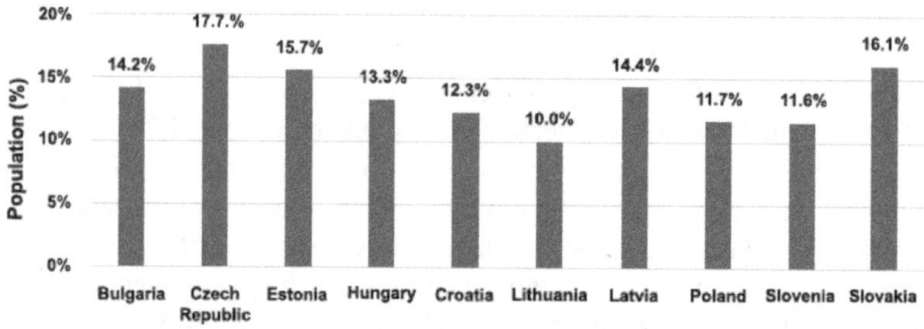

Note: first quintile group represents 20% of the population with the lowest income.
Source: Eurostat (2020d).

Figure 2.4 *Percentage of income for first income quintile devoted to household energy expenses in 2015*

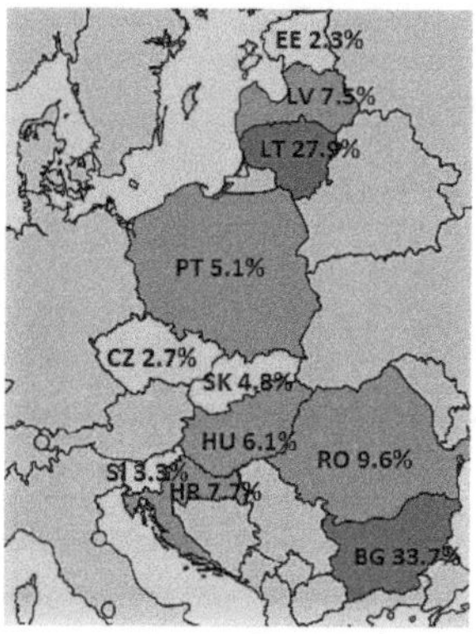

Note: EE = Estonia; LV = Latvia; LT = Lithuania; PT = Poland; CZ = Czech Republic; SK = Slovakia; HU = Hungary; SI = Slovenia; HR = Croatia; RO = Romania; BG = Bulgaria
Source: EU Energy Poverty Observatory (2019a).

Figure 2.5 *Inability to keep homes adequately warm | household (%) | 2018*

entations that split nationalists and pro-EU political parties. Economically, there are also regional differences in Eastern Europe; the Baltic states and the CEE region are most developed in terms of income and GDP (Eurostat 2020a, 2020c). Joining the EU in 2004, they are ahead of the membership of Romania and Bulgaria in 2007 (which also had limitations placed on them). Both the Baltic and CEE regions were at the forefront of privatizations in the energy sector. Countries in the southeast have made strong economic strides, with Croatia joining the EU and Romania and Bulgaria showing strong economic growth and efforts to diversify and cooperate in areas of gas exploration and interconnectors. Belarus and Ukraine are dominated and consumed by events and actions precipitated by Russia acting in its near abroad, such as the annexation of Crimea and military actions in Eastern Ukraine. Uniting most countries in the region continues to be reliance on, or the pursuit away from, Russian gas and nuclear technology, thereby interconnecting energy security and social policies while attempting to realign to EU market requirements.

2.4 ENERGY DEPENDENCY AND INDEPENDENCE IN EASTERN EUROPE

The energy systems in Eastern Europe are marked by high political involvement and can take the shape of maneuvering to restrict the independence of regulatory authorities (LaBelle and Georgiev 2015). Broadly speaking, energy regulators may not serve out their terms in office, either being removed or choosing to resign. Energy companies are controlled either through classification as strategic assets and owned by the state or through restrictive regulatory environments, with strong limits on profits or the inability to reclaim for investment costs. Perceptions and real cases of corruption persist; at a minimum, these undermine public trust while also lending a cloud of suspicion to new initiatives in nuclear and renewable energy projects. In Lithuania and Hungary, nuclear power deals are viewed as a method to siphon off public money (personal communication, Nagevičius 2018; Deak 2016). Regulated household energy prices are effective means for politicians to stay engaged in the energy sector. The region straddles the resource power of Russia with the market authority of the EU. The region struggles with the central question of how to deliver power in a low-cost manner (like within the Soviet model) with Russian sources, but in a competitive market environment structured by the EU.

On January 1, 2009 gas flows between Russia and Ukraine ceased. The dispute between the two countries not only dented Russia's reputation as a reliable supplier but brought to the fore the high gas dependency of the former USSR satellite countries. Gas flows nearly stopped to Bulgaria and Slovakia, which had no alternative supply routes, while Austria, the Czech Republic, Slovenia, Hungary, Poland, and Romania (in this order) were most heavily affected for imports (Pirani, Stern, and Yafimava 2009, 54). While the event was weathered by these countries, it served as a wake-up for proponents of a single European gas market. The Soviet-era system which had limited gas interconnection between countries and low domestic reserves was deemed no longer compatible with the Single Energy Market (SEM). The emergence of the EU's Energy Union is an attempt to build Europe's gas network into a more diversified and flexible system (European Commission 2015b).

Overall, by 2013, Eastern European countries were importing less gas than in the 1990s. Lower demand, economic restructuring, and higher prices are cited as the reason (The Oxford Institute for Energy Studies 2014, 4). Geographically, there are different methods to diversify away from Russia, but the results are apparent in the physical diversification away from Russia. In December 2019, the Balticonnector between Finland and Estonia was inaugurated. Alongside other network improvements, the Baltic countries will connect Finland and Poland, thereby enabling an EU-based gas network to interlink LNG terminals and the broader European gas network. Finland and Estonia have explored the option to build an LNG terminal as a way of reducing their Russian gas dependency (Molin 2014). Lithuania has already demonstrated its push away from Russia by building an LNG terminal to open the country to the global LNG trade (Chapter 3). Lithuania was at the forefront of demonstrating that the old Soviet energy system is replaceable by building electrical interconnectors to Sweden and switching from oil and gas to biomass for district heating.

Further south in Europe, the southeastern Member States of Romania and Bulgaria demonstrate self-sufficiency but also an inability to reform their energy markets. Romania produces its own gas for domestic consumption and does well producing electricity, while also exporting both hydro and nuclear power to neighboring countries. The energy sector is a mix of private and public ownership in distribution companies. Nonetheless, Bulgaria has high energy poverty rates and inconsistent energy policies. The constant changes in Bulgarian energy policy saw it order and then cancel a contract with Rosatom for a new nuclear power plant. Now the country must repay Russia 550 million EUR for cancelling the project (Pitchford 2016). In 2013, Bulgaria was selected to be the landing site of the new Russian South Stream gas pipeline. However, this was later cancelled in favor of a Turkish route. Constant leadership changes in the energy regulator and state-owned firms leave the energy sector in a constant state of flux (LaBelle and Georgiev 2015).

The four Central European countries comprising the 'Visegrad Four' – Czech Republic, Hungary, Poland, and Slovakia – each have their own stories. The Czech Republic has shifted its gas sector by importing from Germany and Austria (Net4Gas 2018). Domestic coal is an important source for heating (as well as gas) and is used for electricity production (DBDH 2015) along with nuclear power. Overall, due to its proximity to Germany, diversification of infrastructure has linked the German and Czech energy markets. During the Communist period, when Slovakia and the Czech Republic were one (Czechoslovakia), nuclear power plants (NPPs) were built, with one being shut down in exchange for EU membership (like Lithuania's conditions). In 2020, a new NPP built as a joint venture between Italian Enel and the Slovak state, attempted to begin operation after years of cost overruns and safety concerns (*Power Technology* n.d.). Further south, Slovenia shares a nuclear power plant with Croatia, and both countries have diversified gas imports, receiving imports mainly directly from Russia or Austria, which imports between 75% to 100% of its gas from Russia (Eurostat 2019). Figure 2.6 shows the share of imported gas in final energy consumption compared with the share of renewable energy in consumption. In all countries there is a significant reliance on imports compared with consumption from renewables, demonstrating the significant efforts necessary to increase renewables as a viable source to displace imported gas.

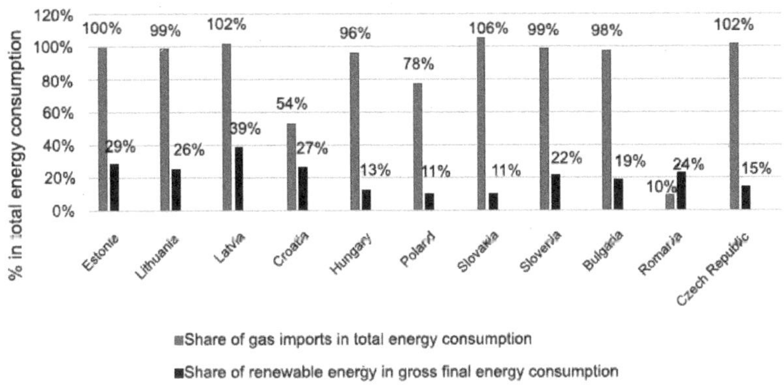

Source: Eurostat (2018b, 2019).

Figure 2.6 *Share of gas imports to final energy consumption compared with renewable energy in final energy consumption*

In Eastern Europe, the past and future energy system revolves around four energy technologies and resources: coal, gas, nuclear, and hydroelectricity. Overall, the region is marked by high energy import dependency, ranging from 76% of total energy consumption in Lithuania, up to around 23% in Romania in 2017, with the exception of Estonia with a small dependency of only 4%, and with some countries heavily dependent on electricity imports from the post-Soviet states of Russia, Belarus, and Ukraine of around 25% (Eurostat 2018a). The exceptions are the Czech Republic and Poland which produce and export solid fuels (lignite) and hard coal. For natural gas, only Romania has significant production, with only around 2% of gas imports, and Hungary, producing nearly 30% of its own gas. Other countries import more than 95% of their demand for gas. The percentage of renewable energy in the mix ranges from 11% in Poland to 39% in Latvia in 2017 (Eurostat 2018b), with Romania's hydroelectric generation capacity accounting for 7% of electricity production, and with overall renewables accounting for nearly 30% of electricity generation in 2015.

Eastern Europe displays a roughly homogeneous collection of resource-poor countries dependent on Soviet and now Russian gas, along with Soviet and Russian nuclear technology. Domestic coal production remains, and a limited willingness to build renewable energy generation. Energy intensity and consumption are highly based on industry and households' inefficacies. Households are price sensitive due to low salaries, compared to the households of older EU Member States (see above). Energy prices are kept low for household consumers, continuing the Soviet-era practice of subsidized utility costs matched with lower salaries. The prices of coal, gas, and electricity from nuclear power and hydro are four categories that directly influence the prices of home heating and electricity consumption, with gas and electricity network costs an important fifth price component affecting consumers.

2.5 COMPARATIVE STUDY AND CASE STUDY SELECTION

Each new member to the EU was required to meet similar conditions to join. For some, this meant shutting down nuclear power plants while for others it required disconnecting from the Soviet-era electricity transmission system facing the Commonwealth of Independent States. Each country also went through multiple rounds of privatization with the infusion of FDI. There was no standard model, and just as each country has a diverse set of energy mixes, so their experiences are variegated in terms of implementing EU reforms and retaining state ownership depending on natural resources and the technological legacy of the Soviet-era energy system (Bouzarovski 2009, 461). This diversity is essential to understand – and appreciate – when selecting which countries to compare with regard to post-unification experiences and transformations.

There could be an obvious comparison of energy import and export levels between Member States or a comparison of changes in Russian gas flows to the former COMECON countries. Selecting a country based on quantitative indicators is a viable option, and one that is moderately weighted in the country selection. However, in selecting case studies for this book, a qualitative consideration is given to strong narratives of pro- and anti-EU policy alignment. If Eastern Europe is the site of a variegated post-Communist landscape, then it is also a place of diverse stories that communicate the unique national and international energy cultures. Therefore, the idea was to identify countries with unique examples that exemplify the acceptance or rejection of a Russian- or EU-oriented energy system.

Looking for and using unique stories provides a means to:

> communicate with, influence, and engage audiences; they serve as artefacts to be investigated in terms of content, actors, relationships, power, and structure; they can be used to gather information, provide insight, and reframe evidence in ways that more science-ordered formats miss. (Moezzi, Janda, and Rotmann 2017, 1)

Stories and the narratives around policies and infrastructure building provide a means to examine culture and the contestation that creates energy cultures in Eastern Europe. Table 2.1 provides a broad description of characteristics exemplifying potential case studies that can expose underlying social, political, and economic contestations within national energy systems. These broadly align with the three categories descriptive of energy cultures (described in Chapter 1). By understanding that both the social and physical energy systems require representation and necessitate analysis, then country selection can also be informed by the role of contrasting relations within the case studies.

Table 2.1 *Characteristics for country case study selection*

Empirical characteristics	Conceptual energy cultures description
Political support to honor social pact to maintain low energy prices or retain/reject culturally significant technologies and resources from the communist period within the 'social energy system'	**Social Energy System:** Energy cultures are broadly relationally transformative (relations)
Social and political support to maintain or reject Communist-era technologies and resources, or embrace an EU-oriented track of renewables, energy efficiency, and security of supply described in the Energy Union strategy	**Physical energy system:** Energy cultures are a physical expression of relations (explicit)
Acceptance or rejection of EU and/or Russian objectives in transforming the national energy system towards a Single Energy Market	**Power:** Energy cultures are socially and economically transformative and reliant on power relations (implicit)

The physical orientation of a country's energy system can be seen in countries building new energy projects, which either break from or continue the Soviet legacy of resource and technology dependency on Russia, and which also accept or reject EU market, resource, and technology preferences. Energy technology is at the center of an energy system and represents choices affecting security, social, environmental, innovation, and economic impacts within each country.

The social orientation of a country's energy system rests on the accepted rules and regulations informing the operations of a national energy system. Here, pricing and social dialogue or political commitments reflect deeper structural relations within the energy system. Respect for or rejection of the EU's governance system, or the assertion of nationalistic sentiment on defending or dismantling energy infrastructure, reflects deeper power relations within society. The social energy system provides a strong influence on the orientation and operation of the energy system and needs to be considered in the selection of countries.

2.5.1 Country selection: the trajectory of secure and interlinked energy markets

There are three countries that provide a unique and strong perspective on rejecting and accepting energy technologies and market conditions. The governments of Hungary, Lithuania, and Poland have made strong financial commitments to building energy infrastructure (such as LNG and nuclear) that is functionally symbolic of their orientations. Lithuania's decision to lease an LNG ship and convert district heating to domestically source biomass, Poland's decision to build an LNG terminal and continue high levels of coal generation, and Hungary's agreement with Rosatom to expand the Paks nuclear power plant provide the foundations of a new energy system in Eastern Europe. Each LNG and nuclear project has regional dimensions affecting the energy markets and security for its neighbors. These technology decisions reverberate throughout Eastern Europe, through the EU's Single Energy Market, thereby increasing reverberations of policy decisions. Lithuanian LNG benefits all Baltic states, while Hungarian nuclear power displaces renewables, gas, and coal.

These three case studies differentiate from efforts in other Eastern Member States, such as the Czech Republic, Slovakia, Romania, Bulgaria, and Slovenia, which also seek to build interconnectors for electricity and gas and improve the internal energy market (IEM) while boosting the security of supplies. In one sense, diversification through a network approach is an underlying strategy of this group of countries. What sets the three case study countries apart is their financial and political commitment to building 'primary' energy facilities in the form of LNG and nuclear facilities, along with grappling with similar domestic social and political issues underlying Eastern Europe's conversion to a market economy within the EU.

In the area of nuclear power, excluding Poland, each of these countries also has Soviet era NPP. They now need to consider renewing their fleets of nuclear reactors, and they will need to decide the nationality of the company that can build new nuclear facilities. Slovakia is the furthest along in building a new NPP, with Italian Enel – demonstrating a Western orientation in its power sector. However, Hungary is the only country in the EU that chose to continue its Eastern orientation by choosing Rosatom to build the new NPP, thereby continuing the previous technical relationship with Russia. Therefore, Hungary is unique in prolonging the Soviet-era technological and scientific relationship with Russia. This is a decision that other Eastern European countries are in the process of deciding on, therefore it is important to understand how and why Hungary made the decision to continue cooperation. In contrast, the shutting down of Lithuania's Ignalina NPP, as a condition of EU membership, is reflective of common experiences of other post-2004 Member States. Thus, this is representative of wider experiences and it is important to understand how the country adapted to the removal of 90% of its domestic electricity generation. While this is an extreme example, it also reveals the necessary steps the country needed to make in a short period of time to maintain a high level of security of supply and long-term energy security. As other countries in Eastern Europe are forced to shut down aging nuclear and coal power plants, Lithuania's experience can assist in understanding how a country adapts to new generation technologies and network expansion fostered by the EU's effort to build a Single Energy Market (SEM).

Diversification efforts in the EU also include building new gas interconnectors between countries and tapping into LNG facilitates. The European Commission laid out this strategy in the 2015 Energy Union strategy (European Commission 2015b) by citing energy security challenges as necessary to reduce external supply disruptions and build the SEM – multiple supplier points and facilitation of gas flows to 'gas islands', as the EU Commissioner for Climate Action and Energy, Miguel Arias Cañete stated:

> After the gas crises of 2006 and 2009 that left many millions out in the cold, we said: 'Never again'. But the stress tests of 2014 showed we are still far too vulnerable to major disruption of gas supplies. And the political tensions on our borders are a sharp reminder that this problem is will not just go away. Today's proposals are about a reliable, competitive and flexible system in which energy flows across borders and consumers reap the benefits. They are about standing together to protect the most vulnerable. (European Commission 2016b)

Poland and Lithuania were and are vulnerable to gas supply disruptions and demonstrate an alignment with the EU in diversifying by building LNG terminals and expanding their gas networks. These two countries are the only ones in Eastern Europe to have built LNG terminals that can enable all of Eastern Europe to benefit from diversification as the gas network expands. Therefore, these countries are at the forefront of gas diversification and can demonstrate both the financial investment into diversification and the price paid for improving energy security. Therefore, it is important to understand and look more closely at each country to understand why diversification and breaking away from Russian gas was so important. These case studies can highlight the economic and political costs of diversification. In contrast, Hungary remains wedded to Russian gas, either shipped via Ukraine or Austria. Therefore, it provides a contrasting example of limited diversification from the previous political era of Communism.

Coal remains a dominant generation force in Eastern Europe. Phasing out coal is meeting with resistance, with the European Commission acknowledging the challenges by introducing a European Green Deal, which vows to spend 100 billion EUR between 2021–7 on a Just Transition Mechanism (JTM), to assist a social-facing energy transition. Poland provides an effective representative case study to address issues around phasing out coal. Half of all coal-related jobs in the EU are in Poland, followed by Germany and then the three Eastern European countries of the Czech Republic, Romania, and Bulgaria (European Commission Joint Research Centre 2018, 2). Whether it is phasing out or building new coal-fired power plants along with expanding mining operations, Poland provides an example of a country both grappling with and seeking ways to sustain or transition away from its use. The Polish coal sector is the largest in Europe. Over 100,000 workers are employed in direct jobs in mines to power plants. In comparison, Germany is second with 35,700 jobs (European Commission Joint Research Centre 2018, 21). Poland provides an information-rich case study to understand why and how a country attempts to retain coal, but also meet EU requirements of a net-zero emissions future by 2050.

Choosing the case study countries requires consideration of quantitative data which demonstrate unique characteristics of the energy system, such as production statistics or financial costs. However, the qualitative aspects, and consideration of narratives and the ability to convey the challenges of integrating into the EU's SEM, also emerge as important considerations. Therefore, the choice of Hungary, Lithuania, and Poland provides a cross-section of issues involving political, financial, and social commitments. Selection of other countries would expose other unique aspects of EU integration efforts and a switch away from the Communist-era energy system. The selection of these three case studies is intended to represent deliberate choices in large-scale infrastructure projects which also must contend with social and cultural elements that influence the development of the energy system. The EU's commitment of 100 billion EUR for a social-facing energy policy is indicative of the importance society now plays in shaping the EU's energy system. Discussed next is a general overview of the three case studies to better understand the embeddedness of the Soviet-era energy infrastructure and the transition towards the EU's Single Energy Market.

Data collection for the case studies relies on secondary and primary sources. Understanding the impact of policies along with the future development of the energy system required the use of both qualitative and quantitative data collection methods. In-person interviews were conducted in each of the three countries between the spring of 2018 and the spring of 2019. Lithuania was visited once during a two-week period in May and June 2018, when 24 in-person interviews were conducted. Follow-up interviews were also carried out. Poland was visited multiple times, with two distinct field research trips occurring in November 2018 and April 2019, with a total of 17 interviews conducted. However, this author's background provides substantial research experiences in both Poland and Hungary. In a previous study, 27 interviews were conducted in Poland (LaBelle 2017a); other research publications also included a substantial amount of time traveling in Poland and conducting in-person interviews and internet-based interviews and correspondence (Goldthau and LaBelle 2012; LaBelle 2012a; 2012b; 2018), mainly over a ten-year period. Likewise, the author's experience of living, working, and researching in Hungary over a 15-year period is reflected in multiple publications on the country (Kaderjak et al. 2007; M. LaBelle 2006; LaBelle and Kaderják 2008; LaBelle 2009; LaBelle and Deak 2015; LaBelle and Georgiev 2015), which lends further depth to the analysis.

Providing a full methodological breakdown is possible to fit a normative framing of formal data collection methods such as in-person interviews or analysis of Eurostat datasets. And these methods and proper data analysis are carried out and reviewed in the chapters. However, it is also important to account for the subjective experience of the researcher. Drawing on experience for a book on energy culture enables this researcher's anthropological experience in the region to inform the overall analysis of energy transition. This experience began in 1998 when he was teaching English to RWE German executives managing the privatized Budapest electricity works (ELMU-EMASZ). The meaning of culture, as is framed in this book, can take on a formal and academic form, but this author acknowledges the subjective experience of more than two decades of personal experience in Eastern Europe. This experience works to shape a perspective on geopolitics, culture, and the interplay of society, economics, and politics. The case studies presented next represent both an objective and subjective collection and analysis of data which meets a high academic standard. But there is also an acknowledgment of an almost Eastern European bias towards the dramatic physical and governance changes to the regions' energy system. Besides international attention paid to Polish coal or Russian gas, there remains a void of understanding how Eastern Europeans perceive their energy system. This book contributes to uncovering the relations that make up the energy system in the three countries.

2.5.2 Lithuania: accidental diversity

In 1990, Lithuania's energy sector was characterized by an oversupply of electricity. With collapsing industrial demand the sector was oversupplied, with very little potential to export to neighboring countries going through the economic transition from centralized to market-based economies.
There were three key characteristics of the sector:

- Below market energy prices
- Limited or no metering of energy production and consumption
- Limited incentives for energy efficiency. (IAEA 2004, 11)

The basis for the modern Lithuania energy sector was the Ignalina Nuclear Power Plant in Visaginas. The plant operated from 1983 to 2010. It held two reactors producing 1500 MW each. In 1993, it produced 88% of the county's electricity (Abaraviciene n.d.). The reactor design was the same as the Chernobyl Nuclear Power Plant and, despite investments to improve the safety of the plant, membership of the EU was conditional on decommissioning the plant.

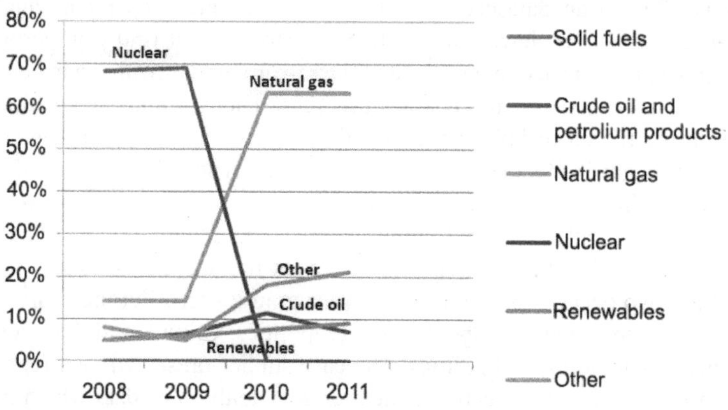

Source: European Commission 2015a, 141.

Figure 2.7 Gross electricity generation mix 2008–11 in Lithuania

In 2012, after the closure of Ignalina NPP, Lithuania became a net importer of electricity, mainly imported from Russia, while imported natural gas replaced domestic nuclear electricity generation (European Commission 2015a). Figure 2.7 shows the shift from nuclear to natural gas for electricity production between 2009 and 2010.

After the closure of Ignalina NPP, Lithuania became even more heavily reliant on Russia for its energy supplies. There were three key infrastructure projects that opened the country to regional electricity markets and the global trade in LNG. Two electricity transmission lines were built. NordBalt has 700 MW capacity (400 kV) stretching from Klaipeda, Lithuania to Nybro, Sweden. The LitPol Link has a capacity of 500 MW (400 kV), linking the electrical grids of Lithuania and Poland (European Commission 2015a, 146). The third project was building a floating liquefied LNG terminal (FSRU) to receive global shipments of gas. This was commissioned at the end of 2014 and has resulted in the country receiving lower-priced gas from Russia. In addition, Lithuania has increased the amount of renewable energy from wind (48% of RES) with plans to reach 23% by 2020 (Ministry of Energy of the Republic of Lithuania 2017). Chapter 3 provides a full account of the Lithuanian case study.

2.5.3 Hungary: political dependence

Historically, Hungary is poor in 'traditional' energy resources. Coal, gas, and oil are extracted but of are poor quality or limited. Hungary needed to boost energy output to grow economically. During the Communist period the state invested heavily into energy projects. Growth in this sector strongly tied Hungary to Russia in the area of oil, gas, and nuclear power. Regional integration with COMECON countries leveled out Hungary's energy imports – including electricity imports. Hungary operates under a 'scarcity' model, so providing for its own energy needs – even during non-market days – was expensive. Therefore, to achieve greater energy independence was viewed as highly expensive and impractical. Joint projects with Russia and other COMECON countries were viable and affordable solutions to Hungary's pressing energy needs.

In 1958, the National Planning Office stated to fulfill the objectives of the country, "must ensure above all ... the development of the energy base" (Berend and Csato 2001, 1:325). 1958 also marked an overall change in approach for the Soviet bloc of COMECON countries, away from national energy self-sufficiency to regional cooperation of COMECON countries (Berend and Csato 2001, 1:326). This decision enabled the building of a regional power grid between COMECON countries (Berend and Csato 2001, 1:327). Hungary became part of the United Energy System (CDU) which was managed in Prague, enabling electricity imports to be better coordinated into Hungary (Bernat 1989, 131).

Importantly, trade balances including either hard currency or the Soviet style of bartering of goods made Hungary's increasing imports expensive by any measure. "Increasing imports [of energy] necessitates increasing exports of agricultural and/or industrial products" (Bernat 1989, 117). Greater electrification of transportation and energy efficiency measures were important to cut oil imports (Bernat 1989, 117).

Hungary's current electricity mix is still dominated by nuclear power and natural gas (see Figure 2.8). In 2015, imported gas accounted for 70% of Hungary's gas consumption (Directorate-General for Energy 2017). Much of this is Russian gas which might flow directly from Russia or be imported to Hungary through Slovakia or Austria. While spot trading of gas is on the increase, and therefore a 'market price' exists, Hungary still maintains a long-term bilateral gas agreement with Gazprom. Visits by Gazprom executives and Russian officials often revolve around well-publicized gas and nuclear agreements. Nuclear power is over 40% of the Hungarian energy mix.

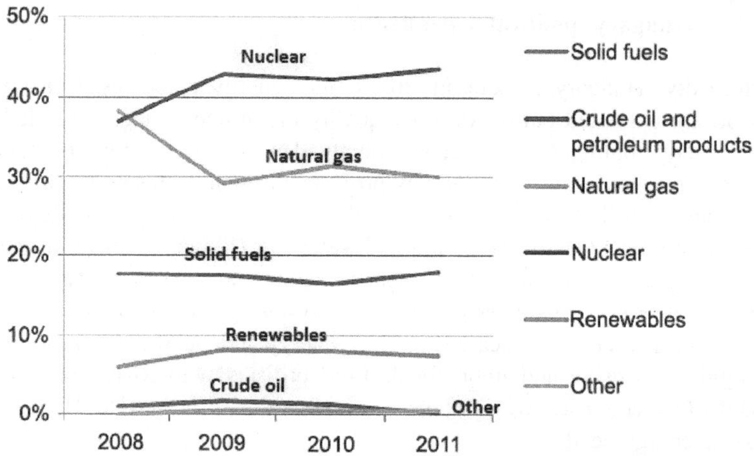

Source: Cited from EU Energy in Figures: Pocketbook 2012–13 (Directorate-General for Energy 2017); LaBelle and Deak (2015, 106).

Figure 2.8 *Gross electricity generation mix 2008–11 in Hungary*

An additional 2 MW are being built by Russia to eventually replace the aging reactors providing nearly 50% of the country's energy supply.

2.5.4 Poland: coal over modernity

Poland maintains a consistent energy strategy with a political vision and economic strategy to retain fossil fuels while constraining the use of RET; this spans political parties and governments. In 2013, former Prime Minister Donald Tusk (2007–14) stated that coal and "soon shale gas" will remain dominant with renewable energy sources remaining "limited as much as EU rules will allow" (PHYS.ORG 2013). In addition, for energy security, "the exploration and production of shale gas seems to be absolutely crucial" (CBC News 2012). In 2015, Polish elections ushered in a new government, under which continuity remains with support for fossil fuels and suppression of RET. Poland's Energy Minister, Krzysztof Tchorzewski, asserted that the EU's pursuit of zero carbon emissions in the power sector by 2050 is impossible to apply to Poland, stating: "we (Poland) reject that, clearly unacceptable." The sacrifices for Poland would be too great to move away from coal. Rather, Poland will pursue an energy strategy that utilizes high-efficiency coal-fired power plants that require less coal for power output. As such, the capacity of renewables should be limited to 10%, as the grid cannot handle more and variable power output reduces efficiency of coal power plants, meaning there is no more room for renewables (Tchorzewski 2016). Therefore, policy continuity in limiting RET and promoting fossil fuels remains.

Poland's future continues to envision a significant role for fossil fuels. Diversification with gas provides a hedge against high carbon prices and a slight greening of the energy sector. Poland remains committed to fossil fuels for socio-economic reasons, subverting environmental impacts to the larger economic and social goals of economic expansion and social stability. The domestic energy sector is centered on state-owned enterprises which are expanding the use of fossil fuels. The latest large-scale project is the state-owned LNG terminal in Swinoujscie, Poland; this is now spurring expansion of the domestic and regional gas network. The terminal contributes to increased security of supply (access to global markets) and contributes to fuel diversification.

2.6 CONCLUSION

The resolve after WWII for the prevention of further military conflicts in Europe led to the creation of the European Coal and Steel Community. Tying together the energy resources and production capacity of the major European countries set the continent on course for a major political and economic realignment. The emergence of the Cold War and the splintering of Europe into two resulted in functionally and politically different economic and social development zones. The development of separate energy cultures is apparent in both the energy technologies and the consumption habits and financial abilities of households. Membership into the EU brought Eastern Member States into new political and economic relations along with revolutionizing the interaction of people. After security of supply brought about by the Ukraine-Russia dispute in 2009, energy security became a driving force attempting to integrate Europe's energy system. This was not always successful.

The focus on the three case-study country's energy mixes demonstrates a continued reliance on Russian resources and technologies, albeit with important shifts towards the EU. As will be discussed in the three following chapters, each country pursues its own unique path towards building an energy system aligned with its energy culture. Poland pursues a strategy of building more coal-fired plants, while Hungary is building new nuclear reactors. Both rely on Russian relations to ensure delivery. Lithuania, after being forced to close its nuclear power plant by the EU, remains friendly, but seeks to diversify away from the EU. Each country chose the energy technologies and resources used to generate electricity and heat. States continue to be able to influence their domestic markets based on choosing electricity generation technologies and areas of expertise to invest in. Only Lithuania has plans to strongly pursue sustainable energy. These descriptions contrast against the role of ACER and asserting power over regulatory conditions and market access. It becomes an expression of government (over infrastructure) and governance (rules and regulations) that drive change. The political intent in each of the three countries is to lower consumer prices, while maintaining authority and independence, despite EU efforts for greater integration.

3. Lithuania: the battle for independence

3.1 INTRODUCTION: FROM THE SOVIET UNION TO THE EUROPEAN UNION

The shifting geopolitical order in Eastern Europe, and even more so in the post-Soviet states of the Baltics, exposes significant shifts in the supply and generation of electricity and heat. This chapter describes Lithuania's turn away from the Soviet-era energy system and the uptake of EU market reforms and diversification of energy supplies and technologies. Of all the countries joining the EU from the Eastern Bloc, Lithuania demonstrates the most dramatic shift away from Russian policies of low gas prices and emphasis on the security of supply to ensure greater independence. Policy makers, entrepreneurs, and society chose democracy, transparency, and a transition towards an economically affordable and environmentally sustainable energy system. Lithuania captures the story of the level of independence achievable by investing in technologies and supply diversification while dealing with historical infrastructure and cultural attributes of the previous political-economic energy system.

Discussed next is how Lithuania left the Soviet Union and its centrally managed economic system and 15 years later joined the EU and the push for an open and competitive Single Energy Market (SEM). The closure of the Soviet-era nuclear power plant and network integration with Sweden and Poland opened routes for low-priced electricity. Firms and state institutions found innovative ways to break from Russian dependence, such as utilizing biomass for heating, building an LNG regasification port with its floating regasification ship, and tapping into neighboring markets for electricity. This chapter describes how in less than a decade the country's energy system was dramatically transformed from total reliance on Russia for resources and technology to a diversified electricity system networked to neighboring countries, able to receive LNG shipments, and converting biomass to supply 80% of district heating needs. More recently, as will be described next, Lithuania has shifted from this 'war of independence' towards building a long-term sustainable energy system integrating with the EU Single Energy Market.

3.2 SHUTTING DOWN THE SOVIET ERA

Lithuania is a country that was tightly integrated into the Soviet Union, with armed conflict and occupation by Soviet forces, with the battle for political independence only achievable in 1991. Since its 2004 EU membership, this country of 2.8 million people adapted an open EU model for energy diversity. In the 1990s, Lithuania's energy sector produced an oversupply of electricity. With collapsing industrial demand, the energy sector had below-market prices, limited metering of consumption, and limited incentives for energy efficiency programs (IAEA 2004, 11). The country was set for a dramatic change in its energy infrastructure if it wanted to join the EU in 2004.

The basis for the modern Lithuania energy sector was the Ignalina Nuclear Power Plant in Visaginas. The Soviet-era plant operated from 1983 to 2010. It held two reactors producing 1,500 MW each. In 1993, it produced almost 90% of the county's electricity. The reactor design was the same as the Chernobyl Nuclear Power Plant, with an MKB reactor, and despite investments to improve the safety of the plant, membership of the EU was conditional on decommissioning the plant. In 2009, after the closure of Ignalina NPP, Lithuania became a net importer of electricity, mainly from Russia. Figure 2.7 (in Chapter 2) shows how imported natural gas for electricity production replaced domestic nuclear electricity generation after 2009 when there was a dramatic decline from nearly 70% of the electricity mix produced from nuclear power to zero in 2010 (European Commission 2015a, 141).

From a local perspective, membership to the EU and the requirement to close Ignalina "killed the golden goose", as stated by the (now former) mayor of Visaginas, Dalia Straupaite. From her perspective, if Lithuania was a nuclear-powered country, then it should stay one because it was an "achievement" that brought the best scientists from the Soviet Union to the country (personal communication, Straupaite 2018). For Straupaite, and more than a few Lithuanians, the 'killing' of Ignalina was too high a political price to joining the EU, as the technology was viewed as functioning well, with a built-in life expectancy until 2022. Also, the human capital and infrastructure to maintain the existing power plant was available and there was even sufficient capacity to build a new nuclear power plant (personal communication, Janeliunas 2018). Nonetheless, decommissioning the plant, which operated for only 29% of its expected life, required employing the same people that built it; we are "using the manpower that built it, using know-how that's in their head," as there is a lack of documentation and sub-standard construction (personal communication, Sabaitiene 2018). Views on Ignalina represent a broader social conflict on nuclear power.

After an agreement was signed with the EU in 1999 to close Ignalina, the country sought ways to build a new nuclear power station. However, continuing with nuclear power failed for two reasons. First, nuclear power became politicized, not over safety but over support or opposition by political parties. Politicization came in the form of two referendums on nuclear power. The first, held in 2008, failed due to low voter turnout, while the second, held in 2012 – alongside national elections, was a non-binding referendum where 63% of voters stated they did not want additional nuclear capacity to be built (World Nuclear Association 2017). Concerns around potential corruption and the environment, along with party politics, influenced this vote (personal communication, Nagevičius 2018). Second, the ability to import cheaper electricity from neighboring countries through existing connections with Russia and Belarus, along with the newly built interconnectors to Sweden and Poland, made new nuclear uncompetitive on price alone. The 'golden goose' that supplied the country with low-priced electricity and high scientific knowledge was irreplaceable.

3.3 HOUSEHOLD HEATING

Domestically, the social price of energy, and in particular heat, appears to be very high for many households in Lithuania. Figure 3.1 shows the percentage of households in Lithuania that have trouble keeping their homes adequately warm in the winter. Around 30% of homes in 2016 had trouble, with about 10% of households behind on their utility bills. The 2011 spike of gas generation coincided with higher Russian imports and an increase in gas prices. In September 2010, Lithuania paid an estimated 30 EUR/MWh; by January 2012 this had increased to more than 40 EUR/MWh (Pakalkaite 2016, 15) with a strong increase in 2011. This price increase coincided with homeowners' difficulty in paying their utility bills and a big jump in keeping homes adequately warm, as shown in Figure 3.1. Collectively, the price of electricity and gas and the final conversion to home heating holds a social impact. As will be described below, Lithuania took steps to diversify away from Russian resources and technologies to improve the social impact of energy.

Since Lithuania earned its independence from the Soviet Union, two periods mark the transition towards integration into the EU. This statement was released in May 2018: "The previous energy strategy was a wartime energy strategy. This has changed to a new peacetime energy strategy" (personal communication, Janeliunas 2018). The 'wartime' strategy picked up speed in 2008 when the Lithuanian government and parliament decided to 'fight' the Gazprom monopoly by fighting for and adopting provisions in the EU's Third Energy Package which would allow diversification requirements and ownership unbundling. The result was the perceived retaliation by Russia in the

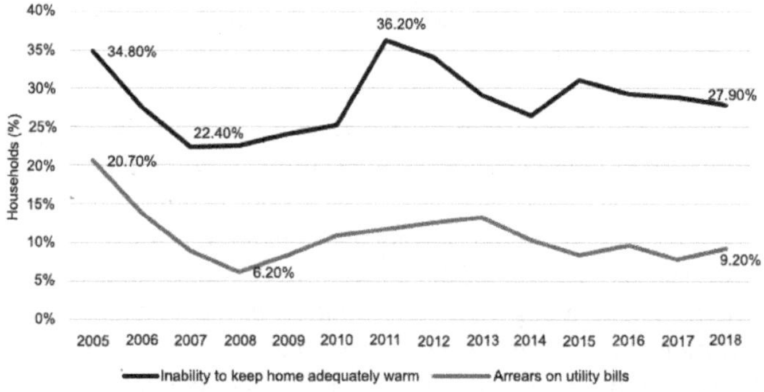

Source: Eurostat (2020a, 2020b).

Figure 3.1 *Inability to keep homes warm and utility arrears 2005–18, Lithuania*

price of Russian gas, which increased in Lithuania by 30–40%; "even Latvia had 20% cheaper gas" (personal communication, Lithuanian Energy Ministry Official A 2018). Nonetheless, as discussed next, the long-term result was lower-priced gas and electricity for industry and households.

The second stage began in 2018, with the adoption by the Lithuanian Parliament (Seimas) of the National Energy Independence Strategy. The revised strategy focuses on further integration with Poland and more local power production using biomass, solar, and wind (Ministry of Energy of the Republic of Lithuania 2018). The side effect of modernization is that the end-user price will likely increase. Drawing on interviews with government officials it is clear there is an awareness that prices will need to increase to prompt investments into domestic (green) generation. High electricity imports, marked by low prices, from Nordic countries, along with 30% from Belarus and Kaliningrad, raises the awareness of the need for incentives to stimulate construction of domestic generation (personal communications, Lithuanian Energy Ministry Official A 2018; Molis 2018). Nonetheless, as will be described next, the 'wartime' energy strategy had diversification as the primary objective with the knowledge it could remove the monopolistic position of Russian companies and (with luck) bring in lower prices.

3.4 FROM ENERGY DEPENDENCY TO INDEPENDENCE

Lithuania is shifting the sources of its energy supplies away from Russia. Diversification efforts are dropping Russian-sourced energy supplies "from 80% in 2012 to 55% by 2016 and 35% in 2020" (World Nuclear Association 2017). This diversification achievement was largely accomplished by three important infrastructure projects that have integrated the country regionally and globally: (1) in 2015, two electricity transmission lines came online linking neighboring countries. NordBalt has 700 MW capacity (400 kV) stretching from Klaipeda, Lithuania to Nybro, Sweden. The capacity of LitPol Link is 500 MW (400 kV), linking the electrical grids of Lithuania and Poland (European Commission 2015a, 146); (2) in 2014, a floating liquefied LNG terminal (FSRU) was stationed in Klaipeda to receive global shipments of gas; and (3) by 2020 there is a 23% RES target, marked by over 80% of district heating being based on biomass and wind already accounting for half of RES production (Ministry of Energy of the Republic of Lithuania 2017). Further diversification is planned to link Lithuania's gas system with Poland's by 2021 and to end the frequency synchronization with Russia's electricity system (for back-up assistance) by interconnecting with the EU system through Poland by 2025. These diversification efforts, taken together, changed the network, resource, and technology orientation of Lithuania away from Russia and towards neighboring EU Member States.

Historically, as part of the Soviet Union, Lithuania's electricity sector was fully integrated into the USSR and then the Commonwealth of Independent States (CIS). With EU membership, the development of Nordbalt and LitPol allowed diversification and expansion into two regional markets. Network integration was an explicit choice by Lithuania to integrate into the EU's electricity network and diversify generation. As described above, the next step is for the country to synchronize the frequency of its electricity system, which differs between the European system and the Soviet-era system that connected all of Eastern Europe. To interconnect with the rest of Europe, Lithuania and the other Baltic countries need to build a network of back-up power stations and physically disconnect from Russia and other former CIS states. Diversification of the gas system, as discussed next, is not reliant on physically altering the network; rather, diversification relies on a maritime strategy.

3.4.1 Diversification of gas supplies

The *Independence* is a Floating Storage and Regasification Unit (FSRU) facility squeezed into a ship the size of three football fields. The 'LNG ship' and its immense land-based infrastructure sit at the Klaipeda Harbor, located behind a spit of the Baltic Sea, and a UNESCO protected nature area, in Lithuania. Sixty km further along the spit is Kaliningrad, Russia. The river-fed harbor has strong currents that keep it open year-round, enabling LNG deliveries even in the freezing Baltic winters. The task of the *Independence* is to idle in the harbor and unload up to 4 bcm a year of gas cargo from LNG tankers. The ship is a working symbol of the cost of Eastern Europe's energy dependence and independence.

The ship can meet 90% of the Baltic's yearly gas consumption. There are two options for the unloaded LNG cargo: distribute it by smaller LNG ships in the Baltic region or pipe it to the underground storage facility in Latvia. The cargo directly competes against Russian gas. Financing of the LNG facility comes from a surcharge on bills placed on all industrial and household consumers. The purpose of the *Independence* is to break Gazprom's monopoly and introduce price competition. In 2014, Lithuania paid Gazprom 48 EUR/100 kg, before the LNG facility; in 2016, it paid 25.98 EUR/100 kg (Hinchey and Mikulska 2017). While the global price of gas also dropped during this period, the higher price Lithuania paid compared with its neighbors – before the *Independence* – indicates that diversification also drives competition and lower-priced gas for Lithuanian consumers (Pakalkaite 2016, 15).

The fight for gas independence began in 2008. After the Baltic states joined the EU in 2004, it was the explicit strategy of Gazprom to raise gas prices to Western European levels by 2007 (Pakalkaite 2016). Further, as Lithuania worked against Russian interests and ownership, it regained ownership of its domestic gas companies by strictly applying the EU's Third Energy Package. The impact of this independence strategy is in 2011 gas prices: Lithuania paid 15–20% more than Latvia and Estonia respectively, who did not work against Gazprom (Pakalkaite 2016, 15–16). Exacerbating this relationship – compared with the limited antagonistic attitudes of Estonia and Latvia towards Russia – were the diversification efforts of the LNG regasification ship and terminal, along with the use of biomass in DH, rather than gas.

It is important to consider the role of the Third Energy Package in the government's political maneuvering to regain control of Lithuania's gas sector from Russian and German ownership. Supply and distribution were controlled by Gazprom and E.ON Ruhrgas, with the Lithuanian state essentially locked out by the ownership arrangement and backing of the two foreign governments. The arrangement in the Baltic states, before the Third Energy Package, is best described by Pakalkaite:

> Gazprom, together with E.ON Ruhrgas, has a stake in the form of shares in the local transmission system operators, which themselves hold dominant or near dominant

> positions in transmission, distribution and supply businesses in Estonia, Latvia and Lithuania. (Pakalkaite 2012, 12)

The Lithuanian state used EU directives (which it pushed during the drafting stage) in the Third Energy Package and Security of Supply Regulation to liberalize and break Gazprom's monopoly over gas supplies, and push for their sale, thereby gaining indirect ownership over the gas companies. This was done to fulfill the interpretation by the Lithuanian government of its obligations under EU Directives. In Lithuania, national politicians, in consecutive governments, supported diversification and plans for the *Independence*. The diversification battle began in 2008 and can be said to have been symbolically concluded with the installation of the FGRU *Independence* at the end of 2014, and only just in time as the long-term contract with Gazprom ended in 2015.

Finally, the *Independence* FSRU is a symbol of the success of EU integration, as much as Ignalina is a symbol of Soviet scientific prowess. The immense cost of the ship was secondary to the security perspective, however; after a long process of negotiations with neighboring countries and the EU, the government negotiated a ten-year lease agreement with Norwegian Hoegh LNG, with the right to buy. Ownership may eventually pass to state-controlled Klaipedos Nafta after the lease expires in 2024. Importantly, the lease agreement broke the resource dependency on Russia. Hanging over the handover of the *Independence* was the 2014 Russian invasion of Crimea. The invasion of Ukraine was a stark warning of Russia's leverage on gas debts (personal communication, Janeliunas 2018). The security concern is there because the precipitation for the invasion of Crimea was disputes around Ukraine's gas debts to Russia. Due to terms connected to gas debts owed to Gazprom by Ukraine, Russia was able to station troops in Crimea, which later ultimately took control of Crimea for Russia in 2014 (Grigas 2017). Lithuania was not close to a direct threat of invasion or gas cut-off, because the pipeline supplying Lithuania also supplies Russia's Kaliningrad, therefore any gas cut to Lithuania would also cut deliveries to Kaliningrad. Nonetheless, Gazprom's dominant position and potential debts to Russia pushed Lithuania to make strategic moves to utilize EU tools to break apart the German-Russian monopoly and build an LNG facility, demonstrating the power of EU membership in diversification away from the historical orientation of the Lithuanian energy system.

3.5 SECURITY, ENTREPRENEURSHIP, AND RENEWABLES

Lithuania's energy strategy, approved in June 2018, envisions 100% local electricity production and 80% of energy requirements from non-polluting GHG sources by 2050. Renewable energy is set to make the country secure in the short and long term. The short-term goal is to have an "energy-secure state" by 2020, the mid-term goal envisions the lowest and most competitive energy prices in the CEE and Scandinavian region by 2030 (built on RES), while the long-term 2050 goal is to establish an energy independent state with 100% local energy production (The Republic of Lithuania Seimas 2018). Despite this long-term goal not conforming with EU SEM expectations, the emphasis is to build a competitive low-cost energy market with a range of renewable energy technologies. The potential for Lithuania to expand its renewable portfolio to increase its energy security and affordability of energy services holds precedents in the country's heat sector. This next section will focus on how the country built up its biomass heating system and market to diversify away from Russian gas and produce an entrepreneurial base of companies exporting biomass market knowledge and heating technologies.

3.5.1 Diversification in heating

The privatization and modernization of Lithuania's only oil refinery – Mazeikiu Nafta – in the late 1990s and early 2000 resulted in a shift away from the use of heating oil and towards biomass as a replacement fuel. For district heating (DH) systems, which most municipalities in Lithuania use, the alternative was in gas and biomass and some waste incineration. In looking for alternatives, Scandinavia served as the inspiration and resource for retrofitting DH systems with biomass boilers. Lithuania received some financial and technical resources (such as used boilers) from Denmark and Sweden to gain knowledge and experience (personal communication, Lapinskas 2018; Ramanauskas 2018). Lacking the funds to buy new boilers at a large scale, Lithuanian companies and scientists worked together to begin local production of boilers and related technologies used for biomass in DH (personal communication, Ramanauskas 2018).

The rise of the biomass heating sector is remarkable for its consistent growth over time and the displacement of (Russian) gas from the heating sector. When heating oil dominated, only 1.7% of heat was produced from biomass in Lithuania; by 2020 this is expected to be 85%, with electricity production expected to be 12–15% from biomass boilers (personal communication, Lapinskas 2018); the future goal is 90% of all heat production produced from renewables by 2050 (Ministry of Energy of the Republic of Lithuania 2018). Lithuania demonstrates an effective path for heat source diversification that occurs over time with a strong awareness of the long-term cost savings for consumers.

There are two dominant reasons Lithuania switched to biomass in DH. The first is the low upfront cost of converting existing heating systems, that once burned oil, to burn biomass. The total cost of conversion was projected to cost 300 million EUR, with funding split between 100 million EUR from EU sources and 200 million EUR from domestic sources. The annual yearly savings of 200 million EUR are almost the same as the initial conversion cost (personal communication, Ramanauskas 2018). The increasing use and competition for biomass is affecting the perceived low cost of biomass. End users in the 2016–17 heating season experienced a 4% increase in costs due to a 25% increase in the cost of biomass fuel. Nonetheless, compared to a higher increase in gas prices, this was viewed as moderate (personal communication, Molis 2018).

The focus on the low cost of conversion and the cost of fuel also drove local politicians to choose biomass over gas. In the 2005–6 period, gas prices were increasing, and security concerns expressed by NATO were also accumulating, enabling an environment to develop that would have long-term effects on the choice of technologies local mayors were making to use the DH plants. While the local mayors felt pressure from Gazprom to use gas, they were also pushed by the voters to reduce costs. This 'war footing' described above, enabled decision-makers to provide subsidies and develop a transparent online auction-based marketplace for biomass. With bilateral contracts illegal, the level of transparency is high, with the perception that the biomass market is well developed and ensures competitive prices (personal communication, Ramanauskas 2018; Lapinskas 2018). Nonetheless, for technical reasons, gas still needs to be used in the heating system in cases of extreme weather and as a back-up source. The growth of biomass in DH and the development of a biomass market enabled Lithuania to keep the money in Lithuania rather than pay for Russian imported gas.

The development of biomass technology in Lithuania also describes the growth of a new renewable energy sector. In 1997 and 1998, there was a lack of money to buy new boilers, so local production of boilers began (personal communication, Ramanauskas 2018). Now, Lithuanian companies are exporting to Italy, France, and Ukraine, and are involved in projects in Poland. The development of a biomass industry in Lithuania is not solely an entrepreneurial business, but also one of national security – aligned with the 'battle for independence.' In developing the technology, Remigijus Lapinskas, at the time the president of the Lithuanian Biomass Energy Association (Litbioma), told scientists working on biomass technology that it was not only good science and business, but that they were "guarding the country" (personal communication, Lapinskas 2018) by developing biomass as a domestic industry. In this regard, the scientific and business effort in biomass would ensure the economic development of the energy sector after post-Soviet independence and ensure both resource and financial independence from Russia. By using biomass for heating, the threat from gas as a tool for dependency would be reduced.

3.6 CONCLUSION: THE WESTERN OPENING

Reflecting on the repolarization of the Lithuanian energy system away from Russia and towards the EU demonstrates the significant legal (Third Energy Package), technical (new networks and routes), and political (policy implementation) will that delivered an energy system that retained lower-priced energy. The pursuit of low-cost heating, compounded by security concerns, was the force behind converting DH into biomass facilities. For Lithuania to succeed in the battle for the *Independence*, the country turned to the sea for not only LNG but to build undersea electric cables to Sweden, thereby breaking away from the inner-continental dependence on Russia. This wartime strategy which utilized EU membership to break apart monopolies and diversify its energy network demonstrates the consistent effort required for reorientation of the energy system from its historical roots.

The closure of Ignalina was the impetus for the systemic change. It is hard to conceive of such a dramatic change if Ignalina had continued to produce most of Lithuania's electricity. EU membership for Lithuania required the closure, but it also forced the country to decide which energy system the country would choose. Choosing Russian gas and electricity provided through the existing infrastructure would ensure a monopolistic supply situation, with potential price disputes tied to political conditions. While this was the choice of the other Baltic countries, the fact that Gazprom charged Lithuania more for gas meant that energy independence held a financial and political cost. Without the use of biomass in heating, the increased price of Russian gas would need to be covered by households, thereby increasing household utility bills and the potential for the political dissatisfaction of voters.

On the other hand, the closure of Ignalina forced Lithuania to build interconnectors and cooperate with neighboring countries on network diversification. In one sense, Lithuania was unable to straddle the fence, because any new infrastructure would reduce the electricity and gas monopoly from post-Soviet neighbors. The pursuit and docking of the *Independence* were the clearest signals that Lithuania would finance and pay for greater security of supply, which wouldn't exclude Russian gas but would create competition. The use of EU processes built into the Third Energy Package and other avenues in the EU meant that Lithuania was an active participant in the EU, shaping policy and engaging in an institutional battle for independence from both Russian and German dominance of their energy system. It is an interesting contradiction between a neoliberal policy era of privatization and competition that the state then used even more competitive regulations to squeeze back control of the energy firms. National (in)direct control of the energy firms enabled Lithuania to pursue a diversified and competitive energy policy rather than remaining with monopolistic suppliers and distributors. With this taste of energy independence Lithuania is now pursuing a sustainable and independent energy system by 2050.

4. Hungary: the geopolitics of household utility bills

4.1 INTRODUCTION: EXTENDING THE SOVIET FRIENDSHIP

In the late 1970s, resource-poor Hungary made the decision to build a nuclear power plant and import Soviet gas. This former COMECON country shifted away from coal and embraced the Soviet energy program. By the mid-1980s half of electricity production was from nuclear power and gas was the primary resource for urban heating. These infrastructure and resource ties continue today. The collapse of Communism in 1989 and Hungary's membership into the EU in 2004 set Hungary on a neoliberal economic path in the energy sector. The 2010 parliamentary elections brought in the Fidesz political party, led by Prime Minister Viktor Orbán. Key legislative efforts were made in rewriting the constitution and electoral laws, and by 2020 the country had transformed from a liberal economic model to an 'illiberal' model where banking and utilities have significant state ownership and foreign manufacturing is an important source of employment. Part of the early policy efforts were made to lower utility rates for households. In short, after 2010, a new period of state centralization occurred which brought the state back into a stronger relationship with household consumers and also with Russia.

This chapter first describes the effort to reduce energy prices for Hungarian households after the 2010 parliamentary elections and the installation of the second Orbán government. There was a concerted political drive to lower the utility rates household consumers were dealing with after years of price increases. The result was a new political-economic system that placed the state at the center of the energy system, rather than market actors overseen by the energy regulator. A historical picture is developed in section 4.3, which describes Hungary's growing reliance on Russian gas and nuclear power, thereby placing energy both as a social and a geopolitical issue. Hungary's EU membership efforts are discussed in section 4.4 which provides a description of privatization efforts and the implementation of the EU's neoliberal market structure. The end of the chapter provides the international context to Hungary's efforts to keep prices low for household consumers. Section 4.5

describes the trade-offs Hungary made with Russia and the EU to ensure the maintenance of low utility prices for households. In Hungarian energy policy, there emerges a linear relationship between domestic politics and economic policies along with the international policies adopted by the Orbán government. Social energy policies are also geopolitical strategies.

4.2 ILLIBERAL ENERGY SYSTEMS: CUTTING THE UTILITY BILLS

In 2011 the era of neoliberal economics was declared dead by Prime Minister, Viktor Orbán. "While we have put an end to the basic principles of a neoliberal era, we have yet to build up the non-liberal economic policy of the 21st century, in terms of planning, coordination and practices," Orbán said (MTI 2011). The political-economic order changed with parliamentary elections in 2010. The political coalition, Fidesz-KDNP won elections with a two-thirds majority. In 2020, state institutions and both private and public companies work in tandem in all sectors of the economy; they fulfill a centralized, ideologically driven 'illiberal' economic order supported by a cultural right-wing reformation. In the energy sector, previously privatized utilities are now state owned, and where there was once a mosaic of Western European utilities active in the country, now only the German firm E.ON maintains a significant presence in the country. The remaining companies have been returned to Hungarian state- or privately-owned Hungarian companies. The illiberal economic model places the state center stage in the relationship between energy consumers and the international supply of energy resources and technologies.

The political-economic transformation began in 2010 with the removal of price-setting authority from the Hungarian Energy Office (HEO) and the transference to the National Development Ministry. However, a parliamentary committee holds dual power in price setting, which tightly controls the methodology outlining the final consumer price. The legislation enabled the committee to place a price cap on gas and electricity, after consultation with the HEO. In 2011, Parliament passed a law altering HEO regulation to one based on end-user pricing (thus establishing a price cap, running counter to EU Directives) (Felsmann 2014). In January 2013, Parliament passed a law stipulating that household consumers receive a 10% reduction in electricity, gas, and district heating. Nonetheless, it was the HEO that would implement the change. The cost of the reduction would mainly come from foreign-owned electricity and gas providers.

The 10% reduction was challenged in court by electricity and gas distributors. The courts found the 10% reduction unfounded. Immediately after this court ruling Parliament passed another law abolishing the HEO and preventing court appeals on network usage, and only allowing appeals to Hungary's constitutional court in certain instances (Hungary Around the Clock 2013). At the same time as the creation of the new Hungarian Energy and Public Utility Regulatory Authority (MEKH) Parliament began discussion on a further 11% cut in utility prices. In October 2013, passage of the 10% cut co-occurred with a second cut of 11%. The third cut of 5.7% in electricity and 6.5% in gas was passed early in 2014. Each price cut took place just before national elections (April 2014) and local elections (September 2014). Altogether, electricity prices fell by 25% between 2011 and 2014 and have remained relatively flat since, although the practice of delivering lower energy prices to voters continues, with the Prime Minister ordering the delivery of 'utility' vouchers for 2.5 million eligible pensioners ahead of the 2019 municipal elections. Each voucher is worth 30 EUR, to a total cost of HUF 4.3 billion (1.3 million EUR), with 40% spent on gas bills and 60% spent on electricity bills – paid to the state-owned utility (Hungary Around the Clock 2019b).

In 2018, it was clear that the earlier price reductions and ownership transformation (discussed below) held limited benefits for Hungarian household consumers. Not only were household consumers unable to benefit from the global drop in gas prices after 2014, but the earlier lowering of utility rates resulted in consumers using more energy (Sebestyén Szép 2017). The impact was also broader, making it harder for Hungary to achieve its strategic goals of improving energy efficiency. With households consuming more energy, they were still spending relatively the same amount as before, negating the overall financial savings for households. In real terms, Hungarians spent 5–6% more on energy services in 2015 than in 1996 (Energiaklub 2015; cf. Sebestyén Szép 2017). The impact of the lower utility rates reduced the financial advantage of consuming less energy and investing in energy efficiency measures (Sebestyén Szép 2017).

The increase in consumption undermined Hungary's strategic energy goals, including an increase of energy efficiency by 2030. It was expected that there would be a decrease of 40 PJ in residential energy consumption between 2010 and 2030 (Sebestyén Szép 2017, 69). Nonetheless, due to the price reduction there was a proportional increase in additional consumption of energy of 36.75 PJ from all energy carriers (including gas, electricity, and district heating). The result of the price drop? Negating a 20-year energy-saving goal in less than four years.

Households increased consumption due to lower prices. In the first year of the household price reduction there was an increase of 17.02 PJ attributable to excess consumption, with later years registering 14.54 PJ in 2013–14 and 5.21 in 2014–15 (Sebestyén Szép 2017, 69, 74). In proportion to the higher consumption levels, the price of energy (due to the utility rate cuts) was mirrored in the politically induced price decrease: "In 2013, it was 7.3% (this is the size of the price effect relative to the energy use in 2013), in 2014 it was 6.6%, in 2015 it was 2.4%" (Sebestyén Szép 2017, 70). In other words, Hungary's increase in energy was almost proportional to the percentage of the price reduction. In turn, Hungary's lower energy prices had a minor impact on household budgets but a significant impact on energy-saving efforts. Overall, because of shifts in economic activities and population effects, overall consumption declined, but the households bucked a decreasing consumption trend and instead increased consumption, attributed to the lower utility rates (Sebestyén Szép 2017, 74).

In addition, the price cuts did not reduce the number of households that had difficulty paying their monthly utility payments. Hungarian households still have a harder time meeting their utility payments than before the financial crisis of 2008. Based on income levels, the top two most populated income categories – representing 66.4% of households – indicated a rate above 30% of households in these two categories being "unable to pay [their utility bills] on time due to financial difficulties" in the previous twelve months (Figure 4.1). Five of the nine income categories also demonstrated increased difficulty paying utility bills from 2006 to 2016 (EU Energy Poverty Observatory 2019b). So, despite lower utility costs Hungarians still find it difficult to pay their utility bills.

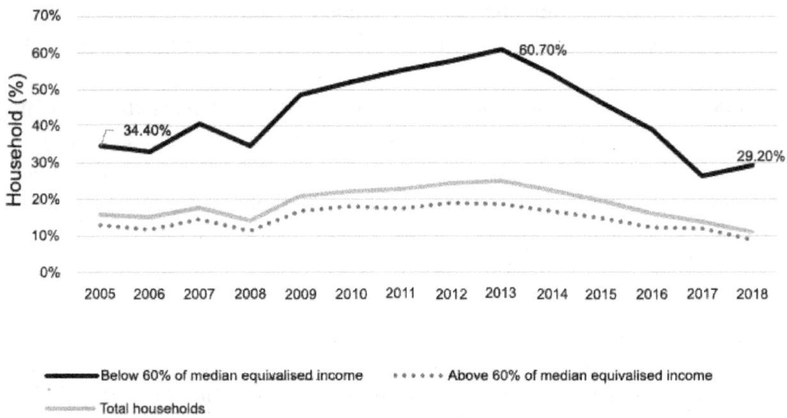

Source: Eurostat (2020a).

Figure 4.1 Arrears on Hungarian household utility bills 2005–18

Demonstrating the depth of energy poverty in Hungary are the numbers of deaths from hypothermia. Since 2016 the state no longer collects statistics on winter hypothermia deaths (with the national statistics office under the authority of the office of the Prime Minister). In response, the Hungarian Social

Forum developed an informal network across the country to assist in collecting the number of people dying of hypothermia in public spaces, during transportation to hospital, and in unheated homes. The number has increased each year. In 2015, 137 cases of hypothermia deaths were recorded, while in 2018 there were 200 cases: 106 in public spaces and en route to the hospital, and 94 people dying in unheated homes. The deaths included a baby in 2018 and an 11-year-old child in 2017. Between 2005 and 2018, 3,063 people did from hypothermia (personal communication, Simo 2018). Tragically, the universal cut in utility prices is not having the expected social impact that would enable households to pay their utility bills in a timely manner. Despite the effort to quasi-nationalize utilities and set the price of electricity and gas for social and political reasons, there remains deep poverty, with no effective policies to address those households unable to afford energy services. Discussed next is Hungary' attempts internationally to secure energy resources and technologies to ensure low prices across the board.

4.3 THE SOVIET MODEL: LAND, RESOURCES AND PEOPLE

There are three observable energy generation eras in Hungary. These help to frame the transition from one type of generation resource or technology to the next while also accounting for the changing political philosophies. This section outlines the history of natural resources and Hungary's shift towards cleaner-burning gas for heat and the regional network integration with neighboring countries. This provides the necessary background to understand current shifts from a market-oriented approach to a centralized government perspective.

In the first post-WW II energy era, Hungary's limited natural resources constrained its economic potential. Hungary is poor in 'traditional' energy resources, such as coal, gas, and oil; these were extracted but were of low quality or were limited. During the second energy era, in the Communist period, energy projects required heavy state investment. Growth in this sector tied Hungary strongly to the Soviet Union in the area of oil, gas, and nuclear power for technology and knowledge transfer. Regional integration with COMECON countries leveled out Hungary's energy imports – including electricity imports. Hungary, in the past and currently, operates under a 'scarcity' model, that is, it is dependent on energy imports. Therefore, energy independence was viewed as highly expensive and impractical. Joint projects with the Soviet Union and other regional COMECON countries were viable and affordable solutions to Hungary's pressing energy needs.

Today, EU climate change policies emphasize a shift away from coal. In Hungary, the transition occurred largely in the 1970s and 1980s and shifted the country towards gas. The decision was driven by both environmental and financial costs. Nowadays, gas both provides heat and produces electricity, along with complementing Hungary's use of solar power. The shift from coal to cleaner-burning gas began in the mid-1960s and marked the second energy era, occurring until the oil crisis of 1973 (Bernat 1989, 123). The shift away from coal was dramatic, particularly between the years 1965 and 1981, when coal dropped from 66% of the energy mix to 30%. This same period saw a dramatic increase in natural gas, from 6% in 1965 to 26% in 1981 (Bernat 1989, 116). As Hungary's energy demand grew, so did the internationalization of the energy system

In 1958, the National Planning Office stated that to fulfill its objectives Hungary "must ensure above all ... the development of the energy base" (Berend and Csato 2001, 1:325). This same year also marked an overall change in approach for the Soviet bloc of COMECON countries, away from national energy self-sufficiency to the regional cooperation of COMECON countries (Berend and Csato 2001, 1:326). This decision enabled the building of a regional power grid between COMECON countries (Berend and Csato 2001, 1:327). Hungary became part of the United Energy System (CDU) based in Prague, and coordinating electricity imports throughout the region (Bernat 1989, 131) Hungary benefitted from increased imports. Later, with the fall of Communism, this coordination would be reduced, and only picked up with EU membership. In 2012, a new regional power exchange reunified the electricity markets of Hungary, the Czech Republic, and Slovakia. As under the Soviet system, Hungary continues to import large quantities of electricity from Ukraine, meeting around 25% of its annual demand.

Prompting the shift into Hungary's third energy era in the mid-1970s was the sustained global rise in energy prices (Bernat 1989, 123). The effort by central planners for energy self-sufficiency after WW II was based on the widescale use of low-quality lignite coal produced at almost two and a half-times the cost of oil (Berend and Csato 2001, 1:325). Expansion of domestic and Soviet sourced oil and gas replaced the dirtiest and least efficient coal plants. Gas from Hungary's Great Plains was piped into Budapest, thus replacing coal and establishing the country's gas industry. Nonetheless, energy imports reached 50% by the early 1980s (Bernat 1989, 116). Further, new lignite-fired power plants came online in the last half of the 1970s, maintaining some self-sufficiency (Berend and Csato 2001, 1:327). Importantly, trade balances including either hard currency or the Soviet style of bartering of goods made Hungary's increasing imports expensive by any measure. "Increasing imports necessitates increasing exports of agricultural and/or industrial products" (Bernat 1989, 117). Greater electrification of transportation and energy efficiency measures were important to cut oil imports (Bernat 1989, 117).

This third energy era, as will be described next, still operates today, with gas, nuclear, and domestic lignite – along with electricity imports – underpinning the contemporary energy mix. Figure 4.2 demonstrates how Hungary's current electricity mix is still dominated by nuclear power and natural gas. In 2015, imported gas accounted for 70% of Hungary's gas consumption (Directorate-General for Energy 2017). Two-thirds of household energy consumption is for heating (IEA 2017, 54), and a large majority of heating is done with gas. Much of this gas, as will be described below, is purchased from Gazprom, which flows from Russia through Ukraine, although it may also flow through Slovakia and Austria before coming to Hungary. Hungary's energy system operating in the 2020s reflects the design from the late 1970s and early 1980s, a 40-year-old energy mix. Hungary continues to be reliant on Russian gas and nuclear technology to meet its electricity and heat production needs. As described in the following section, Hungary is set to continue its future energy path by maintaining this historical reliance on Russian natural gas and nuclear power. The next section discusses the political ramifications of this dependence.

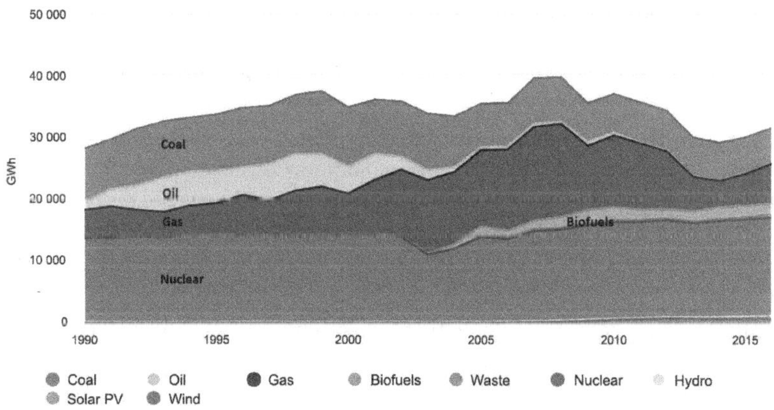

Source: IEA (2018). All rights reserved; as modified by the author.

Figure 4.2 *Hungary's electricity generation by fuel 1990–2016*

4.4 NEOLIBERAL ENERGY: PRIVATIZATION AND HIGHER PRICES

The weakness of the Communist-era energy system lay in ensuring sufficient funds were spent on maintaining and improving the system. Communism delivered below-cost prices, but it would be the private sector that would step in to invest and improve the infrastructure. Hungary's preparation for and subsequent EU membership would establish a neoliberal regulatory market structure. The operating model would change from a politically controlled system to one with private actors and competition delivering electricity, heat, and gas to households. Between 1989 and the 2010 parliamentary elections, the liberal regulatory model transformed and upgraded the Hungarian energy sector. As this section outlines, this led to societal tension, as it became harder to devote more household income to utilities. The story of energy poverty and the necessity of low energy prices is central to Hungary's conversion back towards a politically managed energy system after 2010.

Communism had not even officially ended and the Hungarian energy system was already being prepped for privatization. This point in time is important because it was not joining the EU in 2004 that prompted the privatization of electricity and gas distribution companies. Rather, privatization was carried out to both finance the state's day-to-day operations and ensure long-term investment in the energy system. The privatization of Hungary's energy assets began in 1989. Eight generation and six regional distribution and supply companies were created. The Hungarian Transmission System Operator (TSO) was also established. Each generation company had a mix of two to three power plants: "Thus big enough to sell but not too big to dominate the market" (personal communication, Nagy 2014). State-owned MVM remained the 'middleman', buying power from generators and reselling to distribution companies, and it continues this role today. Its original purpose was to balance expensive generation with lower cost generation, ensuring that consumers paid the least amount; the company still performs this role today.

In 1995, private foreign owners began operating in Hungary. ENEL, EDF, RWE, and E.ON each owned both generation and distribution. The operational efficiency of the distribution companies was improving before privatization. Within a few years of privatization, operational efficiency had reached the same levels as Western European DSOs (personal communication, Nagy 2014). The structure of bills in Hungary reflects the lower consumption levels and smaller population; this translates into higher network charges, since fewer people still need to pay for system maintenance, compared with more densely populated countries. This is important, as will be discussed below, when network charges are compiled and international comparisons are made, because network charges are a higher percentage in final bills in Hungary (personal communication, Nagy 2014).

Reflecting the characteristics of the third energy era in Hungary, the country is tightly connected to a regional CEE market. Hungary imports around 20–30% of its electricity, with 50% of domestically produced electricity produced by the Paks Nuclear Power Plant. Domestic prices are influenced by imports and the capacity of cross-border infrastructure. The Hungarian electricity market is now coupled to the Czech, Slovak, and Romanian markets, and traders are active. Hungarian industrial and business consumers have a competitive market to purchase power. Within the EU the price is near the middle for non-household consumers who pay €.75 cents per kWh, just below the EU average (€.79 cents per kWh) (Eurostat, European Commission 2018).

The story is different for Hungarian households. They pay the third lowest price for electricity, at €.11 cents per kWh in the EU (Eurostat, European Commission 2018). Competition for Hungarian households does not exist, with a parliamentary committee setting the price for households (discussed above). In 2009, the Third Energy Package rules were transposed, and consumers were given the legal right to choose their supplier. Nonetheless, only Magyar Telecom began to offer electricity services as a bundled telecom package (later this was discontinued once government-imposed prices began). Foreign-owned distribution companies did not compete for household consumers, thereby maintaining a monopolistic market environment (Horvath Kadar 2012). This lack of competition or ability to compete on price would later serve as justification for government intervention.

The overall story of Hungarian gas distribution companies is a similar one of privatization and foreign ownership, with a distinct lack of competition in the household market. Nonetheless, while the price of electricity rose steadily each year, the price of gas shot up after 2006, placing significant strains on household budgets. Figure 4.3 shows the deviation of gas prices from other categories such as electricity, firewood, and wages. The significant rise is down to three reasons. First, the global price increase of gas and oil resulted in significant increases, with import prices rising over 250% between 2004 and 2011 (Bouzarovski et al. 2015, 9). Second, regulated household gas prices ended in 2006, so market rates would need to be charged. Third, additional government charges were added, including payments for improving Hungary's strategic gas storage (following both the 2006 and 2009 Russia-Ukraine gas disputes) and a 7% rise in the VAT rate. In short, the price of gas quickly shot up during a period of market liberalization, making it socially and politically difficult to make the transition to a competitive market model – and ripe for a political attack. For both electricity and gas this came in 2010 with a change in government. The installation of the second Orbán government held a political philosophy of centralization of politics and the economy along with an anti-neoliberal energy strategy.

4.5 WAR AND THE RENATIONALIZATION OF UTILITIES

The dissolution of the Hungarian energy regulator in 2013 and the end of neoliberalism, as declared by Prime Minister Orbán, began a long battle to

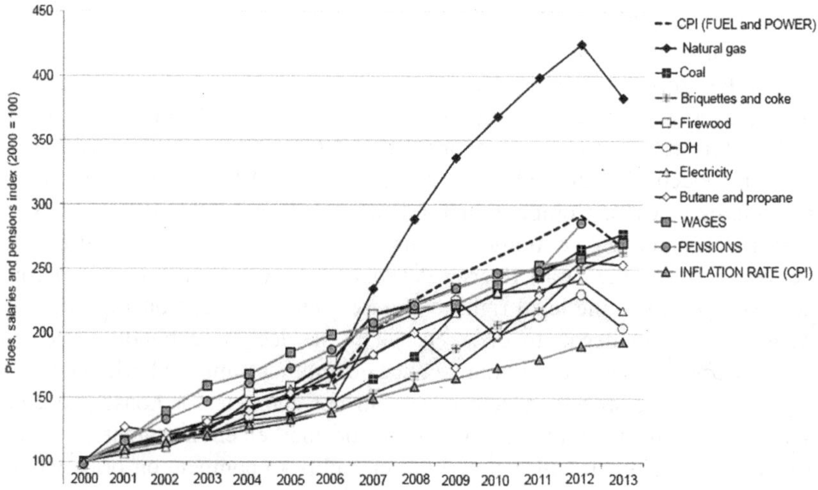

Note: 2000 = 100
Source: Bouzarovski et al. (2015).

Figure 4.3 *Changes in prices of energy carriers, main household income sources and the CPI in Hungary, 2000–13*

push the foreign utilities out of the country – without outright nationalization of the companies. In 2013, after the first legal victory by the private utilities, the Fidesz political party began a nationwide petition that ultimately collected 2.3 million signatures, under the banner, 'Hungary Will Not Give In!' (Magyarország Nem Hagyja Magát!). The slogan and political action referred to the court actions and the EU Commission's reservations on the utility price cuts (The Orange Files 2016). A nationwide billboard campaign was also launched during the 2014 election year heralding the price reductions and the 'fight' against foreign utilities and the European Union.

The war on the foreign-owned utilities went beyond political communication in media advertisements, it extended to 'energy savings' statements on bills. These statements are provided in an orange box (which is technically specified to match the exact party color of Fidesz). The box contains itemized cost savings related to the campaign against the utilities and how much money each consumer has saved each month, and since 2013 when the cost reduction campaign started.

The seriousness of displaying the cost savings is reflected in seven utilities being fined HUF 56.5 million (185,000 EUR) by the National Consumer Protection Authority for not properly displaying financial savings on bills (The Orange Files 2016) – including for using the wrong color of orange. While the cost savings are real for households, system wide they are fictitious, as according to the IEA electricity is supplied at below cost for households with "sector-specific levies and taxes … not fully passed through in the final regulated prices paid by household consumers." This below-market price is sustained by channeling 80% of household consumer electricity from state-owned MVM, which likely incurs losses and cross-subsidies from profitable parts of the business (IEA 2017, 83).

The price reduction was politically driven and economically arbitrary as it placed a greater burden on the industrial sector, as the cost of the consumer price cuts was shifted onto industry. Network charges increased for industry, while being lowered for households. Table 4.1 demonstrates the shift in network tariffs away from households and to industry. Figure 4.4 shows the inverse relationship between lowered household gas prices and increased industrial prices; with the first charts reflecting the percentage change, and the second the price change. By 2014, Hungary had the highest price increase and second highest gas prices for industrial consumers in the EU. This is contrasted with the second lowest price for household gas – with only Romania, with large quantities of domestic gas, placing first. The high industrial prices, therefore, are not solely due to the price of gas, but to the network charges the government places on industry – which has access to gas in a competitive market and therefore follows the international trends in gas pricing.

		Change From 01.2010. to11.2013.	Net change in tariff (FT/kwh)
Connection to transmission lines		44,4%	0,68
Connection to distribution lines	High voltage connection	29,3%	0,65
	High/medium voltage connection	26,7%	0,99
	Medium voltage connection	29,9%	1,70
	Medium/low voltage connection	30,5%	2,34
	Low voltage I. (profiled)	-8,0%	-1,24
	Low voltage II. (controlled)	-3,7%	-0,28
	Low voltage III. (non-profiled)	9,7%	1,37
	Average	1,7%	0,16

Industry: connection to transmission lines through medium/low voltage connection. Households: low voltage I. (profiled) and low voltage II. (controlled).

Source: Felsmann (2018, 63).

Table 4.1 *Development of network access fees xain Hungary, 2010–15*

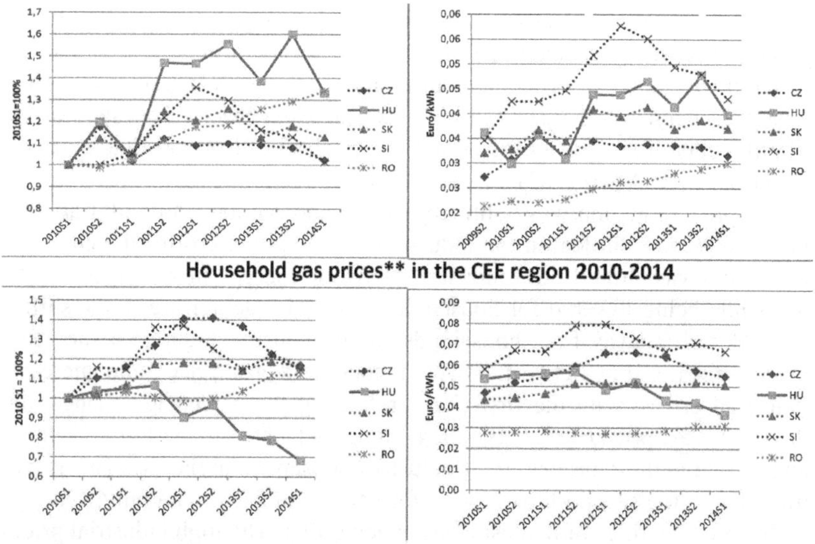

- Consumers between 10000 and 100000 GJ, excluded VAT.

** Households between 20 and 200 GJ.

Source: Felsmann (2018, 65).

Figure 4.4 *Industry and household gas prices 2010–14*

The price cuts occurring in the second Orbán government were also matched with three additional taxes on utilities. (1) A pre-existing ‘Robin Hood’ tax, implemented by the previous Socialist government of 11% on profits, was increased to 31%. In addition, corporate income tax stood at 19%, making the total tax burden 50% at the end of 2013 (US Department of State 2013). (2) In 2010, the so called ‘crisis tax’ was introduced which set a 1.05% tax on energy companies’ taxable revenue. However, (3) this crisis tax was replaced in 2013 with a tax on public utilities networks, such as, water, natural gas, telecoms, electricity. This was set at HUF 125 (€.44 cents) per meter (Schonherr Legal Insights 2013). Thus, large additional revenues flowed to the state through numerous sectoral taxes.

The utility sector’s operating profits as a whole inverted from a profit of HUF 224 billion in 2009 to a loss of HUF 119 billion in 2012 (LaBelle and Deak 2015). Nonetheless, it is clear that the firms adapted to these tax changes. The average level of corporate tax paid by foreign energy firms in 2010 was HUF 719 million, in 2013 this dropped to HUF 443 million (Felsmann 2014). However, restructuring of tax liabilities within firms may also play a role in the overall decline (personal communication, Felsmann 2015). In short, *private firms adjusted internal operations by outsourcing and making less investments, thereby reducing both profits and taxes* (Felsmann 2018, 15).

According to Felsmann (2014), the private utility sector (both gas and electricity) responded in three ways: (1) to sell – or offer to sell – companies to the state; (2) to cut investments, increase operational efficiency, and perform capital extraction by increasing the dividends paid to shareholders (often foreign mother companies); (3) to allow taxes and lowered revenue to financially scuttle the enterprise, thus eroding its capital position and destroying its value (Felsmann 2014). Paid dividends doubled between 2010 and 2013 (Felsmann 2014) while sector investment declined from HUF 247 billion in 2010 to HUF 148 billion in 2012. By 2015, there was virtually no profits to be had for Hungarian electricity and gas companies (Figure 4.5). For gas and mixed utilities (electricity and gas), profits before taxes stood at a loss of −0.9% (Felsmann 2018, 14). After 2013, the financial conditions of state-owned electricity and gas firms (FOGAZ and MVM) deteriorated, the initial 2011 taxes and utility reduction were meant to favor domestic firms; and by 2013, after further price reductions, the whole sector was flat, with state-owned firms in negative territory. The sector was now ripe for the government to take ownership of these firms and become the only universal service provider to all Hungarian households.

The groundwork for the government's takeover of the utility sector was already laid in 2014, when FOGAZ, the gas utility for Budapest, was bought from RWE. In January 2015, the Hungarian government established the First National Utility Service Company (Elso Nemezeti Kozmuszolgaltato – ENKSZ). Later, its name was changed to NKM, Nemzeti Kozmuvek. The intention was that, "The public company will beat the present market actors with good prices and good service," as stated by government minister János Lázár (Hirsch 2015). In 2015, the response of the private gas service providers was clear: they all returned their universal service license which required them to sell gas to all households. In response, the Hungarian state made FOGAZ the universal household supplier. Other distribution companies were sold so that, by 2018, the state had paid at least HUF 226 billion for gas distribution companies. In 2017, Italian owned TIGAZ was bought by Hungarian owned (and government favored) MET, thereby leaving E.ON as the last foreign-owned gas distribution company. A similar strategy occurred in electricity distribution companies with state consolidation, and with E.ON as the sole remaining foreign-owned utility.

Since 2011 the Hungarian government had pushed to reclaim ownership, by forcing financial losses on firms, lowering their profits, and ultimately selling electricity and gas directly to households. The only major holdout was E.ON, which maintained its distribution assets in both gas and electricity. In 2020, E.ON finalized the takeover of the distribution assets of RWE, leaving only

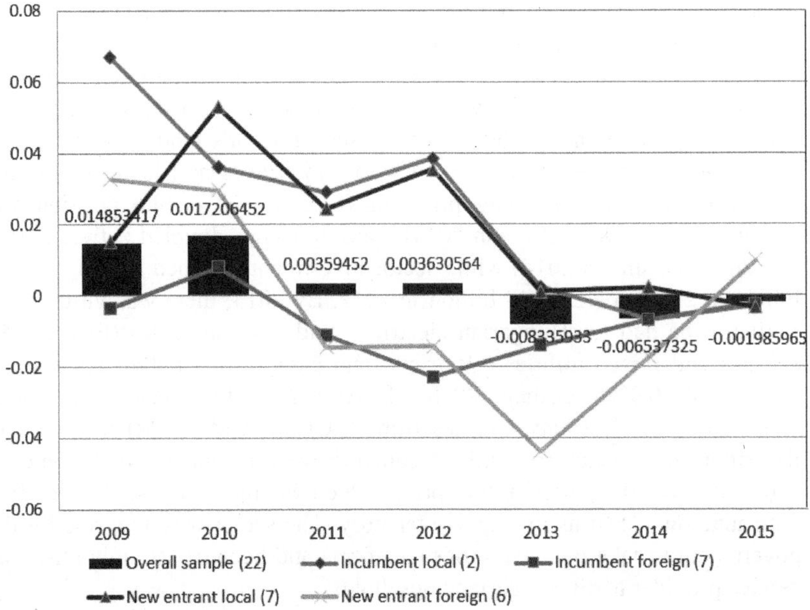

Source: Felsmann (2018, 118).

Figure 4.5 Profit margins of energy traders, 2009–15

E.ON, Hungarian-owned MET, and state-owned NKM as substantial players in Hungary's household electricity and gas sector. In 2017, the state became the sole universal service provider for all households and fostered either state or Hungarian ownership of a considerable amount of distribution, import, storage, and trading assets. The next section will outline how the Hungarian state centralized state ownership of gas assets, returning to the Communist era of state (or Hungarian) ownership and centralized management of the energy system.

4.6 GAS: THE RUSSIAN WAY

1989 may have been the year when political reform changed Hungary from Communist to democratic, but this change did not apply to gas pricing agreements. Low import prices were maintained until 1996 when a new contract with Gazprom was signed. Even in 1994, Hungary comparatively had significantly lower gas prices compared with Western European countries. Italy paid the most at HUF 56.9 per cubic meter, France paid HUF 38.3 and Great Britain paid the least at HUF 29.1, whereas Hungary had to pay Russia only HUF 9.8 per cubic meter (Bogel et al. 1997).

During the post-Communist years, the energy system was the subject of many political tricks. Before December 1994, the Communist-era company Mineralimpex held exclusive rights to import gas from Gazprom. In October 1994, the Hungarian government forced MOL to become the owner of Mineralimpex and made it obligatory by law to buy gas from the company. MOL was then was compelled to sell gas to all consumers in the Hungarian market, which forced it to absorb any loses, and with a similar logic to MVM, not make a profit. In 1994, Mineralimpex was projected to have profits of HUF 82 million on revenue of HUF 68 billion (Bogel et al. 1997, 69) and without any risk of losses. This arrangement – based on a long-term contract with Russia – must have been profitable for companies besides MOL.

However, a few months later – at the end of 1994 – a new Russian entity, Panrusgas, which served to act as a middleman between Gazexport (Gazprom) and Mineralimpex, was created. This was pushed by the newly elected Socialist government which passed legislation forcing the change. Panrusgas served no purpose but to facilitate the transactions and extraction of profits (Orbán 2008, 46). It was 65% owned by Russians (including 50% Gazprom) and 35% by MOL (whereas Mineralimpex was 100% Hungarian owned). By the end of 1994, Panrusgas replaced Mineralimpex as a middleman between Gazexport (Gazprom) and MOL. "The company did not add any real value to the supply" (Orban 2008, 46). Reminiscent of the earlier episode of the Hungarian Parliament of forcing MOL to buy Russian gas, the same method was used a year later. In 1995, the Hungarian government legislated MOL to buy gas from Panrusgas and then sell gas on the domestic market at below cost. While profits from sales accrued in Russian-controlled Panrusgas, all losses were accrued by MOL. In 1996, a new 20-year gas contract was signed with Panrusgas (later extended to 2019 and 2021) for Gazprom to supply Hungary.

From the very start of the Panrusgas-MOL contract it was apparent that losses would mount for MOL. In 1996, MOL projected losses of HUF 70 billion from its natural gas operations because it was forced to sell to the five private regional gas distribution companies (at a loss), which then sold to consumers (Bogel et al. 1997, 69). However, these losses were not new. In 1994, MVM lost HUF 1.3 billion as a result of underpricing imported gas to industrial consumers (Bogel et al. 1997, 70), while in the same year Mineralimpex had revenues of HUF 68 billion with profits of HUF 82 million (Bogel et al. 1997, 69). In addition, domestically produced gas was sold below the border price of Russian gas – despite its international commodity status (The World Bank 1999, 50). All losses would be borne by Hungarian energy companies, while Gazprom extracted profits.

This history of political involvement in setting up companies and legislating how they operate provides an example of how the energy system in Hungary works. Rather than operating the energy system to deliver lower prices for households or industry over the long term in a financially sustainable manner, the system is set up to shift money between companies and incur losses in one firm but deliver profits in another. This system runs counter to EU assumptions of competition and transparency in the marketplace, of a regulated energy market where consumers benefit from efficiencies created through a market system. Nonetheless, it is important to state that the arrangement of the companies and money flows does not indicate corruption, as that is beyond the remit of this research, but rather that it indicates the style of political-economic arrangements between governments and companies in the energy sector. The state, through parliamentary actions, legislates which firms will have losses and which will have profits. It is the Hungarian Parliament voting to create these arrangements. The structure is a political arrangement and even if a state-owned firm loses money, and a foreign firm earns a profit, it exemplifies relationships and politically accepted arrangements within Russian-Hungarian energy relations. This type of relationship is discussed in further detail in the next section, which describes the attempt by MOL to extract itself from this unprofitable Russian-Hungarian 'friendship.'

4.6.1 Shifting financial losses in Hungarian gas

By 2004, MOL decided to sell much of the domestic gas business that was causing the company large losses. MOL sold three companies to E.ON, Panrusgas, and MOL's gas storage and wholesale trading companies (MOL Földgáztároló and MOL Földgázellátó); the sales were finalized in 2006. When the deal was announced between E.ON and MOL – including its 50% holding in Panrusgas, the debt was said to be more than HUF 150 billion (€600 million). From this total in 2006, it is clear that the gas distribution companies supplying households were not paying the full gas import price and MOL was still balancing the financial losses with profits in other areas of their business.

The sale of gas assets to the foreign firms did not last long; with the second Orbán government, a new energy strategy developed that sought to reclaim and further Hungarian ownership of the gas assets *and* re-establish the direct energy relationship with Russia. The Orbán government, in respect of its national consolidation of the energy sector, bought back the trading and storage companies from E.ON in 2013 and Panrusgas in 2015. MVM (traditionally an electricity company) became the owner of these three companies (to circumvent EU regulations, since MOL still owned the transmission operator). Hungary would now own its national gas assets – and debt.

Between 2004 and 2015, despite private ownership, the financial hole surrounding the gas trading and storage companies only got bigger. The Hungarian government (through MVM), paid E.ON HUF 261 billion (€881 million) for the two companies. By then the debt had ballooned by more than double in the intervening years. Just as E.ON had assumed the earlier debt of HUF 150 billion in 2004, MVM would assume a company that had a negative net worth of HUF 355 billion (€1.2 billion) (Atlatszo 2014). In addition, MVM bought back the 50% shares held in the Russian-linked Panrusgas for HUF 940 million in 2015 (Alexander's Gas and Oil Connections 2015). In 2014, other gas storage units were bought back by the Hungarian Development Bank (MFB) for HUF 140 billion (Isaacs and Molnar 2017).

The story of the Hungarian gas sector is one of yearly financial losses for Hungarian-based firms (including MOL and E.ON) and profits for firms with Russian ownership interests. The Orbán government's political narrative demonizes private ownership as extracting high profits from households, while projecting the role of the state working in the interests of households by delivering low energy prices. Nonetheless, the history of the Hungarian gas sector demonstrates a growing balloon of financial losses passed between companies while Russian firms, and the owners of intermediary firms such as Mineralimpex and Panrusgas, consistently extracted yearly profits.

The trail of financial losses for gas firms may be shifting due to the international drop in gas prices and political maneuvering by the Hungarian government. Figure 4.6 demonstrates the shifting import price of Russian gas compared with the regulated household price. The 2008 financial crisis resulted in a decline in gas prices and consumption in Hungary. Nonetheless, since 2015, household prices are no longer following the downward trend of Russian gas prices, which means that households are now paying more for gas than historically justified by the cost curve. By 2018, the price differential was enough for E.ON to re-enter the household market offering prices 10% below the regulated rate – just before the 2018 parliamentarian elections. Political attacks were launched on E.ON and the company withdrew its offer for lower-priced household gas. Nonetheless, due to the substantial level of debt in the Hungarian gas sector the state can benefit from keeping prices high. Contradictorily, with no competition on the household gas market, the government can extol the 'low' prices printed on every household's gas bill measured from 2011 and not from recent year's lower market prices.

The building of Orbán's "non-liberal economic policy" of the twenty-first century (MTI 2011) was done by rebuilding the vertically integrated monopoly of the twentieth century established under Communism. The immediate removal of authority and later transformation of the Hungarian Energy Office into a restricted regulatory entity reversed the liberalization and organizational efforts occurring in Hungary since 1989. By 2018, only E.ON was the substan-

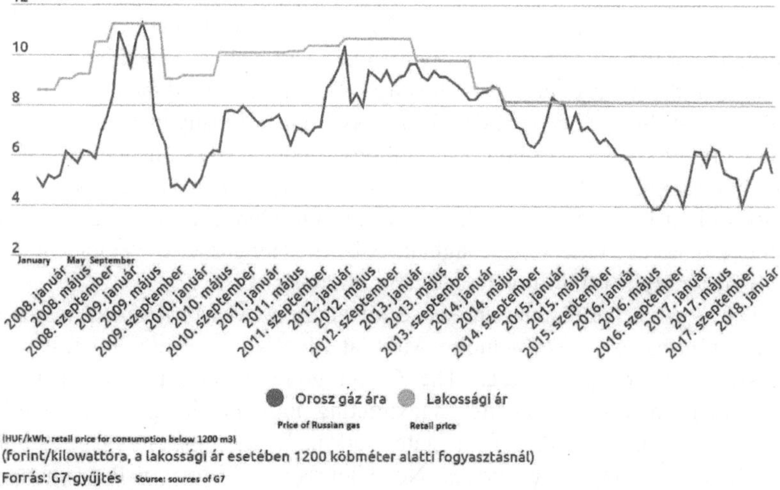

Source: Jando (2018).

Figure 4.6 Price difference between Russian gas price and regulated Hungarian household price

tial holdout from the liberalized era. Ownership of Hungary's energy assets would lie with state and private Hungarian companies. Energy prices for both industry and households would no longer track shifting commodity or network charges. Cross-financing would occur in two areas: first, by industry to subsidize household network charges, and, second, by state and private Hungarian ownership in a range of energy companies, from generation to distribution to universal supplier of households. Financial losses (and profits) can either be absorbed or shifted between entities and customer groups.

Examination of Hungary's international relations with Russia indicates a broader realignment with the Communist-era energy system of COMECON. Discussed next is the development of Hungary's efforts to secure low gas prices to stop the large financial losses stemming from subsidizing household gas prices. To reduce the financial losses, Orbán would need to agree to expanding Paks Nuclear Power Plant (NPP), originally constructed with the assistance of the Soviets and the COMECON countries. By signing onto Paks 2, pushed by the Russian government, Orbán placed Hungary's energy system into the hands of Gazprom and Rosatom for generations to come.

4.7 REBUILDING THE SOVIET MODEL OF GAS AND NUCLEAR

Between 2012 and 2014, the Hungarian government and other state companies (such as MVM) took commercial steps and signed agreements with the Russian government and Rosatom to build two 1,200 MW reactors at the Paks NPP. This activity came after a 2009 vote in Parliament supporting preparation for expanding Paks. Nonetheless, the final intergovernmental agreement cementing the partnership was signed in secret in Moscow between Orbán and Putin in January 2014. After a secret night flight by Orbán to meet with Putin outside of Moscow, for anyone not in the room the signing came as a shock. It came as "a bolt of lightning out of the clear blue sky," with no communication preceding the meeting (Deak 2016, 324), nor was an agreement expected for many years. Less than a month later, in February 2014, the Hungarian Fidesz-dominated Parliament passed support for the international convention on nuclear cooperation between the two countries, cementing the ties on Paks 2.

Hungarian experts would later decry the agreed financial conditions. The agreement signed and now underway requires Hungary to pay Russia 12 billion EUR for building the plant, 80% (10 billion EUR) of which will be covered by a Russian loan with Hungary paying 20% of every invoice. Payments on the loan are already underway even before construction has begun. The completion date continues to slip, but the first reactor may come online in early 2030.

Building Paks 2 alongside the existing Paks 1 capacity of 2,000 MW can be viewed both as a continuation of Hungary's energy policy in completing the original plans of Paks from the 1970s, and a justifiable effort to build domestic generation in a resource-poor country. Nonetheless, the original agreement signed between Putin and Orbán in 2014 should also be seen in light of Orbán's domestic reforms and renationalization of the energy sector. At the time of signing, the energy sector was hemorrhaging financial losses as a result of the re-centralization of the energy sector and delivering price cuts to household consumers. A snapshot provides a partial perspective on these financial losses:

- Privately owned universal service providers for domestic electricity made HUF 20 billion in losses in 2011 and HUF 13.5 billion in 2012 (Portfolio.hu 2014), due to the government's price reduction.
- The privately owned gas universal service provider TIGAZ had a combined loss of HUF 29.5 billion 2011 and 2012, due to the government's price reduction. By 2013 losses were still mounting, at HUF 20 billion (Felsmann 2014, 17).

- Financial losses in all energy utilities were projected to be over HUF 100 billion in 2012 (International Consulting Firm 2013).
- Between 2009 and 2013, investments by utilities were cut by 65% (International Consulting Firm 2013).

The January and February signing of the Paks 2 into Hungary's energy system preceded the April 6, 2014 national parliamentary elections. In seeking a third term, Orbán and his Fidesz party rode on a second utility price cut of 11%, delivered in the fall of 2013, and a third of 6.5% coming in early 2014. As Andras Deak (2016) points out, the timing of signing the Paks contract – before the elections – puts Orbán and his Fidesz party in an awkward position. They would need to defend committing Hungary's future generations to the previous Russian occupiers. Importantly, the pre-election signing of the agreement demonstrated Russia's distrust of Orbán, "the agreement prior to the elections rather suggests that the Russian side feared that Orbán, following reelection, might back out of the plan to expand Paks" (Deak 2016, 336). The linking of the delivery of lower-priced Russian gas with the building of Paks 2 meant Orbán could continue with delivering lower-priced energy to households while receiving Russian investment money into the energy system, where once Western European money had flowed.

In agreeing to building Paks 2 and to lower gas prices, both governments struck a complimentary bargain. "The two were obviously part of the same transaction" (Deak 2016, 334–5). For the price of gas, they managed to publicly settle on $260 tcm compared with a European hub price of $270 tcm, and a much lower price than the former $440 tcm oil-indexed price of previous contracts. Conditions were nearer those given to Bulgaria, which was also committed to building a new Rosatom plant (LaBelle 2015). Russian energy, as in the past, still represented a low-cost future for Orbán, as he himself stated in 2014, "if Europe fails to do its utmost to secure Russian energy, I am not sure how it is going to supply its economy" (AFP 2014). For Orbán, Russia provides the resources and technology to power households and industry at an affordable level.

Overall, striking a deal with the Russians in early 2014 occurred in an international environment with increasing oil and gas prices. High oil prices in 2013 and early 2014 had driven up the oil-indexed gas contract price with Gazprom (Sebestyén Szép 2017, 66). In addition, the state resources required to fill pre-winter gas storage were also significant (since the state now owned gas storage). In 2016, this amounted to 0.4% of state debt, which the government tried to hide from its official statistics, with Eurostat ruling in 2019 that this must be accounted for (Hungary Around the Clock 2019a). The repurchase of companies by state- or privately-owned Hungarian firms could also be seen as strategically shifting state debt away from the government's books.

4.8 CONCLUSION: MEETING SOCIAL COMMITMENTS THROUGH SOVIET DEPENDENCY

The sustained rise of global oil prices in the 1970s prompted Hungary to switch to Soviet nuclear power. Likewise, in 2014, increasing oil and gas prices pushed Hungary to sign up again with Russia to complete the Soviet-era planned expansion of the Paks nuclear power plant. The pursuit of low-cost energy for a resource-poor country pushed the Hungarian government to continue the previous Soviet model of nuclear power and gas for electricity and heat. The increase in energy consumption by households paralleled the price reductions, and thereby increased the energy intensity of the country. This increased consumption drove further dependency on Russia, making consumers more vulnerable to future price increases in both gas and electricity. Politically, Orbán delivered low-priced energy by continuing the political agreements between Russia and Hungary. Rosatom and Gazprom were able to continue their traditional role in Hungary to provide the technology and resources to keep operating the country. Financially, Hungary chose a third era with Russia to transition away from Western European ownership of the energy assets. The choice was to reject EU market pricing for household consumers and expel foreign utilities in exchange for a geopolitical realignment with Russian for accessing resources and technologies. Sustaining Orbán's utility price cut was dependent on this geopolitical reorientation.

After the 2010 election Orbán set out to delink household utility prices from market forces. The financial pain for households after the 2008 financial crisis became a key social policy which could put more money in the pockets of households and turn foreign utilities into enemies of the people. Later, the utility price cuts became an election promise, politicized in the 'war' against the EU and foreign utilities. This became an effective script (later repeated in the battle against the EU and migrants) and was essential for Fidesz's social policy in the battle for Hungarian national independence from global capital (which was viewed as causing the 2008 financial crisis and previous rises in utility prices). The experience of increased household utility prices under EU market conditions was used to motivate voters to sign up to Orbán's vision of low power prices – however financially unsustainable these were.

After 2010, the method and size of state intervention into the energy sector was robust enough to drive foreign utility owners out of the country. However, the departing companies also left behind the accumulated debt accrued since the end of Communism. With the lower utility rates, increasing global prices, and accumulated losses for firms, the pressure built for Hungary to seek relief through the Soviet-era system of patronage to Russian resources and technologies.

Just as the Soviets delivered relief in the 1980s in the form of non-market based nuclear and gas, so did they come to the 'rescue' of Hungary in the mid-2010s with a new energy package that would tie Hungary to Russia for generations. Hungary remains in the EU, and within the interlinked regional security of supply markets, but it lies outside the governance space of consumer markets and a regulatory structure for incentivizing investments.

The interlinkage between energy geopolitics and domestic politics is demonstrated in the embrace of an illiberal economic model, reliant on Russia but with access to EU markets. Low household and industrial energy prices make Hungary affordable and competitive and assist in keeping Fidesz and Orbán in power.

Long term, this interlinkage of geopolitics and domestic energy prices is set to play out for the next few generations of Hungarians. If fair elections are once again conducted in Hungary (currently they are not) (Office for Democratic Institutions and Human Rights 2018), thereby removing the Orbán government, any opposition government has its hands tied. Russia would be able to exert financial pain through Paks 2's onerous financial obligations along with existing and future gas debts. For Hungary to 're-enter' the EU's competitive and transparent energy market, backed by an effective independent energy regulator, Hungarian society's expectations and need for low energy prices must be addressed. The expectations of the last three energy eras are based on the Communist formula of in-built inefficiency and low price. Hungary's domestic energy system, in both demand and supply, is reliant on the upstream relations between the EU and Russia. An effective political and energy transition must tackle these interlinkages.

5. Poland: the other side of the European energy transition

5.1 INTRODUCTION: ENERGY ON THIS SIDE OF THE WALL

Towering on both sides of the entrance to the AGH University of Science & Technology, Krakow, are two pairs of miner statues, with one set holding a Davey lamp and a pickaxe. The four-meter-high statues represent the intellectual and physical strength of coal mining in Poland. The statues stand at the Faculty of Geology, Geophysics and Environmental Protection, housed within one of the most prominent and grand buildings of the university. There is no doubt about the position of mining in the Polish educational system and the state resources expended to support the sector. As Professor Kasztelewicz of the AGH UST Department states, "this is the *other side* of the Berlin Wall"; signifying that Germany can afford a low-carbon transition but the history of the Polish energy sector is based on coal (Kasztelewicz 2019).

Just as the Berlin Wall separated two different socio-political and economic systems, this old division is sustaining a division in the Polish energy system. This chapter describes the Polish government's pursuit to improve energy security and maintain low prices through a fossil fuel strategy reminiscent of the Communist era. The emphasis is on energy inputs and economic output by building gas networks and retaining coal to fuel industry and low-priced heating and electricity. This contrasts with a more localized and EU-oriented sustainable energy strategy that emphasizes cooperation between individuals, businesses, and regional and local governments in Poland. This local energy strategy, as will be described, relies on investments in technologies in energy efficiency and renewables that are linked together in an energy management system within local energy clusters. This chapter explores these different energy strategies: first, how a geopolitical approach retains fossil fuels to sustain low energy prices, and, second, a more recent push to build community-based energy systems that address both sustainability concerns and meet the everyday requirements of citizens and businesses.

This chapter addresses the perception that Polish fossil fuels contribute to a secure and affordable energy system. The narrative around coal and gas in

Poland, examined in the first half of this chapter, retains a Cold War narrative of providing a secure and affordable energy source. This storyline holds both an international element, with the argument that coal, along with gas, provides greater security against Russian resource dependency, and delivers domestic benefits in the form of low energy prices and jobs, including votes in a political swing region (Kureth 2015). Internationally, this position is expressed as Poland drags its feet with EU climate change goals and slowly enacts climate change policies. In 2016, the Energy Minister from the ruling PiS party, Krzysztof Tchorzewski, pointed out that moving to a zero carbon economy as prescribed by the EU is "clearly unacceptable"; the sacrifice for Poland would be too great (Tchorzewski 2016; LaBelle 2017a). Coal – and gas – will remain the central pillar of the Poland's energy mix.

Regardless of the central government's position on coal and gas, progress in other cleaner technologies is progressing. An opposition member of Parliament, Krzysztof Sitarski, a former miner himself and representing a mining region, co-authored a prosumer act and supports renewable energy. He states, "a miner is fighting for renewables" (personal communication, Sitarski 2019); however, he continues to back coal. Nonetheless, in Poland support for coal does not mean a contradiction, rather it demonstrates the nuance of a more informal energy policy reliant on local community and business expertise to build up a new sustainable energy system. As will be shown in the second half of this chapter, at the local and regional levels there is a clear movement towards building integrated sustainable energy clusters. These local initiatives are not waiting for the national government to adjust its policies away from coal and gas. The basis of local investments into both energy efficiency measures, and renewable energy are meeting a social call for improving air quality and keeping consumer prices low.

The East-West division on energy resources and technologies emphasizes the division between a geopolitically secure system and a socially and environmentally focused energy system. This chapter delivers a nuanced accounting of how two different energy systems are developing in Poland. Rather than being shown as contradictory and diverging from previous energy eras, the evolution of Poland's energy system follows international trends of the collapse of the coal sector and the rise of renewables. This chapter accounts for this transition and outlines how localized energy clusters deliver a socially based energy system.

5.2 POLISH ENERGY MIX: SECURE AND DIRTY

In the twentieth century, Poland ranked in the top five countries producing hard coal, alongside the United States, USSR, the UK, and Germany. After WWII, the sector was nationalized and functioned as part of the barter system of the Soviet Union. Production distortions occurred with a record output in 1979 of 201 million tons, an overproduction that enabled further investments to meet a non-existent demand (Global Studies Initiative 2018, 2). After 1989, the coal sector collapsed and was privatized, with the state unable to sustain a massively unprofitable industry. Between 1990 and 2015, there was an 85% reduction in miners, with much of this occurring before 2002 (Global Studies Initiative 2018, 2, 3–4). Despite high output, in both the past and the present, Polish coal remains unprofitable and continues to shrink in capacity and profitability. The future is not bright.

Nonetheless, the argument for retaining coal emerges from both a technological and historical perspective. "For 50 years our energy system was based on coal." The neighbors have nuclear, but Polish society was not that easy to direct or rule (Sitarski 2019). Poland rejected nuclear for the influence the Soviet Union could wield over the country (with the Solidarity Movement beginning at the time of a widespread roll-out of nuclear power in Eastern Europe). Instead, according to this member of the Polish Parliament, money was spent on the Palace of Science and Culture, the towering university building sitting at the heart of Warsaw. For these reasons, "our energy is based on coal" (Sitarski 2019). Polish coal runs on Polish technology, to diversify means giving up the technical capability of Poland to have the know-how to generate its own electricity (Kasztelewicz 2018).

To understand the drive to preserve Polish coal and different options, it is important to separate the different types of coal. Poland possesses both hard coal and lignite mines. Hard coal is mined under the surface, with Polish miners increasingly having to go deeper and deeper to find new seams to exploit. This raises the cost of extraction (WISE 2015). Hard, black coal holds a lower sulphur content, so it is relatively cleaner to burn and more energy dense. Financially, it is profitable to transport this over long distances and accounts for 51% of Poland's installed capacity for power generation. In contrast, 21% of the installed capacity of Poland is composed of lignite-fired power plants. Lignite coal is extracted from open cast mines on the surface of the land. Extraction and burning is technically cheaper (excluding environmental costs); however, burning it produces more CO_2, sulphur and other greenhouse gases. Discussing Poland's energy mix comes with this differentiation in relation to different technology and environmental policy solutions and costs.

The Polish energy mix is heavily reliant on both types of coal, which together account for 52% of overall energy consumption, followed by oil at 26%, natural gas at 16% and renewable energy only accounting for 5% (US Energy Information Administration 2016). Of installed electricity production capacity, 48% comes from hard coal, 31% from lignite, with renewables accounting for 14% (Forum Energii 2017, 13). Heat production is also heavily reliant on coal use, with 89% of heat produced from coal (World Energy

Council 2016) (discussed further below). Coal is highly integrated into the overall Polish energy mix and needs to be assessed within the electricity and heat markets. Poland's continued heavy reliance on coal reflects both domestic resources, social policies, and available and affordable alternatives.

5.2.1 The growing decline of Polish coal

Innovation of new energy technologies sits at the heart of Poland's 2040 energy strategy. Over the next 20 years significant innovative technologies need to come online to boost coal as a profitable and environmentally safe fuel source. Currently, the Polish coal sector suffers from high costs and high inefficiencies, and it causes significant environmental damage. The sector resembles the decline and crash of the Western European coal sector. Figure 5.1 demonstrates the alignment of the decline of coal production alongside the UK, France, and Germany (WISE 2015). The continued use of coal is dependent on fostering a competitive, innovative technological renewal of coal in Poland. Underpinning the justification of coal are: (1) low cost, (2) high security, and (3) social support. Each of these pillars of support is threatened if high imports close Polish mines.

Polish coal must be internationally competitive to remain as a domestic fuel source contributing to energy security and as a low-cost fuel. Polish hard coal must contend with lower-priced imported coal, and extraction in Poland must become cheaper. "Innovations in coal mining and use must be put in place to improve the competitiveness of Polish coal compared to that from imports and other fuels" and reduce negative environmental impacts (Polish Ministry of Energy 2018, 3). The continued use of lignite also depends on new technologies, as it becomes increasingly "burdened" by the costs of complying with the EU's climate policy; therefore, "exploitation of new deposits will depend on the development of innovative methods" (Polish Ministry of Energy 2018, 3). For Poland's coal sector to remain a viable source of energy production, substantial innovative methods must be implemented for both hard and lignite coal due to low international prices and high environmental costs. However, as described next, there are four issues that make Polish coal more expensive and that undermine the 'cheap' energy label.

First, the long-term financial viability of Polish coal requires high upfront costs. The closure of loss-making mines, the opening of new mines in productive seams, and investment into machinery and fewer employees require more financial investments. The average productivity of coal extraction is now 700 tons per employee for 80% of production, a level equal to old subsidized Western European mines to be closed in 2020 (WISE 2015, 22). Productivity will need to increase to 1,650 tons per employee to become profitable by 2050 (WISE 2015, 27). The only mining group performing above this, and with

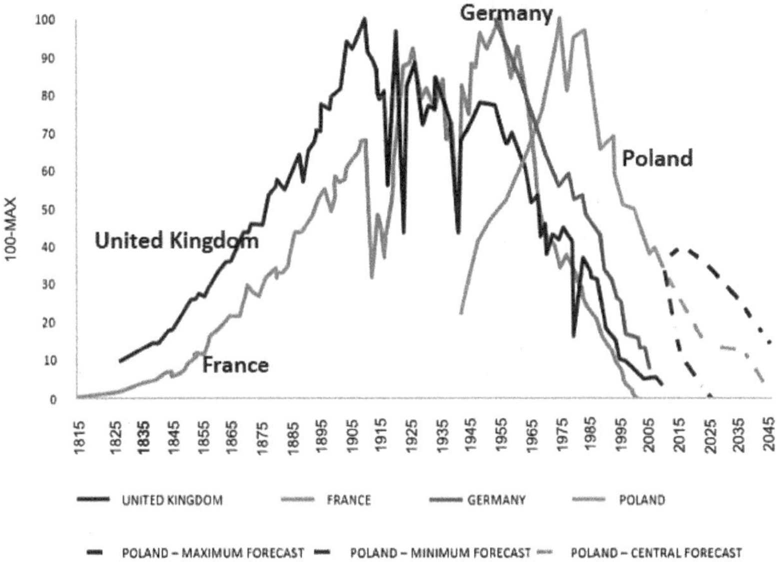

Source: WISE (2015, 37).

Figure 5.1 *'Peak Coal' extraction of coal in Western European Countries and in Poland*

a profit, is the Bogdanka coal mine in Lublin, which has a different geological structure from the Silesia region. Based on the geological structure in the Silesia region, lack of long-term investment, and historic inability to make a consistent profit, it seems unlikely Poland will be able to sustain present output in a financially viable manner (WISE 2015).

Second, subsidies will be necessary to retain coal as a source of energy security. Along with the above reasons for high upfront costs in modernization, socially there is a need to sustain support for closing mines, job losses, and higher costs associated with investments in new technologies. In 2015, Poles supported the closure of unprofitable mines rather than state subsidies to keep them open, with support for renewables higher than for coal (WISE 2015, 43–5). However, 65% of Polish society supports subsidizing the domestic coal industry by buying expensive domestic coal for power production to ensure energy security. Therefore, coal for energy security holds social support (WISE 2015, 43–5) while state subsidies should not be given for social reasons. In the end, there may be a fine line with 'justifiable losses' at a certain level acceptable for society.

Third, the building of new coal power plants shifts the economics of energy production, resulting in higher prices for both heat and electricity. Communist-era coal plants are profitable due to their continual life extensions and lack of debt. The European Commission gave Poland until 2020 to decommission these power plants that are now only 33% efficient. Poland is bringing new power plants online, but at a much higher cost. In 2017, there was the largest increase in new generation. The new Kozienice coal-fired power plant produces over 1,200 MW a year. In addition, Combined Cycle Gas Turbines (CCGT) in Wloclawek, Gorzow, and Torun added an additional 729 MW to electricity production (Forum Energii 2017, 9). These new sources have higher CAPEX; while gas is more expensive than coal to burn they are both necessary to modernize the energy system but at present are unable to recoup their costs under the current power structure. New coal plants operate at a loss of 770 EUR to 1,000/MWh (Smolen 2018). Further renewal of Poland's coal power plants may be shifting. In 2020, the 1 GW Ostroleka C coal power plant unit – once planned to be online in 2023 – appears to have been canceled, and the site revamped for a gas power generation unit under the new ownership of PKN Orlen (Edwardes-Evans 2020).

And, fourth, the cost of burning coal is increasing due to EU emission allowances and coal prices. These higher prices could be seen in 2019, when prices were projected to substantially increase by 30–40%. An industry group complained in 2018 that they pay more than in Germany to burn coal (S.A, Telewizja Polska 2018), with complaints of 34 different types of taxes on the sector (Adamowicz 2019). In 2018, it was projected that prices would increase 50–70% between 2017 and 2019 (Olszewski 2018). To prevent this rise, in the final days of 2018 the Polish legislature voted to reduce taxes on the sector to absorb the price increase and compensate energy companies for their losses at a total cost of over two billion EUR. An additional 230 million EUR was put into a green investment fund to reduce CO_2 emissions (Polska Agencja Prasowa SA 2018). With the outlook for higher costs associated with coal generation, previous justifications are now questionable. The next section addresses the health and environmental costs of coal generation, lending justification as to why there is another local and regional energy strategy developing that reduces the use of coal (discussed in section 5.3).

5.2.2 Staying with coal: the social and environmental cost of coal

The split in public support for coal can be seen in the emergence of air quality as an important public and political issue. Air quality in Poland is the worst in Europe. Thirty-six of Europe's 50 most polluted cities are in Poland. A significant reason for this is attributed to the use of coal in power plants, industrial production, and heat generation in both district heating facilities and homes. In the early 2000s, nearly 45% of building space and water heating consumption was attributed to coal. Heat consumption alone is responsible for 43% of Poland's total annual SO_X emissions and 62% of PM_{10} emissions (3CSEP 2012, 11). Industrial air pollution continues to be dominated by the energy sector. There is a large share of pollution from the energy sector releasing a range of toxic pollutants, carbon dioxide, mercury, nitrogen oxides, and sulphur oxides (European Environment Agency 2018). There is also a significant division between Poland and the rest of Europe in terms of air quality (European Environment Agency 2019). Poland leads Europe for poor air quality, which also creates considerable health impairment with a projected 6,000 winter deaths caused by poor air quality attributed to heat production (3CSEP 2012, 14).

Building a description of those who are energy poor in Poland highlights factors that indicate a higher propensity towards an inability to afford energy services, rather than use of coal. An adequate heating level is hardest to meet by those using electrical and gas heaters (Instytut Badan Strukturalnych 2015, 13) rather than using coal stoves or wood. In Poland, income poverty and energy poverty are largely separate experiences. "Only 20% of individuals afflicted with energy poverty are also stricken by income poverty" (Instytut Badan Strukturalnych 2015, 16). Nonetheless, using the definition of energy poverty there is a significant level, with 34% of Polish households, or 17.2 million people in 2013, spending 13% of disposable income on utility services (Instytut Badan Strukturalnych 2015, 19). Most affected are people living in single-family detached or terraced houses which are occupied by single persons or either single or married parents with one or two children (Instytut Badan Strukturalnych 2015, 19).

Progress is made each year in the ability of homeowners to keep their homes adequately warm in the winter. Figure 5.2 demonstrates the significant drop over time, from above 35% in 2005 to below 10% in 2016. With over one-third of households extremely price sensitive for energy services (Figure 5.3), the price of electricity has remained constant over a ten-year period since 2007, at below €15 cents per kWh (Eurostat 2020a). Many Polish households, therefore, are highly price sensitive.

The price of Polish electricity and heat may be among the cheapest in Europe, but the price sensitivity also means policy makers tread carefully over pricing issues in the energy sector. The dramatically high levels of pollution and poor health effects of Polish coal producing electricity and heat requires a thoughtful energy transition. Nonetheless, it is clear from the statements of policy makers that they are not prepared to move towards a higher mix of renewable energy sources. The country's decision-makers maintain a consistent fossil fuel-based energy strategy with a political vision and economic strategy.

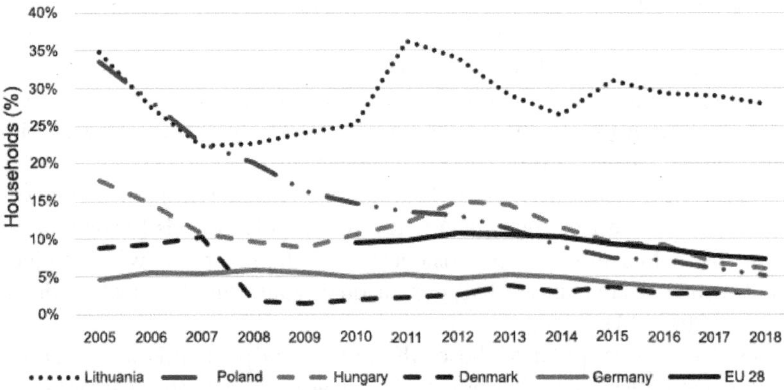

Source: Eurostat (2020b).

Figure 5.2 *Inability to keep home adequately warm 2005–18: Lithuania, Poland, Hungary, Denmark, Germany and EU 28*

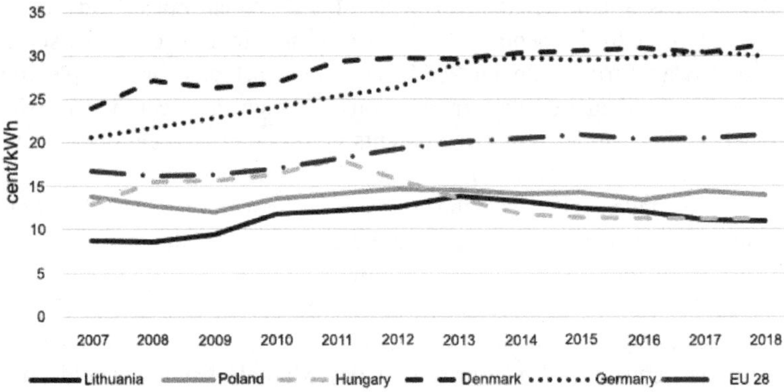

Note: includes all taxes and levies.
Source: Eurostat (2020a).

Figure 5.3 *EU household electricity prices of selected countries*

Regardless of political party, the strategy is to retain fossil fuels while constraining the use of RET. In 2013, former Prime Minister Donald Tusk (2007–14) said that coal and "soon shale gas" will remain dominant, with renewable energy sources remaining "limited as much as EU rules will allow" (PHYS.ORG 2013). In 2015, Polish elections ushered in a new government, under which continuity remains, with support for fossil fuels and suppression of RET. Poland's Energy Minister Krzysztof Tchorzewski asserted that the EU's pursuit of zero carbon emissions in the power sector by 2050 is impossible to apply to Poland, stating that: "we (Poland) reject that, clearly unacceptable." The sacrifices for Poland would be too great to move away from coal. Echoing that, both the financial cost to consumers and energy security would be too high to leave coal behind.

Nonetheless, the Polish energy system needs to evolve and two visions are emerging of how Poland will meet its energy needs in the future. As the next section outlines, the future energy mix is based on both a centralized gas and coal strategy along with a decentralized – locally controlled – program utilizing energy efficiency and small-scale renewables to power local and regional economies. The local energy clusters sit in contrast to the centralized vision of high efficiency coal-fired power plants and suppression of renewables (Tchorzewski 2016). The final section describes how these diverging systems are being set up.

5.3 POLAND 2040: SETTING A NEW TECHNOLOGICAL TRAJECTORY

> The objective of the Polish energy policy is to provide energy security, while ensuring competitiveness of the economy, energy efficiency and reduction of the environmental impact of the energy sector, and with optimum use of Poland's own energy resources. (Polish Ministry of Energy 2018, 2)

The objective of the Polish energy policy up to 2040 and beyond is focused on energy security through diversification of production sources. In 2018, a new medium-term energy strategy was drafted outlining the Polish energy sector to 2040. The biggest shift in the objective is the building of a 6–9 GW nuclear power plant to become operational in 2033 with full capacity reached in 2043. Electricity generation from coal is expected to remain high at 60% by making coal production and the operation of powerplants more efficient and profitable through innovative technologies (discussed above).

In 2017, renewables accounted for 19% of installed capacity, with onshore wind accounting for 13%, which was essentially banned after the PiS government came into power in 2015. Renewables are expected to account for 21% of final energy consumption by 2030, with solar PV and offshore wind accounting for the biggest increase. Biomass, energy storage, and gas CCGT are expected to assist in the operation of the renewable market. Overall, there are significant planned changes to Poland's energy mix. The next section provides an overview of this strategy and its reliance on new infrastructure, innovation in both gas and renewables, and the emergence of local leadership in a sustainable energy transition.

5.3.1 The quiet revolution: Polish gas

If the argument to retain coal is due to energy security concerns, then the pursuit of gas emerges as a strong, cleaner alternative. Poland holds specific designs on importing and producing large quantities of gas that equal the amount of gas imported from Russia. Diversification of sources and routes represents a robust geopolitical strategy by the government. There is a three-pronged energy strategy for the use of gas in Poland: shale gas, LNG, and new import routes.

Currently, the Polish gas sector meets 16% of its needs, with conventional production dropping as reserves are depleted, leading to higher imports. In 2016, 84% of gas was imported and came largely from Eastern sources (i.e. Gazprom). Industry is the largest user (45%), followed by households (24%) (Forum Energii 2017, 35–6). Gas is viewed as important both for industrial processes (chemicals) and for future electricity generation, with a 20% market share expected (Polish Ministry of Energy 2018). Headlines around Poland's gas sector involve its 'failed' attempt to produce shale gas and its inability to block Nord Stream 2, the Russian-German Gazprom pipeline. A look at these headlines demonstrates significant infrastructure projects going forward despite the headline setbacks.

In 2012, the Polish shale gas revolution became front page news when the country's vast shale gas deposits became known. However, from 2007 there had already been exploration of Poland's potential. Nonetheless, the apparent success in the US demonstrated the profound impact shale gas could make to a country's gas supplies. In 2011, the US Energy Information Administration released a report claiming huge and significant potential in Poland (US Energy Information Administration 2011). US and Canadian oil and gas firms set up camp in Poland to explore and hopefully extract deposits holding up to 250 years' worth of Polish demand, with 2.5–5.5 times more shale gas deposits than conventional gas (Goldthau and LaBelle 2016; KPMG Global Energy Institute 2012; Polish Geological Institute-National Research Institute/ Państwowy Instytut Geologiczny-Państwowy Instytut Badawczy 2012). The flood of interest was underpinned by the perception that the price of shale gas could undercut Russian gas.

Gas firms rushed to file for exploration concessions from the Polish state. In 2012, 115 exploration concessions were awarded, which began producing a long administrative backlog, despite Parliament attempting to speed up the administrative process (LaBelle 2017a, 201). The height of the shale gas revolution was reached in 2015 when 70 gas wells were drilled for research purposes to assess the viability of shale gas. However, only 25 of the wells used hydraulic fracturing technology to test the ability to extract gas (Kureth 2015). By 2015, over $2 billion was invested into Polish shale gas with no commercially viable gas being extracted.

However, by 2016 the 'revolution' was over. Eighty-four concessions were returned, with mainly state-owned firms remaining active; international firms lost interest due to a range of factors and left the country (see Goldthau and LaBelle 2016; LaBelle 2017a). Ultimately, Polish geology was different than in the US and required different technological solutions to commercially extract the gas (Buckley 2012). Foreign companies that quickly arrived in Poland to explore the potential were also quick to move on. ExxonMobil, Talisman, Marathon Oil, Total, Chevron, and ConocoPhillips had all pulled out by 2015. Different explanations were offered, such as better prospects elsewhere, and certainly the international fall of natural gas prices played a role.

The enthusiastic rush for Polish gas is over, but the energy security and demand for gas in Poland is not lessening. More significantly, the country is turning towards a long-term strategy that holds greater potential to deliver gas to meet environmental and security requirements. Polish firms PKN Orlean and PGNiG stuck out the technological challenges and are now producing results with hydraulic fracturing and seismology – the core shale gas technology. In 2018, a joint effort by both companies resulted in a joint discovery of a new gas deposit along with a test well confirming good potential for production. This adds to previous findings in other deposit regions of Poland (PKN ORLEN 2018a). Further efforts by PKN Orlean using the "latest technologies in seismic imaging" and data analysis enable horizontal drilling to find further gas deposits (PKN ORLEN 2018b). A domestic shale gas industry assumes a significant role in contributing towards a more secure and cleaner energy system. Discussed next is how imports will also be contributing to the larger role of gas in Poland.

5.3.2 Poland diversifies gas import routes

The geopolitics of gas place Poland right in the middle of Russian and German imperialist history. The Molotov–Ribbentrop Pact which divided Poland between Nazi Germany and the Soviet Union provides the historical weariness of Poland to foster a more integrated course in its modern energy relations. Reliance on Russian gas extends back to the Soviet period when Poland imported 65% of its consumption, 8 billion cubic meters, annually from Russia (Rosicki 2015). Because of this high dependency, Poland is diversifying its gas import routes through new ground and sea networks and using LNG. There are now three strategic import routes, with two of these routes under the project name, North Gate; this seeks to build a Northern European gas supply route independent of Russia (Figure 5.4). This includes the Swinoujscie LNG terminal and a Norwegian and Danish gas corridor with undersea and land-based pipeline networks bringing Norwegian North Sea gas to Poland and other Eastern European countries. The European Commission is assisting in the finances for the project (Warsaw Institute 2017b). The Baltic Pipeline connects with Lithuania and has a capacity of 10 bcm, thereby fostering supply and route diversification for both LNG terminals (with the Klaipeda LNG terminal) and an alternative route for Russian-sourced gas. The projects are expected to be operation in 2022, when Poland's long-term contract with Gazprom ends (AFP 2018).

Source: Warsaw Institute (2017a).

Figure 5.4 *The North Gate project, composed of an LNG terminal and large pipeline network*

Polish distrust of Russian and German intents is compounded by the building of the Nord Stream 1 pipeline between Germany and Russia under the Baltic Sea and completed in 2011. Previously, there were plans to expand the Yamal I pipeline that opened in 1999. This pipeline traverses Belarus and Germany.

The route was viewed as secure, since it was thought unlikely that Russia would turn off gas to Germany. However, once Nord Stream I went online, then the risk that the pipeline could be shut down for political purposes was viewed as higher. Further, Russian efforts to diversify its import routes into Western Europe went beyond Nord Stream 1 by building a second pipeline (Nord Stream 2). In short, Nord Stream demonstrates the antagonistic relationship between Poland, Germany, and Russia over gas flows (Georgi 2015). Breaking the imperialist geopolitical isolation, Poland is taking independent action and expanding beyond these two neighbors to create new sea and land delivery routes.

5.3.3 Local self-sufficiency: energy clusters

The increasing cost of power and the environmental impact of dirty coal used for heating is motivating local authorities in Poland to also transform their local energy systems. Energy clusters, an integrated local network of supply and energy efficiency technologies and practices, are a means for local and regional authorities to ensure the power system functions at the local level. Officially, these systems were launched in 2016 and enable small-scale investments into renewable energy and energy efficiency (personal communication, Lipinska 2018). In 2019, there were over 60 local energy clusters formed after a government initiative. Clusters are also outlined in the 2040 national energy strategy. This section reviews and identifies how some local organizations are cooperating to lay down the future local energy system. This community-based system brings together neighbors within an energy cluster framework to deliver affordable and clean energy to households and businesses.

The examples for energy cultures differ between each community. One municipality is pushing residential solar PV, biogas, and biomass as well as the renovation of public buildings, and providing educational assistance to households (Adamowicz 2019). Another example is a 20-km-long valley with the longest village in Poland which is building up its solar PV capacity. The valley is susceptible to power outages during storms. Eight hundred houses out of 2,200 now use solar PV to produce electricity for hot water and heat (Kopec 2019). Energy clusters build resilience in the system even as long-term solutions are implemented by the national government. The future holds the potential for prosumers in this energy cluster model.

The energy cluster model fits both the demand side and the supply side where there are strong movements to integrate and transform at the local level. This is apparent in the discussions and actions between community leaders and large Polish energy companies. In 2015, Tauron produced over 80% of its energy from coal (Tauron 2015); the company is now setting up a special unit to focus on energy clusters (Kopec 2019). According to Rafal Soja, President of the Board of Tauron, large energy projects are now too costly (Soja 2019). Instead, the company is focusing on energy efficiency and small-scale production in Polish communities. For Soja, there can only be one strategy that the whole sector "must follow," and that is meeting the energy needs of communities through solar, energy management, and efficiency, including more R&D and innovation (Soja 2019). This is a monumental shift, as even the largest Polish coal company sees coal as a dead-end business, with growth prospectus only in the clean energy field.

This switch for the company is echoed by a local mayor, who had stated in the past that Tauron was not interested in cooperating with the municipality. In 2017 the company really changed its attitude when it started to build large-scale solar farms; now it is interested in other energy projects that benefit the community (Adamowicz 2019). The mayor of 35,000 citizens of a commune in Eastern Poland, who was last elected with an 80% majority, takes the view that citizens are not interested in reducing carbon emissions, "but [in] the money left in their pockets" (Adamowicz 2019). For this, they are developing their own energy cluster in cooperation with Tauron, meeting and managing the energy demands of the community in a variety of ways. This strategy of ensuring money stays in consumers' – and voters' – pockets underlines the financial and social benefits deliverable through energy clusters.

5.3.4 Focusing on demand

A regional energy manager in Gdansk views energy clusters as energy islands that provide local generation of electricity and heat; they are both small systems with connections with the larger national centralized system (personal communication, Kumiega 2019). Those participating in an energy cluster include private and state-owned businesses along with energy companies. The idea is not to compete against companies, but to work with these companies for local solutions (Adamowicz 2019). Currently, municipalities can point out the problems with the energy system, but there remains an information gap on the solutions (personal communication, Kumiega 2019), with information campaigns necessary to increase awareness and interests in energy efficiency and solar systems (Adamowicz 2019).

Building a cleaner future for electricity and heat production can occur at the local level. Local communities are building solar and biomass projects for public and private buildings, but without government support (personal communication, Mateusz 2018). In the Miedzyrzec Podlaski Commune, schools were a priority project; money came from external sources rather than the government to build a passive energy gym, install LED lights, and modernize the heating system. Even if in the end these projects benefit the central budget by reducing energy consumption, there remains limited government support (Adamowicz 2019).

Regional and local governments are taking over the operations of the central state in other areas. Air pollution is a driving force in the regional cluster initiatives. Normally, environmental issues are under the authority of the central government ministries and agencies (personal communication, Lipinska 2018). But here too local communities have stepped up efforts to reduce air pollution through integrated energy systems approaches which focus both on the physical energy system and the social needs.

In the Pomorskie Region, including Gdansk, Sopot, and Gdynia, the regional and municipal authorities are building a regional macro perspective by producing an energy audit that will assist in planning and integrating a regional energy system (personal communication, Lipinska 2018). The audit includes assessment of companies' needs and the services offered by companies. The scale of change is modest but important at the regional level.

The interests in energy efficiency are different at the local and national levels. The National Energy Strategy of 2040 outlines the constrained role of efficiency measures in which "savings need to be compared to inputs" (Polish Ministry of Energy 2018, 5); that is, energy efficiency is expensive and producing more energy may be a cheaper option. However, as one city energy manager remarks, the rising cost of energy and air pollution requires actions in energy efficiency. Improving the energy efficiency of a residential building with ten apartments holds a return on investment (ROI) of 60 years (personal communication, Tobolewicz 2018). Therefore, it does require large upfront costs that are only amortized over a very long period. Nonetheless, the direct impact on air quality, lower utility bills, and displacement of new generation (for wasted energy), along with health and environmental impacts, holds significant value (3CSEP 2012).

For example, assessing energy savings from buildings over the long term means that not only are the financial benefits apparent but the system benefits are considerable. Figure 5.5 demonstrates renovation scenarios in Poland. These 'S-DEEP' scenarios outline the long-term energy requirements for heating, based on the extent of renovation in dwellings. In this scenario, upfront costs for renovation are higher but the long-term impact holds substantial energy-, societal-, and system-level savings. The 'lock-in' of energy – that is, the amount of energy 'wasted' – is between 43–60%. This perpetual lock-in of wasted energy corresponds to a highly efficient building renovation (with 60% savings) over no renovation or a less-than-effective renovation (3CSEP 2012, 6).

There are two energy systems under development in Poland. The first is based on expanding the physical infrastructure to import more gas and ensure security of supply for the industrial and energy base. The second system integrates the local social contexts of the energy system to assess and build an interconnected regional and local energy system. These two approaches utilize different politics and economics, with the latter assuming the failure of the planned upgrade of the centralized energy system. Diverging perspectives also fuel diverging approaches, with the biggest difference over energy efficiency and air pollution. It seems oxymoronic for the state to support the long-term import of gas but not place the same weight on energy efficiency.

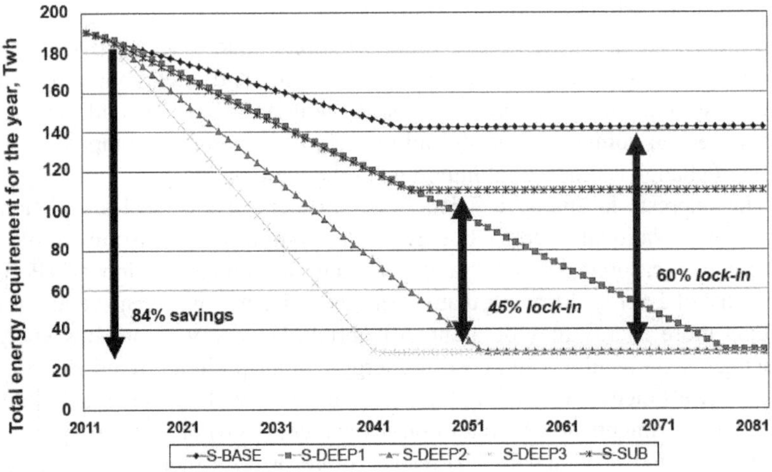

Source: 3CSEP (2012, 6).

Figure 5.5 *Potential total annual energy savings (TWh/year) of the Polish building stock*

This Soviet-era model of production output continues to dominate Poland's energy strategy. It is only at the local level, with the lack of resources, that a system-wide approach is taken. Discussed next is how these two approaches combine with the future of coal to expose how geopolitics and social activities shape Poland's energy system.

5.4 CONCLUSION: CLUSTERS OF CHANGE

The miner statues standing at the entrance of the AGH University in Krakow represent the strength and place of Polish coal within the nation. However, society is quickly changing around it. Air pollution, political mistrust, and climate change are forcing the policy adjustments necessary to build a new energy system. The justification of coal, accepted by both society and politicians, is based on energy security concerns and the historical imperialist policies of Russia and Germany. Even with EU membership, Poland pursues a neighborhood policy of integration with a global strategy of supply and technology diversification. Coal is neither environmentally nor socially economically sustainable for Poland. The shift towards gas requires both new delivery routes and new technology requirements. At the national level, gas appears to be the long-term solution combined with an emotional attachment to coal that is devoid of economic reality.

The building of energy clusters shifts the country towards a renewables future, with energy efficiency reducing the need for a bigger or more efficient fossil fuel generation. The projected failure and high costs of coal mining, combined with high operating costs for coal power plants, means that local industry, governments, and social groups pursue a low-cost strategy of efficiency improvements and synergies. Delivering 'money in the pockets' of consumers and voters enables local politicians to benefit from advances in technology and meet the demands for a cleaner (and more sustainable) environmental policy. Poland provides an effective case to examine the creation of both a new physical and social energy system.

The energy system in Poland is influenced by the social pressure, or rather the acceptance, to sustain coal. Polish society accepts coal mining as a way of life; nonetheless, it is also demanding cleaner air. The Polish government is delivering, and has plans to continue coal mining on a financially sustainable manner; even though most indicators suggest that the enormous efforts and cost required to raise the productivity of Polish mines means that the domestic industry is unlikely to survive. Probably, the best indicator is the comments and investments of the coal companies themselves, who are both shifting investments and canceling projects. There are at least initial steps to shift investments into working with communities to deliver clean energy in local clusters.

Poland lives and breathes coal. The task ahead is how to separate these two. Nuclear power, international gas networks, and renewable energy combined with energy efficiency efforts produce a cleaner energy system while addressing social concerns. The heritage of coal feeds the socio-political dialogue but a managed phase-out of mines and power plants is necessary from both an economic and social perspective as well as a financial one. If Polish society and politicians choose to retain coal, for security or social reasons, a more robust and environmentally-aware plan needs to be developed. Rather than watching the terminal decline of this resource- and human-intensive sector, a longer-term environmentally sustainable perspective can deliver a socially more sustainable transition.

6. The power of energy cultures

6.1 INTRODUCTION: CHOOSING OUR ENERGY RELATIONS

The flow of gas and delivery of electricity represent established political and economic actions built over decades. Lithuania, Hungary, and Poland each display efforts to deliver secure and affordable energy to consumers. Conversion technologies emerge as contentious points of domestic and international struggles. The energy relations of society, politics, and economics is about controlling the site of combustion (Dalby 2018, 720). For Ostwald, it is the task of a responsible society to manage this process in the most efficient manner (Ostwald 1907, in Stewart 2014). An energy culture reflects societal values and norms, which shape practices and the material well-being of society; these are perceptible in the physicality of the energy system present in the landscape.

Our physical and social relations create energy cultures. Sites of rapid and pronounced cultural transitions can expose a juxtaposition of cultural practices, thereby making the cultural milieu of Eastern Europe a rich landscape for case studies of economic, political, and social transition. Lithuania, Hungary, and Poland provide rich case studies to understand cultural choices within the energy system; thereby exposing the clash of energy cultures, interpretations of justice, and the convergence and expression of a geopolitics of cultures. This chapter largely focuses on the delivery and interpretation of particular energy justice where the cultural traits of each country provide an overriding influence on the perception of justice.

The linking of the particular perceptions of justice is connected to common experiences within the new EU Member States in Eastern Europe. Here a new 'geopolitics of energy' emerged after the collapse of Communism. Efforts to open up and integrate energy markets relied on a neoliberal agenda of privatization and regulatory governance (Eberlein 2008). The energy system itself required a significant inflow of foreign direct investment (FDI) preceding many country's memberships into the EU (LaBelle 2009). Eastern European Member States were left with the infrastructure of the Communist planned economy and COMECON era; later EU membership resulted in a regulatory and legislative change for the operation of the energy system. The orientation of both the physical energy system and the socially embedded expectations and practices around energy (cultures) remained similiar to their Communist-era structure, only gradually changing over time. After 2010, Lithuania, Hungary, and Poland built domestic and foreign policies on the orientation of their energy systems. They had two choices: (1) supply diversification utilizing EU Directives to break domestic and foreign monopolistic control over distribution and supply; or (2) retain Communist-era infrastructure and resource ties with Russia to provide heat and power at stable low rates. These two options bring into focus the geopolitics of energy and cultural interpretations of an equitable energy system.

Developing an energy culture framework provides us with the tools to understand the power relations that influence this energy transition in Eastern Europe. Energy justice and geopolitical cultures expose the relational struggles within energy cultures. The creation of culture, according to Mitchell, stems from the struggle, "between the production of 'culture' and its use, where 'culture' is produced, not as a thing, but as a relationship" (Mitchell 2000, xviii). There is overlap between Ostwald's energy and efficiency culture combining with Mitchell's relational struggles fomenting culture: energy cultures are power relationships.

The diplomat securing a confidential gas contract is also securing a position of power for the gas provider. The contractual relationship, reliant on the infrastructure, creates the structural conditions that society and the state accept. Gas displaces other heating and generation technologies. The contract can be done in a commercially transparent manner (soft power) or as part of a political exchange of sovereignty (hard power). The provision and use of the resource require cultural conditions in both the physical energy system, identified in pipelines, and the social energy system, measured in the consumer price. A national energy culture reflects these power relations in the energy system.

Imbalances in power relations reflect relational struggles producing culture. The site of combustion is where the physical and social energy systems collide and produce culture. This is where we can understand how relations create energy cultures in Eastern Europe. Table 6.1 provides a broad description of characteristics exemplifying the case studies that expose underlining social, political, and economic contestations within national energy systems. The social and physical energy systems are structured through relations between society and the state. In the case studies it is possible to see the physical and social structure the EU and Russia use to organize their energy systems. By exposing the relations within the energy system, the culture of energy can be described.

Table 6.1 Characteristics for country case study selection

State and society relations	Empirical characteristics	Conceptual energy cultures description
Social contract: Society transfers the sovereign authority to the state to secure conditions for freedom and equity.	Political support to honor social contract to maintain low energy prices or retain/reject culturally significant technologies and resources from the Communist period and implement a regulated market-based system.	**Social energy system:** Energy cultures are broadly relationally transformative and reliant on power relations (implicit).
Regulatory compact: Society authorizes state to secure a modern energy system with universal access to energy services and resources. Protect the public good.	Choice of political-economic system favoring certain physical artifacts in the energy system. Choice for Communist-era technologies and resources (nuclear, RU gas, coal), or EU supported policies of renewables, energy efficiency, and security of supply described in the Energy Union strategy.	**Physical energy system:** Energy cultures are a physical expression of relations (explicit).

The physical orientation of a country's energy system can be seen in new energy projects. These projects either express an EU and global connection or continue the Soviet legacy of resource and technology dependency on Russia. The choice of the technologies and resources powering an energy system emerges from state-society relations expressed in social contracts (Chapter 1). The contract is an articulation of equality and freedom of the transfer of sovereignty from individuals to the state (Vatn 2005, 28). Whether this is represented in low-priced district heating in Lithuania or low-priced coal in Poland, upholding the social contract is a political duty. The contract requires political action to secure resources and technologies, often through international supply chains, and requires the delivery of energy services at an affordable price to consumers. More substantially, for those citizens on the financial edge, alleviating energy poverty is a political duty (cf. de Vita 2007; Bouzarovski and Simcock 2017, 645). Both the infrastructure and orientation of the energy system need to be built to serve society and fulfill this social contract.

For Eastern European countries, delivery of energy services requires their own 'social contract,' this is either an EU- or Russian-oriented energy system. There are important differences, such as ownership of utilities and whether a regulatory governance system operates or if household prices are determined by politicians. To satisfy this social contract, national and international supply chains with infrastructure and diplomatic activities all need to work with domestic consumers over the use of resources and technologies (just as Ostwald describes). The built infrastructure is connected to social expectations over issues, such as price and upstream sourcing of resources and conversion technologies. The site of combustion – located in the middle of upstream and downstream activities – also sits in the middle of the physical and social energy systems. The next section provides a deeper discussion of the structural aspects to understanding the differences and overlaps between the physical and social energy systems. This enables a fuller perspective of understanding how energy culture is displayed and contested in the case study countries.

6.2 THE STRUCTURAL IMPACT OF ENERGY CULTURE IN EASTERN EUROPE

Space and scale provide an important part in understanding cultural relations in the energy system. By identifying relational struggles within spaces and between scales, there emerges a visibility to 'sites of contested energy relations' – hot points where cultures clash. Within the case study countries, this describes the restructuring of the physical energy systems and the embedded expectations around the price of energy within the social energy system. The importance of energy resources, technologies, and prices emerge as key contestation points that orientate the energy systems towards the EU or Russia and determine the acceptable level of national self-sufficiency. Table 6.2 summarizes issues connected to spatial relations and scaled market activities. It demonstrates the commonality between the three case studies around access to resources, networks, and price. Solutions to these security threats were treated differently based on the orientation of the energy system. Taken together, the energy cultures in the three countries display commonality in their choices around energy system geopolitical orientation and addressing social justice issues to fulfill the social contract.

The spatial and scalar organization of the energy system creates a structure that organizes energy relations. The use of Mitchell's (2000) relational perspective to explain how culture is created enables an ontological division to assist and describe relations interacting between and in scales and space. A geographic perspective highlights interaction in society and the landscape. Relational struggles create energy cultures, therefore understanding the contestation over space and scale assists understanding how culture is created. To provide a greater understanding of the relational struggles creating energy culture, three axioms are developed. These 'truisms' help guide the analysis within the overall structural fragmentation of energy cultures. First, the built infrastructure expresses the characteristics of a country's energy culture. The built environment, with pipelines, roads, power lines, and power plants demonstrates what type of resources are used and the habits of society.

A deductive approach can be taken to understand how society interacts within the energy system, such as how social practices around technologies, the built environment, and government policies enable or deny access to affordable energy services or resources. By maintaining a spatial and scale division of the energy system, a structural perspective breaks down the energy system through the physical and social systems rather than by demand and supply.

In the three case studies, the physical energy system emerges through the use of artifacts, such as LNG ships, gas pipelines extending from Russia and Central Asia to Europe, Polish or Russian coal mines, district heating systems keeping panel houses warm in Eastern Europe, or stoves in single-family homes burning coal and firewood. The expression of energy poverty encompasses this whole supply and demand chain of resources and technologies. Energy poverty emerges through the leaky panel houses and single-family homes and antiquated heating systems. High levels of winter smog choke Polish cities and limited financial assistance from state institutions leaves people vulnerable to the cold. The first axiom summarizes these surface-level expressions of energy cultures:

1. Energy cultures are *spatial* expressions of the social milieu around energy systems and are perceived through physical expressions of artifacts, imaginaries, and inequality of material and environmental differences.

Second, a more conceptual understanding provides a nuanced accounting of inequity and representation of injustices within the social energy system. Space and scale structure power relations which determine the use of networks, technologies, and resources. Here, geopolitics and energy justice identify how Russia uses hard power to extract political dependence from Hungary by 'solving' or perpetuating its high energy poverty level, while the expression of soft power is perceived in how the EU motivates Lithuania to join the Single Energy Market. The societies and politicians of Eastern Europe maneuver between local demands for low-cost energy services but require international interconnections to provide resources and financial relations to connect with supply lines and larger markets. Russia and the EU provide a dichotomy of approaches and power relations which influence the expression of energy cultures. The scaled interactions within the physical energy system exemplify the power relations within energy cultures. An equitable energy system is reliant on power relations in the economics of energy markets and geopolitical positions of producers and consumers. The second axiom summarizes:

2. Energy cultures play out at different *scales* and are both *socially and economically transformative* and reliant on *power relations* between scales.

Table 6.2 Spatial and scale inequality in case studies

Country	Market scale issues	Spatial networks and resource access	Sites of contested energy relations	Orientation of energy system to support social contract
Lithuania	Small market size; dependent on international resources and power sources. Removal of nuclear power forced scaling up of electricity and gas markets, international network expansion fostered import reliance on electricity and gas.	Previously constrained network connections; total dependence on Soviet-era energy network. Higher Russian gas prices compared with Baltic neighbors; limited natural resources for power generation. Perceived security threat due to geographic location. Spatial diversification of gas and electricity networks reduces dependence.	Energy resources and technology; price of energy services; energy security.	Transparency and accountability through national ownership. Ensure affordability by diversification. Implementation of due process through EU governance framework.
Hungary	Small market size; dependent on international resources, technology, and power sources; regional market integration; slow pace of diversification; support for Russian Southern gas corridor.	Limited diversified network able to import non-Russian gas; use of Russian nuclear and gas limits non-Russian technologies and resources. Limited support for Croatian LNG diversification. High share of electricity imports from neighboring countries.	Energy resources and technology; price of energy services; energy security.	Deteriorating financial conditions within the energy system and households resulted in a different energy system to address inequity and affordability. Neglecting transparency and due process; a return to the Soviet-era energy system addressed rising inequity in households, which was not recognized under the neoliberal system.

Country	Market scale issues	Spatial networks and resource access	Sites of contested energy relations	Orientation of energy system to support social contract
Poland	Large market size, dependent on low-priced coal imports. Previous dependency on Russian gas imports, declining gas reserves forces scaling up of supply chain; high production cost for coal and gas, imports ensure cheap power. Different energy strategies at national, regional, and local levels.	Higher Russian gas prices compared with Germany. Previous dependency on Soviet-era gas network drove network diversification. Reliant on cheap domestic and international coal networks to alleviate energy poverty. Perceived security threat due to geographic location.	Energy security; price of energy services; control of technology; energy resources.	Coal is retained to provide affordability for all households in a secure national energy system. Lack of recognition for an equitable generational and sustainable energy system. Long-term affordability and sustainability require a coal alternative.

Source: Author.

Third, there is a deep structure within energy cultures, and it is perceptible in the injustices and poverty within the physical energy system. It is here where we can again invoke Ostwald (Stewart 2014) to understand that energy cultures are relationally transformative and there is a moral imperative to accessing the benefits of our modern energy system. The deep structure is where the relational struggles occur between those attempting to influence the direction of the energy culture and those dominating the social practices around the culture of the physical energy system. For example, Poles or Hungarians are forced for economic reasons to burn coal in their homes, which degrades both their health and the environment. Through a radical activist lens, we see this is where political and social leaders vie for domination and extract political and economic power to control the cultural energy practices, and even the narrative around an energy culture. In Eastern Europe, this plays out through maintaining a Communist-era narrative of (low-cost) resource dependency on coal and gas; thereby enabling geopolitical cultures of fossil fuel dependency to shape foreign and domestic policy. Controlling the technology and resources for combustion translates into political and economic power. The physical and social expression of energy cultures are representative of these power relations. Power is given through culture. Culture holds social, economic, and political value. Energy cultures are relationally transformative due to their influence on the built infrastructure and control over social practices. This enables influence over past narratives around the past, present, and future energy system, along with influence on the choice of future technologies, resources, and practices. Energy cultures transform the energy system. The final axiom represents this influence:

3. Energy cultures are *relationally transformative* in energy systems, including mechanical and thermal, social, political and economic.

Taken together these axioms guide investigations in an energy cultures framework. This approach accounts for implicit and explicit expressions of energy cultures and power relations through different spatial and scale compositions. An energy cultures approach cannot only label and view struggles over cultural representation, but it must provide a path to identify leverage points and ways to end unjust practices built into the cultural practices of the energy system. The next section reviews the case studies using both the spatial and scale perspective on the social contract and applies the energy cultures axioms to each country.

6.2.1 The culture of Eastern Europe's energy system

The Cold War established the long-term division of Europe. In Eastern Europe, the modernization of the energy system in a post-WWII era established new networks, resource flows, and diffusion of technical expertise. As established in Chapter 2, the resource intensity of the Soviet Union carried over into the Soviet satellites of Eastern Europe. Gas pipelines established a flow of gas from the 'center' to the periphery. Nuclear expertise shared in the COMECON countries further integrated the region into the cutting edge of nuclear science. Common assistance within these countries, such as MOL's contribution to building Soviet gas pipelines, along with Polish mining and Czechoslovakian power generation expertise, created a value chain of expertise, resources, and technologies – notable in the case of Lithuania's nuclear city of Visaginas, with Russian-speaking Soviet engineers and their families. These physical systems powered the homes and factories and built an economy from Eastern Europe to Central Asia based on an energy system of barter and trade, rather than market-based prices. Essentially, the energy in this system was nearly priceless.

The social upheaval in Eastern Europe, culminating in the 1989 destruction of the Berlin Wall, set about rapid economic changes and a democratic political system. The Iron Curtain was metaphorically removed. Following this collapse, rapid political and economic changes put society on a different footing as privatization took hold, and a demand economy was built. Along with the collapse of industry, demand for energy also fell. Both the state and industry required foreign investment to improve the energy infrastructure, from network operations to generation of heat and electricity. Privatization in the early 1990s gave way to EU membership in 2004, and the gradual introduction of a competitive and regulated domestic energy market implemented through an EU-based system of governance (LaBelle 2009). This tumultuous period resulted in spatial and scalar shifts – as the EU expanded the Soviet Union shrank then disappeared – and contestation.

Security of supply threats and events culminated in the 2009 Russian-Ukraine gas disruption. The recognition came about that the energy system in Eastern Europe was still tied to Russia and its gas diplomacy. This section will examine the sites of contestation, from resource extraction and network flows to security of supply that rested outside the EU for these new Member States. Each case study will be reviewed for how the social compact is reflected in the energy culture. The rapid integration into the EU failed to account for the social compact between Eastern European politicians and their citizens. Yes, a consumer society and democracy was desired, but on what terms? And how should access to energy services, as a 'public good,' be maintained in the utility sector?

Delivering on the social compact of low prices was essential for politicians. As will be seen in the case studies, the energy cultures (even in other Eastern European countries) demonstrate a reliance on resources, networks, and technologies to supply energy-inefficient homes and industries. The sites of contestation emerge as leverage points for domestic and geopolitical power. Each country has a different geopolitical and resource context. But politicians needed to make a choice: integrate into the EU-accepting network diversification or maintain their Communist-era energy systems and relations. Described next is how each country altered its energy culture within these leverage points to respond to EU integration.

6.2.2 Lithuania: from dependence to independence

During the 1990s and early 2000s, the Lithuanian energy system was still integrated into the Russian (former USSR) energy system. There was significant German and Russian ownership in supply and distribution. After the 2004 EU expansion and the post-2009 Russian-Ukraine gas crisis, Lithuania utilized the EU's Third Energy Package to take control of its energy system. It created a 'wartime' strategy of supply diversification for heating and power generation (Chapter 3). Not only did the spatial supply chain of the network change, but so too did the scale of the source of resources. Developing a domestic biomass sector created local and national supply lines for resources and technologies. The spatial networks and scale of resource delivery shifted to account for greater independence from resources, technologies, and networks that held a political price in the final delivery price. Lithuania shifted towards an internationally diversified supply chain enabling independence and EU interdependence through the EU's energy governance framework.

The reorientation of Lithuania is more a story of geopolitical fortitude to reduce the political leverage Russia held over gas prices. More specifically, it holds a narrative of power relations between the two countries and the pursuit of an equitable energy system by the Lithuanian government to ensure resource access at an affordable price. Lithuania leveraged its geographic location to build a global LNG terminal and an electricity network to neighboring countries. The culture of low-cost energy required the government to act – the built infrastructure and income levels required maintaining low prices. The social energy system embedded with power relations is perceptible in both the domestic relations between society and the government, and the international relations with Russia.

The physical energy system required securing new routes to ensure the flow of affordable gas and electricity. There was a necessity to secure supply routes unencumbered by the Soviet-era gas network susceptible to Russian political leverage. An increase in gas or electricity prices would impact household consumers and both their economic conditions and their political perspectives. The social contract between the Lithuanian government and society required politicians to act to secure lower-priced resources to meet consumer needs. For example, while Hungary reinforced the physical relations with Russia over gas and nuclear, the Lithuanian government chose to diversify and reduce the political leverage held by the Russian government (exercised through Gazprom). Potentially higher heating bills would impact household energy practices and political perspectives. Energy independence was secured by breaking Russia's monopoly over the energy system. Asserting the public good, and utilizing the EU's Third Energy Package, an overhaul of the energy sector was carried out, with the government kicking out Russian and German companies. They were perceived to be operating in their own interests, rather than in the national interest to provide a secure and affordable energy system.

The three axioms demonstrate how energy cultures alter spatial relations at different scales. The spatial expression of Lithuania's energy culture was in the nuclear power plant, gas pipelines, and total reliance on the Soviet-era energy system. Changing the spatial relations through new supply routes (axiom 1) also changed the power relations at different scales (axiom 2). Russia's political and economic leverage was reduced by Lithuania's adoption of a new energy culture that emphasized competition, diversification, and transparent market operations. EU membership enabled Lithuania to choose the EU's liberal market structure reflecting the soft power of democratic norms, rather than Russia's hard power of political patronage in exchange for low-priced gas. Adoption of a new energy culture, characterized by network diversification and market pricing, provided the Lithuanian government and consumers with the ability to fulfill the social contract of low energy prices. Both domestic and international power relations were changed by embracing the EU's culture of energy interdependence and transition away from Russia's culture of energy dependence (axiom 3). Lithuanian energy culture demonstrates that the social (implicit) energy system can highlight power relations and injustice within the energy system and foster a change in the physical (explicit) energy system.

6.2.3 Hungary: returning to a culture of energy dependency

In the early 1970s, Hungary, as a resource-poor country, built both oil and gas networks to the Soviet Union. By the 1980s, nuclear power created total reliance on Soviet resources and technologies. The energy culture developed both around the built environment of energy inefficient housing and industry and non-market pricing for energy resources and technologies. Even after the economic and political system was shifted towards a democratic and market-based system, the previous Communist arrangement of low prices carried over into the 1990s. Hungary's consumers benefitted from low gas prices and low power prices. Successive Hungarian political parties enabled legislative changes to benefit Russian firms, despite the negative effect on Hungarian companies. Nonetheless, the crushing rise in gas prices for Hungarian households opened the door to a political power play by Russia. Putin was able to secure another generation of nuclear power in Hungary by sealing a deal for cheaper gas (Chapter 4). In the winter of 2014, months before the next parliamentary election, Prime Minister Viktor Orbán secretly flew to Moscow to sign the Paks 2 agreement with Putin. The result would enable the Orbán government to be able to afford to provide households with lower-priced gas and proceed with the Soviet-era assumption of cheap nuclear power. In reality, Orbán bartered the country's sovereignty to remain part of the Soviet-era energy system now controlled by Russia. The Communist-era social pact – of low-priced energy, low household energy efficiency, along with resource and technological dependency – would remain in place.

The realignment with Western liberal democracies and neoliberal economic systems – requirements for EU membership – resulted in the financial restructuring of the Hungarian electricity and gas sector. The previous energy culture of low prices, in proportion to the low incomes and inefficient homes, meant that social practices were based on inefficiency. Power relations, as the case of Lithuania demonstrates, were based on upstream political patronage to Russia as the monopolistic seller of gas and oil. Competition and a regulatory governance framework influencing the energy market was rejected. Hungary's commitment to a politically centralized energy system, with only marginal adherence to the technical requirements of the EU's SIM, meant Hungary's pre-1990s energy culture could be preserved.

The social energy system required an equitable solution that accounted for the low incomes and inefficient homes present in the physical energy system. EU membership coincided with and contributed to households feeling the financial rise in energy prices. In 2014 Putin offered Orbán the chance to influence his political power by ensuring household consumers (and voters) would receive low-priced gas and (on the surface) benefit from nuclear power. The Soviet-era energy culture provides complete integration of the physical energy system with the social energy system. With Putin's offer, and Orbán's previous dismantling of a regulatory governance structure, there was the opportunity to maintain the Communist-era energy system and social contract of low energy prices – regardless of the cost to political sovereignty. Hungary, unlike Lithuania, was willing to trade political independence for low-priced energy dependence.

A review of the energy culture axioms indicates how central the political and social relations are to culture. Hungary's adherence to the Soviet-era culture of low-cost energy means that its relations with EU institutions and their liberal energy culture influenced Hungary's decision to return to the Soviet (Russian) model. Hungary's energy culture transformed its relations with the EU and with Russia, by rejecting a governance model and accepting a culture of Russian resource dependency; energy cultures are relationally transformative (axiom 3). Culture is not static but dynamic in its constant reinterpretation of power relations. Scale structures both actions and understanding of social and economic power relations. Orbán took political control over domestic energy pricing for households, but he also secured an international deal with Russia. Energy cultures play out at different scales and are reliant on power relations at each scale (axiom 2). Spatial relations also reveal Hungary's adherence to the post-Soviet model. Hungary's lack of energy efficiency measures in buildings (such as retrofitted buildings with new windows and insulation), and its continued support for Russia's Southern Corridor pipeline from Turkey and the building of Paks 2, demonstrate how the landscape and artifacts represent Hungary's energy culture (axiom 1). Hungary's spatial expression of its inefficient energy culture demonstrate its adherence to a politically oriented energy system based on political and economic dependence on Russia.

6.2.4 Poland: clash of energy cultures

The collapse of the Polish coal sector between 1990 and 2015 resulted in 85% of miners losing their jobs (Global Studies Initiative 2018, 3–4). The centrality of coal to Polish energy culture means that despite the devastation of coal-dependent communities and the continued financial difficulties of the sector, coal remains the dominant source for electricity and heat generation. Energy cultures are about relations, the echoes of the Polish coal era continue to reverberate through the political and economic policies. Nonetheless, there is recognition within Polish society for diversification away from coal. The Communist-era social compact, just like in Lithuania and Hungary, places an emphasis on low-priced energy for household consumers. This has translated into a reduction of domestically sourced coal and an increase in Russian coal imports. This reliance reduces Poland's security of supply. The actions also demonstrate how the importance of coal is represented in the cultural imaginary of the nation, rather than through the economic support for coal mines. The division between Poland's social and physical energy systems is highlighted in the primacy of maintaining the social compact through low energy prices, rather than through the retention of coal jobs in communities.

The complexities of the Polish energy sector are shown in different spatial relations at different scales. There is a clash of energy cultures: two unaligned energy systems operating at different scales. The first system is fossil fuel based and is integrated into an international network of gas pipelines, an LNG terminal, and an international supply line for coal. This nationally supported power system holds a similar strategy as the Lithuanian example, it builds an international energy network. The second energy system is built at the local and regional level. Here, a collaboration between government units, industry, and residences utilizes renewable energy and energy efficiency measures. This ground-up initiative places the power of the energy system within local communities, rather than at a national or international level. Within Poland there is a scaled division of the energy system affecting the relations of all actors.

There is a clash of energy cultures in Poland. The relational struggles produce two different types of culture. The three energy culture axioms help to understand the tension and divisions over the production of Polish energy culture. The first axiom indicates that energy cultures are perceived in the spatial expression of artifacts or inequalities. This applies to Poland's international pursuit of gas and coal along with the development of gas and electricity networks within the EU. Even the social contestation around shale gas demonstrates the social milieu that occurs in the choice of energy resources and technologies. Nonetheless, it is the division between national/international and local/regional cultures that is the source of struggle. The second axiom identifies power relations influencing energy cultures between scales. It is the contestation and disagreement both domestically and internationally that shapes Poland's dichromatic response to building an internationally linked energy system. At the same time, the country is building a locally based energy system disconnected from fossil fuels. The outcome of these struggles indicates power relations and the importance of culture in determining the resources and technologies accepted in a country. As the third axiom indicates, energy cultures are relationally transformative. When Poland's largest coal company shifts away from coal and towards community projects (Soja 2019) or a parliamentary representative also supports renewable energy, there is a cultural shift (Adamowicz 2019). Poland's energy culture demonstrates the continual evolution and relational struggles over technologies and resources that will define the future. The dominant culture attempts to fulfill the social compact through an equitable energy system by delivering low-priced energy.

6.2.5 Case study conclusion: the social compact of energy cultures

The three case studies provide a range of responses to the collapse of the Soviet energy system and integration into the EU's single market. Lithuania demonstrates the physical transformation of the Soviet energy system and reduction of Russia's political power; Hungary exemplifies what it means to retain Russian influence in energy; and both emphasize cultures of geopolitics transmitting both top-down and bottom-up power relations. Poland, on the other hand, demonstrates a domestic clash of local, regional, and national actors. Their spatial and scalar relations exemplify a clash of energy cultures; that is, power relations clashing by asserting different energy cultural practices. The national (political) level is fossil fuel based while regional and local governments, along with firms, are taking decisive steps to build a sustainable energy system. The regional and local authorities are embracing policies and technologies encouraged by the EU, energy efficiency, and renewable energy.

Each country provides an example of how energy cultures project power relations. Utilizing spatial networks and scalar relations within the energy system, social practices take on political orientations thereby influencing resource extraction and financial benefits to those who control the resources, networks, and technologies. An energy culture is not a benign social practice around the materiality of the energy system. Rather, energy culture is a powerful compilation of power relations struggling to dominate both the physical and social energy system. The political task is to develop a geopolitical orientation to deliver the resources and technologies necessary to fulfill the social compact in energy.

6.3 CONCLUSION: THE LEVERAGE FOR A JUST ENERGY SYSTEM

COMECON countries are important for their integrated economic and energy policies, likewise efforts to unify energy policies and technologies in the EU serve as a base for unification of social, economic, and geopolitical goals.

While COMECON countries cooperated in nuclear energy, EU countries cooperate in network integration, and a majority push for greater use of renewables and energy efficiency measures. In an energy culture, the artificial division between demand and supply is eliminated. Rather, the physical infrastructure and the social practice of society are influenced by socio-political struggles attempting to deliver on the social contract of affordable access to energy resources.

Energy cultures emerge from these relational struggles and express attributes such as the use of electric lighting or a gas stove in the home. But this expression needs to be traced back to the decision to extract gas, transport it, set a price for it, and finally the combustion of it into heat or electricity. The site of combustion emerges as the point of contention between the physical and social system, it is where social practices receive the fruit from the political practice of the state. Subjective and objective judgments are based on the successful delivery of the resource along with the environmental, social, or financial cost.

Different energy cultures are comparable between the social, economic, and political practices in the arrangements of COMECON countries and those in the EU energy system. The expression of energy cultures emerges through the power relations embedded in energy practices. Rather than perceiving the energy systems as divided between demand and supply, cultural practices and the provision and protection of the culture enable political and economic action to occur between the gas stove in Budapest and the Siberian or North Sea gas fields. A descriptive 'definition' of energy cultures provides a concise explanation: *energy cultures are the social and physical interactions forming relations in the energy system, extending from resource extraction through technologies of conversion, combustion, and networks, providing society's material and physical well-being.*

The transformative interactions are power struggles over narratives and the material expression of a culture. Together, the social energy system, guided by cultural narratives and the physical energy system, expressed in networks and the built environment, produces our energy system. There is value in energy culture. By transforming energy cultures, the physical energy system and the perceptions and judgments of it are held within the social energy system.

Energy cultures, which expose power relations, also expose injustices in the energy system. By applying an energy justice framing, the injustices of an energy culture expose power relations and the equity of a specific energy system. Likewise, a culture of geopolitics expands the framing of culture to understand how power relations enable the delivery of energy resources and technologies and ultimately determine the price of energy. Hungary, Lithuania, and Poland each provide examples to expose both just and unjust actions that either keep their citizens in energy poverty or lift them out. The next chapter explores this unified approach between energy equity and geopolitical power relations.

7. Justice and equity in the energy system

7.1 INTRODUCTION: VALUES AND JUSTICE IN CULTURE

The attraction to Ostwald's energy culture is in the moral duty the state holds to provide energy services to the people (Ostwald 1907, in Stewart 2014). The efficiency culture he espouses holds an environmental and intergenerational perspective. A moral efficiency culture runs through the energy system's value chain. From the extraction of resources to the hours worked to pay for electricity or heat, there is a financial, environmental, and social cost to the energy system. The energy culture sentiment is also expressed by more recent scholars who perceive a range of everyday experts and consumers holding agency in the energy system (Sovacool et al. 2016, 1). The task in this chapter is to lay down a path for pursuing social justice by identifying injustices within the energy system. Utilizing the 'energy justice framework' along with a 'culture of geopolitics' enables a fuller assessment of injustices and prompt change within the energy system. This chapter equips an energy cultures framework with the tools for a radical critique of injustices and power relations in the domestic and international arena.

The production of culture through relational struggles (Mitchell 2000, xviii) is also the same process that creates a society's judgment of justice and equity. Culture and justice intertwine with human relations. "'Justice' is a socially constituted set of contested configurations of power that have everything to do with regulating and ordering material social practices within places for a time" (Harvey 1996, 330). *Culture is the expression of regulated social practices, while justice is the regulating values of those social practices within a place and time.* The critical task is to identify who is regulating these social practices, and what are society's tools to ensure justice is a regulating value in their energy culture. This will meet the call by Bouzarovski and Simcock, for a "multi-scalar strategic approach to address the mechanisms … [preventing] fair decision-making procedures render[ing] households incapable of meeting their energy needs" (Bouzarovski and Simcock 2017, 646). Addressing the whole energy system brings a practice of 'bounding out' each stage of the energy system. Energy justice does this by providing a holistic perspective of the energy system, thereby engaging at a range of scales, such as, local, regional, and international (Jenkins 2018, 119). Therefore, in the production of culture there is a constant tension and struggle within and between scales.

Cultural practices are a source of power because they transmit knowledge and values. "'Culture' is the pattern of social behaviors by which groups transmit knowledge and values, and it exists at multiple levels" (Nye 2011, 84). Social practices and knowledge of the energy system, both subjective and objective, provide a means to influence cultural practices in social relations. The production of both justice and culture in space and time means those politicians operating on 'the other side of the Berlin Wall' (Kasztelewicz 2019) work through a different cultural lens. The Communist era laid down a particular set of cultural values enabling power relations to structure the energy system through social practices regulated through infrastructure and culture (Bouzarovski 2009; Bouzarovski, Bradshaw, and Wochnik 2015). At the same time, a universal set of perceptions of justice influence the particular cultural practices perceived to be just. Thus, Communism could regulate the economics and cultural practices around electricity and gas systems. Still, the political-economic system strove to deliver a just energy system with near-universal access to energy services – just as capitalist economies did.

Particular and universal energy justice provides the means to understand the tension between culture and justice. Energy cultural practices are socially and physically regulated through both the 'social energy system' with knowledge and values and in the built 'physical energy system.' The multi-scalar perception of securing a culturally justice energy system links both domestic and international practices of energy cultures. But fundamental to the operation of culture is the overriding sense of justice embedded in social practices.

> No society can do without a working and workable concept of justice any more than it can dispense with workable concepts of space, time, place and nature, the way these concepts get constituted through social practices has to be the primary focus of attention. (Harvey 1996, 333)

For Harvey, "the quest for justice" is a means to talk about how to regulate human relations to "achieve a particular set of goals under a given set of ecological, historical, and geographical conditions" (Harvey 1996, 333). Energy culture is a powerful lens empowered by accounting for particular equitable values and also perceiving energy practices through a universal interpretation of what an equitable energy system is. This approach enables the larger goals, such as sustainability and intergenerational equity, to be explored and to understand the leverage points to create a more just energy system. The route to justice through energy culture is reliant on energy justice as a meso-level framing. Nonetheless, as will be discussed below, the development of energy justice – as a conceptual framing – rests too much on a universal interpretation of what is just or unjust (Cloke, Mohr, and Brown 2017). As will be described in this chapter, sharpening the division between universal and particular energy justice (LaBelle 2017c) assists the quest for justice.

This chapter concentrates on the particular interpretation of a just energy system, while the previous chapter provided greater context for a universal energy justice. A universal framing provides the context to develop Ostwald's intent for a social transformation of the energy system (Ostwald 1907, in Stewart 2014). In his view, and as accepted throughout this book, an efficient, sustainable, and just energy culture requires the constant pursuit of social justice in an energy transition.

This chapter makes the argument there are two sides to interpreting energy justice in culture. One side holds a *social regulation of cultural values and social practices* over energy cultures. This influences the perceptions of realities around the energy system, and what is a just energy system based more on particular interpretations of justice. The other side holds a more *radical interpretation of power relations in the construction of energy cultures*, and asks, "whose interests are served by the construction and sublimation" of social reality (Gioia and Pitre 1990, 589). These power relations regulate society's energy system and extend into the realm of geopolitics, where cultural traditions influence the exercise of hard and soft power (O Tuathail and Agnew 1992; Goldthau and Sitter 2015). The integration of a cultural lens on justice and geopolitics utilizes tools for the 'quest for social justice' (Harvey 1996, 333). Social justice can be judged not just from a local or universal interpretation, but also by the alignment of countries to certain energy cultures. The delivery of a just energy system requires addressing the power relations controlling energy cultures.

This chapter provides a critical investigation into the energy cultures of Lithuania, Hungary, and Poland. The focus uncovers how these countries perceive their particular justice as a socially just energy system that recognizes inequalities. Section 7.2 develops a multi-paradigm approach to understand how a more radical interpretation of energy justice gives agency to actors to uncover power relations and foster change in each country. The use of both soft and hard geopolitical power extends energy justice and examination of the energy supply chain beyond national borders; demonstrating a whole systems approach to justice begins from extraction to consumption. Section 7.3 then applies these theoretical frameworks to the three national case studies and understands how particular interpretations of justice work to justify national energy policies. The development of just or unjust power relations in energy systems serves to highlight the tension within energy cultures over who creates culture and who holds power within a culture. Section 7.4 concludes this whole systems approach by bringing together both the energy justice framework and the geopolitics of culture framing to perceive the attempts at building a just energy system in Eastern Europe.

7.2 A MULTI-PARADIGM APPROACH TOWARDS ENERGY CULTURES

This integration of energy justice and geopolitics is essential for delivering on universal rights of energy access and mediating local (particular) interpretations of an equitable energy system. This section describes the conceptual framing energy culture uses to uncover power relations and to instigate change. Since culture itself is the outcome of relational interactions (Mitchell 2000), which serves to differentiate practices and relations, energy justice and geopolitics act as connecting meso-level theories. Bringing energy justice and geopolitics into energy cultures enables the uncovering of deep structures to expose, and if necessary, identify action steps necessary for building an equitable and secure energy system. Energy justice and geopolitics are framed within a cultural perspective using the multi-paradigm approach (Gioia and Pitre 1990). Here, culture describes how different approaches, Interpretivist, Humanist and Structuralist, influence the design of research and assistance in identifying sources of domination.

Energy justice "highlight[s] how domestic energy deprivation is fundamentally intertwined with, and produced through, geographical inequities and flows that are engrained in the economic, infrastructural and cultural make-up of society" (Bouzarovski and Simcock 2017, 640). A whole-systems – energy cultures – approach embraces both domestic (energy justice) and an international political-economy (geopolitical) paradigm to reposition culture to perceive spatial and scalar power relations.

The strength of the energy justice approach also holds its limitations. The framework aims to provide a 'socially just sustainable energy policy' by applying a justice framework to "normatively judge," with moral criteria, injustices preventing this sustainable transition (Jenkins, Sovacool, and McCauley 2018, 67). The threat is that this normative perspective of energy justice becomes static and unbending as the framework develops and society changes. In addition, the approach prevents a more bottom-up (re)interpretation of justice rather than an academically imposed perspective of justice. The threat of this static perspective frames energy justice as normative and positivist. The 'three As' of availability, access, and affordability rely on a normative positivist framing. The framework perceives a problem through three core tenets to understand both the universal nature of injustice and empirically through the 'three As' (Cloke, Mohr, and Brown 2017). Underlining processes are neglected, and the struggle for justice is negated for the more positivist labels of 'just' and 'unjust.' The following quote is an example of the difficulty in labeling what is just or unjust. Here, the benefits and subsidies for electric mobility may obscure more in-depth questions of justice, excluding underlying political-economic struggles.

> changing the performance or engine of a vehicle … does not necessarily change the underlying political economy or power dynamics behind mobility or automobility. Systems of mobility themselves — involving multiple, competing and overlapping technologies, modes, and transport infrastructures — can also be just or unjust. (Sovacool et al. 2019, 214)

A solution to this positivist labeling is shifting energy justice into a more critical and radical terrain. Returning to a multi-paradigm approach elucidated in the physical and social energy system (Chapter 6) brings out the pursuit of social justice within the energy system. Harvey's "particular ideals of justice" (Harvey 1996, 333) enable the actions of society and the state, through an institutional construct, to expose cultural practices and the embedded power relations influencing both a universal and particular interpretation of energy justice. Within particular energy justice lies 'recognition' and 'restorative' justice – the 'two Rs, in contrast to the 'three As'. Energy justice operationalizes energy culture by embracing a more radical critique of justice and particular interpretations of justice. Embracing the particular is at odds with the universal interpretation of justice, highlighting power struggles within and between cultures. The operationalization of energy culture, through energy justice, relies on acknowledging the tension within frames of justice.

Energy justice becomes more than a normative viewpoint within a Sociology of Regulation, to a radical critical approach in a Sociology of Radical Change paradigm (Figure 7.1). Power in the radical paradigm is, "primarily understood in terms of the regulative, cognitive and normative rules underlying socio-technical regimes, and the 'power struggles' between incumbent regimes and upcoming niches"; agency is placed with actors and social groups where contestation, struggle, and resistance against regimes occurs (Geels and Schot 2007; cited in Kohler et al. 2019). Energy justice largely operates within this functionalist/institutionalist order due to the current applications of energy justice by researchers (Fuller and McCauley 2016; Heffron and McCauley 2014; Jenkins et al. 2016). Figure 7.1 demonstrates the shift to the radical and structuralist/conflict quadrant, thereby bringing it into the social energy system. The shift to the Sociology of Radical Change refocuses examination on "deep-seated structural conflict, modes of domination and structural contradiction" (Burrell and Morgan 1979, 17). Social – and energy – injustice is perpetuated through domination and subjugation, not solely through the structure of the energy system. This shift places agency with society to create a radical change to construct an equitable and just energy system. This answers the proposed more radical shift for energy justice scholars to engage in a more activist critique by applying restorative justice (Heffron and McCauley 2017). A social justice framing prompts change and understands interventions into energy systems, which "are about political power, social cohesion, and even ethical and moral concerns over equity, due process and justice" (Sovacool et al. 2016, 5). The energy culture envisioned by Ostwald, where the energy system serves society – not society serving the energy system – proliferates through a radical energy justice framing.

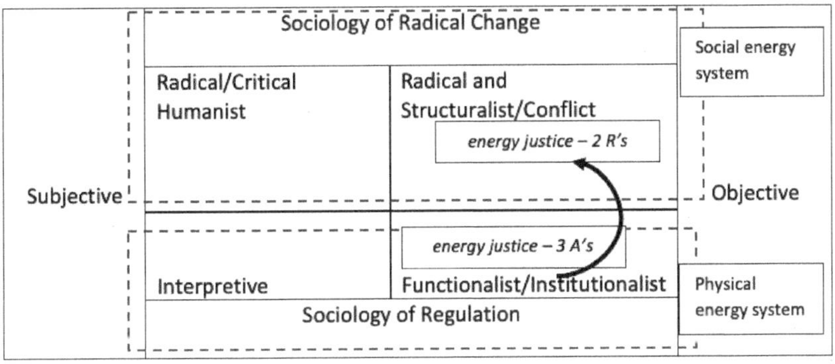

Source: Altered from Burrell and Morgan (1979, 23).

Figure 7.1 *Paradigms of social theory analysis within the energy transitions literature*

By shifting energy justice in a radical direction into the Sociology of Radical Change, it merges into the radical position alongside 'spatial justice' (Burrell and Morgan 1979; Sovacool and Hess 2017), which provides a critical perspective on socially constructed and contested structures. The point of a radical structuralist view is to expose the "existing dysfunctional structural relationships, which can only be changed through some form of conflict … With the ultimate goal of transforming them through collective resistance and radical change" (Gioia and Pitre 1990, 589). Table 7.1 provides a meta-level view of a multi-paradigm approach encapsulated in an energy cultures framing. Energy justice and geopolitics align with the labels created by Burrell and Morgan (1979, 19), which exemplify the differences of perspectives through the two dimensions of the Sociology of Regulation and the Sociology of Radical Change. The two different perspectives, seen through an energy cultures framework, provide a normative critique on institutional actions or identify leverage points in the energy system to end injustices.

Table 7.1 *Energy culture assumptions within the Sociology of Regulation and the Sociology of Radical Change*

Sociology of REGULATION	Energy justice and geopolitics	*Sociology of RADICAL CHANGE*	(Radical/critical) Energy Justice and Geopolitics of Culture
Paradigms: Functionalist/Institutionalist and Interpretative		*Paradigms: Radical/Critical Humanist and Radical and Structuralist/Conflict*	
The status quo	Codified rights and responsibilities; moral authority; e.g. United Nations and Sustainable Development Goals.	*Radical Change*	Power relations exist within society and the state. Changing relations changes power structure, e.g. fossil fuel divestment movement.
Social order	Legal framing; state institutions.	*Structural conflict*	Identify weakness in power structure to create conflict and change.
Social integration and cohesion	State and international formal and informal rules provide structure for stability.	*Modes of domination*	Challenge narratives and social/state structures.
Solidarity	Alliances and social institutions recognized by state and society.	*Contradiction*	Rights for one social group infringe on rights for another group.
Need satisfaction	Provision of energy resources and services from state and societal activations.	*Emancipation*	Freedom from oppression or exclusion through changing power relations.
Actuality	Businesses and state institutions recognize/ neglect social groups.	*Deprivation*	Exclusion and domination cause deprivation.
		Potentiality	Social and individual potential can foster change.
Energy cultures: Critique of how formal and informal institutions are delivering energy services within the physical energy system.		**(Radical/Critical) energy cultures:** Identification of exploitation, exclusion, and injustices within the energy system created by power relations and subjugation in hierarchical relations within the social energy system. *Identify leverage points to end injustice.*	

Source: Categories from Burrell and Morgan (1979, 19); content from author.

By understanding the framing of the energy system around the framing of a

'Sociology of Regulation' or a 'Sociology of Radical Change,' the opportunity emerges to deconstruct energy culture critically. There is a greater ability to understand power relations that perpetuate cultural practices. For example, the concepts of 'class' and 'economic structures' were once socially constructed, now they "are treated as facts or objective realities by the people who live within them" (Gioia and Pitre 1990, 594), even if these are not physically perceived. Likewise, the Communist construct of low energy prices for all members of society perpetuates a social belief of a 'reality' of how the energy system must be constructed. People must accept polluted air, nuclear waste, and cold rooms for low prices; while this is the *structure* of the energy system, it is not the only reality. These constructed meanings of the energy system shape the social practices and perceptions in the energy system, and influence, and are influenced by, the political-economic rationality that organizes the energy system.

The above framing highlights the interrelations between states, institutions, and society in power relations through both a justice and geopolitical lens. From a geopolitical perspective, there is an evolution as well. Figure 7.2 demonstrates the evolution of geopolitics from (a) real *geopolitik* (hard power), to (b) discursive geopolitics, and then (c) to geopolitical cultures (soft power). The shift from discursive geopolitics to a geopolitics of cultures refocuses on liberation within an international order. Discursive geopolitics advances both an ideology of power serving as a lens on national policies and justifying political control over the territory (even control of others' territory). The study of discursive geopolitics "is the study of the socio-cultural resources and rules by which geographies of international politics get written" (O Tuathail and Agnew 1992, 193). That is, from this view, geopolitics helps to write the rules.

In contrast, a *geopolitics of cultures* observe the "tradition of discourse and debate about territorial nation-state identity and its relationship to the wider world" (Toal and Agnew 2002, 457), thereby interpreting and explaining actions through *cultural observations*, rather than utilizing a cultural view to motivate and justify action by nation-states. A more radical interpretation of a geopolitics of culture will likewise examine how structural changes can prompt liberation or emancipation from international power structures that prevent sovereign self-determination. In geopolitics, the division between soft and hard power (Goldthau and Sitter 2015; Nye Jr. 2004) creates an ontological division; this changes geopolitical interpretations of physical and diplomatic actions. Geopolitics is no longer about military might and games (hard power), but also about cultural influences and perceptions (soft power). Due to this reframing, it is more useful to think of a continuum of soft to hard power (Goldthau and Sitter 2015). Figure 7.2 displays how the different geopolitical perspectives (objective to subjective) shift through these paradigms.

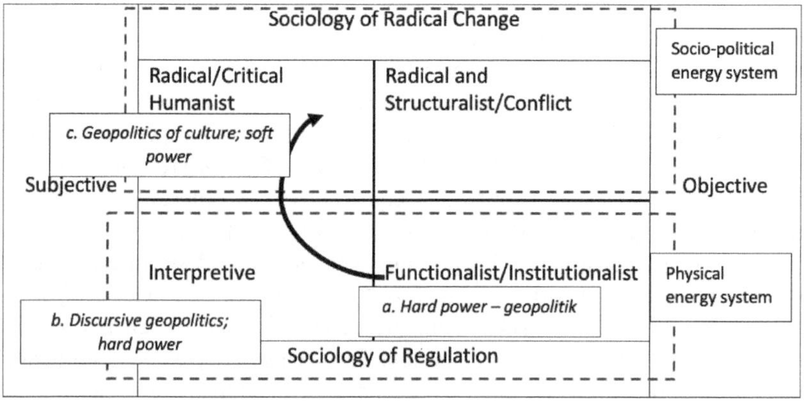

Source: Altered from Burrell and Morgan (1979, 23).

Figure 7.2 *Paradigms of social theory analysis within the energy transitions literature*

Geopolitics is about the study of interpretations of political and physical actions expressing a state's spatial power. In contrast, justice becomes a means to contest and break subjugation within spatial power relations. Bringing the concepts of geopolitics and justice together is done with an eye on the ontological construction of theories. The interpretation of real-world examples requires these paradigms of knowledge (ontologies) within different theoretical approaches. For example, the general dichotomy of interpretivist and radical humanist lenses explains the operation and expression of power:

1. "*Interpretivist theories* are based on the view that people socially and symbolically construct and sustain their own realities, and the goal of theory is to generate thick descriptions, insights and explanations of the complex models of and for action that people share, reproduce, perform, contest and modify." (Sovacool and Hess 2017, 736)
2. "Whereas proponents of interpretive theory building focus on how a particular social reality is constructed and maintained, *radical humanists* focus on why it is so constructed and ask whose interests are served by the construction and sublimation to the deep-structure level." (Gioia and Pitre 1990, 589)

Activating energy cultures as a framework provides a means to develop a multi-paradigm approach that engages with different physical and social structures within the energy systems. Ostwald's concept of energy culture provides an effective goal to justify and prompt a radical change to the operations of the energy system (Ostwald 1907). Delivering a just energy system to the 'working class' requires a radical critique of our current energy system. There must be a deconstruction of the power relations within perceptions of justice and cultural practices. A priority is the use of social justice as an essential end point that needs to be pursued. As Harvey identifies, the quest for justices is a principled way to talk about human relations; nonetheless, it is our collective endeavor, with understanding "embeddedness of particular ideals of justice in particular processes [which] is critical to the endeavor" (Harvey 1996, 333). Energy cultures are reflective of the relational struggles and geopolitics within the energy system.

7.3 ATTRACTION AND RECOGNITION OF SOFT POWER

> The question for justice falls squarely into the middle of the tension between particularity and universalism and does it in such a way as to make it impossible (politically as well as theoretically and empirically) to remain securely lodged at either end of that polarity. (Harvey 1996, 332)

The energy justice framework lodged in the universal and particular framings provides a source of constant tension as justice is universally and particularly interpreted. Chapter 1 (Table 1.2) provides an accounting of the types of justice within the universal framing: procedural, distributional, and cosmopolitan. Particular notions of justice are framed through the lenses of recognition and restorative justice. However, the latter is based first on recognizing groups or the types of injustices occurring; thus, the former must be addressed before restoration of injustice. Nonetheless, restorative justice indicates proactivity on the part of those controlling the structure disseminating justice. In essence, there is an explicit effort made by those controlling the structure to mitigate unjust power relations. "The application of restorative justice ... forces decision-makers to engage with justice concerns ... as any injustice caused by an energy activity would have to be rectified" (Heffron and McCauley 2017, 660). A radical interpretation of particular forms of justice must address power relations. This moves the paradigm of knowledge away from a cohesive view of society, and towards recognizing the fragmented nature of society and the many different social groupings. Chapter 6 provides a fuller accounting of how universal interpretations of energy justice prompt political domestic and international political action. This section focuses on the recognition of energy injustice within the three case study countries by emphasizing the power relations within the energy cultures.

Recognition justice prescribes respect for groups displaying distinguishing features such as social, ethnic, and gender who should be free from devaluation, degradation, and physical threats (Heffron and McCauley 2014; Heffron, McCauley, and Sovacool 2015). As Jenkins notes, it is the 'who' that recognition justice focuses on (Jenkins et al. 2016); it is highlighting *who* is at a disadvantage in relationships which enable energy justice to uncover both the explicit relations (such as ownership) and the implicit relations (political power) within the physical energy system. The injustices around recognition address marginalization and lack of agency to foster change; the relational struggles, including neglect and later application of restorative justice, means the recognition of social groups is a source of cultural acceptance and creating new cultural lines.

Restorative justice sets a forward-looking tone to energy policy because it "makes society think about how to respond to injustices (harms) that have occurred and also in defining what injustices society should give attention to in the first place" (Heffron and McCauley 2017, 660). This framing promotes a priority approach in setting out an energy strategy that addresses the most immediate means to prevent the continuation of a previous wrong – or injustice. Recognition and restorative justice shift energy justice into a radical framing (Figure 7.1) because they identify power relations and the leverage points used in perpetuating – or stopping – injustices. Fulfilling particular energy justice turns into a proactive approach of forward-leaning policy-making. Agency is with actors and social groups who are aware of past injustices and work to reorganize the energy system to prevent further injustices.

Energy justice in the radical paradigm corresponds with the radical framing of a geopolitics of culture. Both paradigms perceive culture as the site of power relations. Culture, along with political values and moral authority, is a form of soft power that attracts or repels other nation-states (Nye 2011). Soft power works by compelling adherence or alignment rather than forcing alignment with the policy aims of a country. Geopolitics of culture, reflecting the soft power approach, motivates alignment through policies connected to historical and geographical context. For example, relational histories, geographic location, or specific geopolitical alignments influence the perception of past injustices. The use of gas by Russia as economic and political leverage (hard power) for alignment could be less for countries located further away or with different historical relations (such as Germany) while for Poland, the construction of Nord Stream 2 is interpreted as a hard power threat. The imposed Communism and the centralized economy during the Cold War motivated countries such as Poland to join the EU because of cultures of attraction towards the liberalized economic and political system.

Accounting for relations through geopolitics of culture requires the recognition of priorities that influence decision-making and wider cultural geopolitical alignment. The benefits of a particular interpretation of justice are framed as a prioritized list of national, local, and cultural needs. Justice is context and place specific. In the case of Lithuania, Hungary, and Poland, the application of recognition and restorative justice provides a localized 'particular' energy justice perspective – one rooted in their own cultural perceptions of their geopolitical position (Chapters 1 and 6). Taking this bottom-up viewpoint exposes deep structural forces perpetuating injustices and which inform energy strategies in an attempt to escape from past injustices. The case studies examined next expose how national leaders sought to transform the physical energy systems to deliver a just energy system free from the threat of security of supply problems (hard power) and conditionally accepted the EU's liberal political and economic system (soft power).

7.3.1 Lithuania: just energy policies

The recognition of Lithuania's independence from the Soviet Union fuels its drive to pursue an independent energy strategy. The country's energy culture is connected to its drive to pursue a just energy strategy – perceived through its paradigms of radical change. "Culture can be an important power resource" (Nye 2011, 84). The attractiveness of the EU stems from Lithuania's acknowledgment of the hard geopolitical power exerted by Russia through the energy system. At the same time, Lithuania's turn from Russia acknowledges Goldthau and Sitter's (2015) perspective of the EU holding attractive values, through the liberal market ideology with a hard edge that forces Gazprom to conform to EU rules to continue its energy relationship with an EU Member State – Lithuania.

Changing domestic perspectives translates into actions within the energy system. The killing of the golden 'Soviet nuclear goose' (personal communication, Straupaite 2018) for EU membership prompted Lithuania to seek out a means to ensure its national sovereignty and satisfy the cultural provision of low-cost energy. Shutting down the Soviet nuclear reactors resulted in Lithuania being *forced* to choose between greater integration with Russia or the EU. Lithuania chose greater integration with other EU Member States by implementing the soft power measures of liberal economic governance. Russia represented a clear hard power play, enforced allegiance, and leverage over Lithuania's inelastic energy market and a say in the political-social power dynamic.

Understanding Lithuania's choice to transform its energy culture lies in the pursuit to address the particular injustices perceived in Lithuanian–Russian energy relations. First, there was the acknowledgment that past energy relations could not honor Lithuania's renewed status as an independent country. Recognition justice provides a means to understand the power relations of distinguishing an independent Lithuania free from political and economic distortion in the price of imported electricity and gas. There is a "cultural rationality" to interpret dichromatic perspectives on energy systems, whether it is communities in natural beauty opposed to wind farms or 'outsider' supporters of wind energy (Heffron and McCauley 2014, 436). Recognizing the power relations within the energy system assists those 'oppressed' or 'opposed' to a power system to find an alternative technical or political arrangement (Heffron and McCauley 2014, 436).

Lithuania ended the external imposition of Russia's political-economic power within the domestic energy system by diversifying away from the Soviet model. It sought out a 'restorative justice' by preventing the continuation of the injustices on its sovereignty through diversification. The EU governance structure was attractive for Lithuania because of the acceptance of an independent and interdependent energy system. Gazprom's increase of gas prices for Lithuania only, compared to regional peers (Chapter 3), indicates the hard power economic pain Russia (and Gazprom) was prepared to inflict on Lithuania's diversification and independence efforts. Likewise, Lithuania's use of the EU's Third Energy Package as a hard tool to break Russian and German ownership of its energy system resulted in the ability to diversify to other EU States and into the global LNG market. The energy culture of the EU was attractive for its ability to grant greater independence to the country and reduce Russia's resource leverage over the political and economic system.

Lithuania's energy culture (of independence) is reflective of the call by Heffron and McCauley that "Energy policy and the goal of energy security increasingly require a nuanced understanding of social justice concerns within energy systems, from production to consumption" (Heffron and McCauley 2014, 437). The spatial understanding is given to social justice to assist in creating a line through energy policy to perceive the link between particular energy justice concerns and foreign policy. The assistance of a geopolitics of culture framing combined with energy justice identifies energy cultures as holding power relations that determine both affordability, access, and availability (the three As) (universal), while also elevating the importance of the two Rs (recognition and restorative) of energy justice (particular). There is visible tension between Lithuania's pursuit of universal justice of liberation to ensure access and affordability against the particular interpretation of how to achieve justice through demanding recognition and respect for its national aspiration of self-determination.

The juxtaposition of universal and particular energy justice emerges as a means to call attention to how energy is consumed in a country and the role that geopolitical relations play in creating an equitable energy system interpreted by local or national societies. For Lithuania, the EU holds a pushed power of attraction and acts as the main alternative to Russia. Russia's energy culture uses gas for political and economic (and military) subjugation in foreign relations. Lithuania's EU membership is based on the attraction of democracy, access to the single energy market, and system of governance aligning with the domestic energy culture (Chapter 3). In contrast, Russia's domestic system of politicized energy culture places politicians (and its leader) at the center of government, thereby creating economic dependency on state institutions and interstate relations to deliver politically determined prices (Högselius 2013). This Russian (and Soviet) energy culture can appeal to other countries (discussed below in relation to Hungary).

The actions to liberate Lithuania from Russia's powerful energy system resulted in the country diversifying towards electricity imports from Sweden. Self-reliance became an important factor in providing heat to households. By investing in biomass technology, with the assistance of Nordic technologies, Lithuania built self-sufficiency into its energy system to meet its citizens' heating needs. Through its strategic planning, and to diversify gas supplies, Lithuania developed its LNG receiving capacity (with the help of Norway). This facility provided a competitive alternative to the higher (politically) priced Russian gas. Lithuanian politicians continued to deliver low-priced energy but through the EU's energy market and by technology transfers. A new energy culture developed that included energy security and independence through market and supply diversification (even by naming the LNG ship *Independence*). Russian energy supplies were not rejected but were forced to compete within the EU market framework with its hard regulatory approach (see Goldthau and Sitter 2015; Andersen, Goldthau, and Sitter 2017).

7.3.2 Hungary: geopolitics as justice

Universal and particular justice of energy cultures are two broad categories to collect a range of philosophical rootings of justice, such as distributional and procedural, and even more applied principles, such as affordability, due process, sustainability, and intra- and inter-generational equity (Sovacool et al. 2016). The case of Hungary shows the transitory nature of politics, which despite the historical context (of previous Russian and Soviet intervention) could be pushed aside for continuity in energy relations. Hungary had the opportunity to adopt an energy strategy similar to Lithuania, transition away from Soviet/Russian nuclear, diversify with Croatian LNG, increase the use of biomass, and build up a greater reliance on renewable energy while scaling up energy efficiency measures (see also Safian 2015). The Orbán government's perception of Russia is opposite to that of Lithuania and Poland. Rather than seeing Russia as a security of supply threat, the inheritor of the USSR energy system is a provider of reliable energy resources and technologies. In contrast to Lithuania's embrace of the EU, Hungary perceives the EU and liberal markets as a threat to national sovereignty, while Putin's centralized and authoritarian political system is an attractive model (Isaacs and Molnar 2017, 113) that has been implemented in Hungary.

Recognition and restorative justice are at the center of Orbán's – and Hungary's – energy policy. In the 1990s and early 2000s, foreign (mainly Western European) utilities participating in privatization owned much of the distribution and important generation companies (LaBelle 2009). The rise in gas prices combined with the economic crisis after 2008 placed significant financial pressure on Hungarian households (Bouzarovski et al. 2015). After the 2010 election of the second Orbán government, the governing perception and the reframing through a populist lens – of the EU and foreign utilities – shifted. Both the utilities and the EU were reframed as exploiters of Hungarian households, causing financial hardship. This resulted in the 'soft renationalization' (Isaacs and Molnar 2017). In an attempt to ensure foreign utilities did not harm Hungarian society, state intervention was seen as the most effective and efficient method to deliver low-cost energy.

This impetus for restorative justice by 'do no harm' to society utilizes recognition justice to provide the historical (and cultural) context of state ownership. The Communist legacy and the operating energy culture of Hungary (Chapter 6) rests on state price controls and ownership, rather than a regulatory governance structure favored by the EU. The 'illiberal state' marks Orbán's contribution to the Hungarian political-economic system. This new ideology projects a revisionist policy towards neighboring countries, along with dismantling neoliberalism by putting "an end to the basic principles of a neoliberal era" (Orbán; MTI 2011). There is centralized political power, nationalization of foreign capital, and implementation of a 'work-based state' (Isaacs and Molnar 2017, 115–16). By 2020, the majority of the Hungarian energy sector was either state owned or in Hungarian hands. These efforts capped a decade of soft nationalization (Isaacs and Molnar 2017; Felsmann 2018; Sebestyén Szép and Weiner 2020). The erosion of regulatory independence and political determination of household energy prices reflect a rejection of the EU's energy governance system (LaBelle and Georgiev 2015).

The paradigms of knowledge are essential to understand the illiberal Hungarian state built under Orbán. Hungary, through this illiberal paradigm, appears to be the victim of the colonization of Western European utilities, with the former state assets secured by EU Directives fit for Western Europe but not accounting for the particular interpretations of a just energy system in Hungary. Illiberal government policy works from a position of particular justice, attempting to restore the broader national sense of justice. The EU institutions (because of the historical mandate) work from a cosmopolitan framing of justice. Market integration and free movement of capital is the cornerstone of EU policy, this is delivered through Directives, like the Third Energy Package, and requirements for competition at the household level. The

EU, by its structure and embedded philosophy of governance, works from a position of universal energy justice.

Nationalists and populists, like Orbán and his Fidesz party, work from the 'opposing' framing of recognition justice. This radical interpretation of justice places the nation and its cultural energy practices at the center of policy-making. The nation and its citizens require respect and liberty from market distortions, and degradation imposed by the neoliberal free market, and the private utilities exploiting Hungarian households. From this particular energy justice perspective, the energy system is not divided between demand and supply, as through a neoliberal framing; rather, the energy-inefficient homes and factories are tied to the rich natural resources and technological knowledge of Russia. Russia – and Putin – provide Hungary with an equitable energy system at a price point that fits the built infrastructure of housing, transport, and social practices. In other words, the energy culture of Hungary remains Communist in both form and function: energy is a social subsidy necessary to provide the *working class* with a sufficient material existence. And only the state, through its domestic ownership and international relations, can utilize its power relations to provide an equitable energy system for its citizens.

The actions, by the Hungarian state, to build the ideologically imposed 'illiberal state' is about a state-controlled energy system with politicians setting the price and cross-subsidization methods between state-owned firms. The dramatic utility price cuts after 2012 that led private and state-owned utilities to lose money was an act of restorative justice. "Restorative justice aims to repair the harm done to people (and/or society/nature), rather than solely focus on punishing the offender – as societies use the legal system for" (Heffron and McCauley 2017, 660). While it is debatable whether the extra tax burden on utilities and shifting cost structure in the sector was punitive or an act of rebalancing the energy system, it nonetheless marked the beginning of soft renationalization and rebuilding of state ownership. The results indicate that Hungarian households reverted to their previous social practices in energy consumption. With the lower utility costs, Hungarian households increased their consumption, thereby spending the same amount of their income on the utilities as before the rate reduction and thwarting energy efficiency goals (Sebestyén Szép 2017). The lower prices discourage investments into energy efficiency, erode the competitiveness of renewable energy technologies, and undermine the security of supply while increasing prices for non-household consumers (Sebestyén Szép and Weiner 2020). Hungary's energy policies are in direct contradiction to EU efforts represented in the Energy Union. However, they align with Russia's (and the Soviet era's) energy culture where financial profits, transparency, and procedural justice are antithetical to a strong centralized state led by a powerful leader. Applying restorative justice through a nationalistic and illiberal paradigm demonstrates the tension of a country inside the EU but operating through a sense of injustice within the governance framework. Hungary's political alignment with Russia serves Orbán's interpretation of Hungary's energy culture.

Ensuring maintenance of the Soviet-era geopolitical energy system also ensures continuity of the Communist energy culture in Hungary. Hungary's realignment with Russia demonstrates the acceptance of both hard and soft geopolitics. Soft geopolitics play out in the attractiveness of incentives towards Russia – even if these are not transparent. The 1995 requirement by the Socialist-led Parliament for MOL (shareholders, including the state) to incur financial losses with gas imports enabled profits for Gazprom and opaque third parties. This action parallels the longer-term actions of the Orbán government's acceptance for Rosatom to build a new nuclear power plant on terms disadvantageous to Hungarians (Chapter 4). Political action is taken only against Western energy firms, rather than Russian firms. In the area of gas pipelines and the exercise of hard geopolitics over resource access, Hungary continues to favor and assist Russia's building of a Southern Gas Corridor through the Balkans, thereby undermining Ukrainian and EU efforts to utilize its soft power through the Single Energy Market. Just as Lithuania feared, these political and geopolitical energy ties with Russia can be used for political-strategic purposes. The election of a party opposed to Orbán could experience higher Russian energy prices, and no doubt as they might seek to pivot away from Russia they would experience higher prices, just as Lithuania did. Russia and Orbán, by controlling the energy culture, control the political and economic future of the country.

7.3.3 Poland: justice on this side of the wall

The recognition that Poland is on "the *other side* of the Berlin Wall" (Kasztelewicz 2019), translates into a different plan to organize the energy system. The EU's Energy Union pushes renewables and a net-zero framework, with limited regard for the greater energy intensity in Eastern Europe (Sebestyén Szép 2016). The Polish national government perceives the necessity to retain coal for both affordability and security, despite climate change arguments. Through the Polish interpretation, the country is building an equitable energy system, one that produces a much smaller percentage of CO_2 emissions compared with Germany (personal communication, Kasztelewicz 2018) at a price that Polish consumers can afford. The Polish perspective towards the EU corresponds to the Hungarian perspective in terms of equity while also being reflective of Lithuania's energy security concerns towards Russia. These differing perceptions of *who is at a disadvantage* creates conflict at a range of scales (Jenkins et al. 2016). Conflict emerges over the East–West fight over controlling renewable or fossil fuel technologies, to cultural preservation in coal mining, to recognizing the impact of air pollution. These fights occur over the greater energy intensity of the CEE region despite the impact on the environment and health.

Understanding the Polish position requires looking at its interpretation of justice. First, recognition justice uncovers who is recognized but also highlights the power of who does the recognizing. In this sense, there is a strong social awareness of vulnerable social groups, from miners to low income households. These citizens rely on coal and require social assistance by having the energy system structured to their needs. Expression of particular energy justice in Poland requires acknowledging the contradictions within the justice framings. In Poland, there is tension between the application of universal and particular forms of energy justice – structural conflict between the built Communist-era energy infrastructure and the necessity for local and regional authorities to improve energy efficiency measures and increase renewable energy generation. Just as Hungary pushed low energy prices, in Poland providing low energy prices results in fewer incentives to move towards a cleaner energy system.

Poland demonstrates a range of scales to the recognition of solutions, from energy efficiency renovations at the local level to planning for more coal mines at the national level (Chapter 5). Efforts in Poland to change the energy culture are wrapped up in creating a 'just transition.' Implementing "a fair and equitable process moving towards a post-carbon society" requires a multi-scalar approach (McCauley and Heffron 2018, 2). Poland's reliance on coal highlights the necessity of recognizing the negative impact of coal but acknowledging local efforts to change. This review of Poland provides a whole systems approach (Sovacool et al. 2016) and the importance of assessing "the entire energy chain, from mining, conversion, production, transmission, and distribution" (Jenkins et al. 2016, 179). Poland demonstrates actions to tackle energy injustices through a multi-scalar approach by highlighting how citizens and businesses participate in the energy system. While national-level energy strategies promote the justification for coal use, there is a churning of energy cultures below the surface.

The promotion and building of energy clusters in Poland demonstrate that when agency is given over to households and local communities, sustainable energy projects can begin. Investments into energy efficiency and renewable energy turn into a bottom-up process led by mayors who actively seek out funding and partnerships. The mayor of the Miedzyrzec Podlaski (Adamowicz 2019) and the parliamentary representative (Sitarski 2019) are both participating in restorative justice by looking ahead and using prevention as the means to address the negative impact of fossil fuels. Energy efficiency measures in houses, or installing solar PV panels on homes, reflect local energy culture-shifting social practices and how people consume energy. Energy justice, by engaging in a critical perspective on energy cultures, provides a means to highlight the decision-making process as leaders attempt to protect or shift their communities in an energy transition. A focus on restorative justice "assists decision-making that is more just and fair, and hence can contribute to restoring increased equality in society" (Heffron and McCauley 2017, 663).

Geopolitically, there is a recognition of the EU as preferable in a hard-geopolitical framing against Russia. However, the EU's soft power with a hard edge, while welcomed in terms of gas security, is also disputed in relation to coal technologies. Nonetheless, there is a great level of contradiction in Poland's coal position. While the national government strives to retain the cultural heritage of coal, the weak financial position of Polish coal requires a phase-out (WISE 2015). The national energy strategy rests on Communist-era assumptions of cheap coal (Nyga-Łukaszewska 2015). Nonetheless, Polish coal is too inefficient and expensive to keep prices low; Russian coal transported efficiently by rail becomes the economical choice. Coal does provide flexibility in sourcing, just like oil; nonetheless, for Poland's national energy strategy to be successful it must rely on low-priced, imported Russian coal (Global Studies Initiative 2018). The interlinkage between the affordability of energy in Polish homes to the sourcing and burning of coal is all intertwined in the multi-scalar energy system.

Tension arises as Poland struggles with the EU's soft regulatory power (such as using ETS and ACER in the energy market (LaBelle 2012)) and the historical threat of Russia's hard power (Högselius 2013; Orban 2008). Poland, similarly to Lithuania's push for independence, also incorporates its particular geopolitical position to inform the diversification of its energy system. The myriad new gas projects, such as bringing in Norwegian gas or increasing interconnectors with neighbors, and the diversification of gas supplies along with expanding its electrical network demonstrate the physical alteration to Poland's energy system. Essentially, the expansion in the Single Energy Market demonstrates Poland's energy security gains within the EU. However, in contrast, its efforts to ensure coal remains part of its future energy mix provide a source of tension with the EU. Coal becomes more reflective of hard geopolitical relations in terms of independence and sovereignty expressed by the nationalistic PiS government. Traditional Polish energy culture retains coal for the social, economic, and security characteristics, just as Hungary retains nuclear power for its scientific and perceived affordability characteristics.

EU membership is attractive for economic integration and network diversification in gas and electricity (Goldthau and Sitter 2015). It is not attractive for protecting national identity and cultural practices that are heavily embedded around the material benefits derived from coal. The local and regional scales in Poland demonstrate acceptance of universal energy justice norms, which also correspond with the interpretations of particular energy justice. By reframing energy transitions in a more holistic framing of restorative justice through prevention, the use of new renewable technologies can address the concerns around affordability and accessibility.

7.3.4 Conclusion: perceptions of justice and geopolitics

The pursuit of a just energy system, in each of the three countries, demonstrates a struggle to continue the social energy system of low energy prices while improving the aging infrastructure. Lithuania embraced the EU's soft power by erecting a hard border with Russia. EU membership for all three countries delivered a more secure and just energy system carried out through diversification. However, Hungarian consumers suffered from high domestic energy prices brought about by a neoliberal economic model. In response, Orbán's illiberal nationalistic regime choose to pursue the Communist-era energy system of Russian dependency. Choosing to shift allegiance to Russia enables a stable supply of low-priced gas and nuclear power. However, this politically dependent energy system rests on friendly relations with Russia to ensure low prices. Poland embraced the security aspects of EU membership, like Lithuania, but pursued Hungary's nationalistic Communist line of retaining the Soviet-era coal infrastructure. Nonetheless, the leaders of each country work to build a socially just energy system as perceived through their particular interpretation of justice.

7.4 CONCLUSION: A UNIVERSAL AND EQUITABLE ENERGY SYSTEM

The state is an articulation of universal human values and rights maintained by a social contract (Vatn 2005, 28). The state is also the articulation of domestic and international culture fostered through relational struggles (Mitchell 2000). The struggles highlight power relations and particular expressions of culture within domestic and international relations. State and social institutions assert territorial power as a means of geographical dominance or agreement expressed through soft or hard power relations. Within the energy system of developed countries, the provision of energy services is the political responsibility of politicians (Bouzarovski and Simcock 2017, 645), which is influenced by geography and particular cultural perspectives within the state.

The expression of energy cultures can take the form of both an expression of human rights enshrined in the Universal Declaration of Human Rights or as a soft power influencing the international alignment of friend or foe. Energy cultures are inherently geographic, and are expressions of power relations perceived through both an energy justice and a geopolitics of culture framing. Understanding power relations is, therefore, central to understand both justice and expressions of culture within the energy system. A radical interpretation (Sociology of Radical Change) of energy justice provides a particular perspective on the recognition and restorative justice a country may deploy to ensure an equitable energy system.

The social commitments of the state to provide access to energy services requires state institutions to deliver a just energy system (Hiteva and Sovacool 2017, 632). Awareness of society's norms and values is tied up into both a universal and particular interpretation of energy justice (LaBelle 2017). The transboundary awareness of energy injustice (Sovacool, Sidortsov, and Jones 2013, 29) highlights the universal interpretation of a just energy system, via respect for procedural, distributional, and cosmopolitan forms of justice. Energy culture draws on the interpretation of the social and institutional order in delivering a just energy system to understand how procedures, distribution of resources, and respect for universal access of energy services foster cultural energy practices and relational structures (Chapter 6).

A more radical framing perceives a geopolitics of culture and energy justice, embracing localized expressions of culture and justice. The domestic cultural relations can serve as a source of attraction for an alignment of other countries along particular (energy) cultural lines. Both the implicit and explicit energy cultures enable justice and geopolitics to embrace a geographic view of the landscapes of energy infrastructure, and power relations influencing socio-political relations. Power relations expose the push for radical change, which prompts structural conflict and alters once established narratives. Table 7.1 provides the context to understand the shift to a radical paradigm exposing power relations. It is this exposure which also displays the weaknesses and opportunities for society and individuals to assert their agency to secure a more just energy system.

The geopolitics of culture serve to encapsulate both domestic and international power relations by utilizing the socio-political relations, responsibilities, and orientation of energy systems. This chapter provides a means to understand the state as an expression of particular cultures that align with more universal concepts of norms and values between states. Cultural alignment emerges as a means of power between and within states. Energy systems, with both their domestic and international connections, are perceived as one system, rather than split between demand and supply. Society entrusts its sovereignty to politicians to deliver equitable energy systems. The protection of individual liberties is assessed through the frames of energy justice. Energy culture assists the expression of both universal and particular interpretations of social practices and agreements within each state.

The assessment through the radical/critical humanist perspective in geopolitics fosters an awareness that culture represents power relations produced from the conflict in the deep structure of the state. This approach contrasts against an interpretivist discursive geopolitics, which considers the state as the container of a socially cohesive society, projecting hard power to retain or gain territory. This is more nuanced than the real geopolitik, which holds state military actions as central to the expression of state power. State actions express power emanating from forces (different political and economic factions) struggling over cultural dominance within nation-states. Soft power is about controlling the cultural narrative and expressed values of these dominant forces (factions or 'regimes'). Therefore, as Mitchell identifies (discussed in Chapters 1 and 6), it is asking the questions 'who is,' and 'why do' they produce culture that enables a radical perspective on power relations to expose deep state structures and *the identities of these deep forces* (Mitchell 2000, 73). These radical interpretations enable us to move beyond calling those controlling cultural narratives 'deep forces,' and enable their identities to be exposed. Each of the case studies has peeled back these relations demonstrating the power motives behind the energy cultures.

The history of geopolitics demonstrates a shift from an assumption of hard power and objective perspectives to understanding the role of discourse, symbols, and social narratives in geopolitical cultures. The geopolitical cultures of Eastern Europe can be framed through spatial relations to provide a greater understanding of the divisions between hard and soft power in the energy cultures of Eastern Europe. This meets the call of different energy justice scholars to assess the whole energy system (Jenkins et al. 2016; Sovacool et al. 2016).

Spatial influence is perceived through Russia's geopolitical use of resources and technologies. The EU's influence is perceptible in its market governance structures required to belong to the EU and to participate in the Single Energy Market. Within the context of this book, with regard to Hungary, Lithuania, and Poland, these countries begin to represent regional examples representative of broader choices that Eastern EU Member States make. There are national differences, but common regional characteristics of the post-Soviet environment are present in the built infrastructure and energy ties. The spatial relations are embedded within different energy cultures serving as attractive or repulsive forces in international and domestic relations. The geopolitical energy cultures of the EU and Russia represent two different types of power projections, marked as 'friendly' or 'unfriendly' towards each nation-state's energy culture. The orientation of each country is dependent on the alignment of each country's energy culture.

Russia can hold soft power by enabling low-cost consumer power. Still, more often, its power is perceived to derive from its hard edge and even harder geopolitical power in maintaining demand for its natural resources. The attractiveness is contained in low-priced gas. The use of natural resources to exert power over Eastern Europe – most explicitly in disputes with Ukraine and the annexation of Crimea (facilitated by a previous gas agreement allowing the stationing of Russian troops, see Grigas 2017) – demonstrates Russia's hard geopolitical position and intertwining of energy and military might. Both the soft and hard power can be a source of attraction and repulsion for the three Eastern European case studies.

The geopolitical energy cultures in these three East European countries demonstrate domestic socio-economic relations influencing choices over infrastructure, resources, and generation technologies affecting international relations. Lithuania's and Poland's gas diversification efforts using EU Directives for building new networks and LNG terminals demonstrate rejection of Russia's energy culture of resource dependence. Hungary's acceptance – and even assistance – of Russian control over gas networks and advancement of nuclear power reflects a domestic energy culture accepting of resource and technology dependency; this dependency is exchanged for assured domestic political power. Low household utility prices provide political power for both Putin and Orbán in their friendly geopolitical relations. This is a deal which an opposition government cannot maintain. An equitable energy system is free from these distortions and leveraged power relations encompassing the whole energy system.

8. Conclusion: building a culture of justice in the energy transition

> We find again and again the statement that energy is merely an abstraction or mathematical function possessing only the particular attribute of retaining its value under all circumstances. This causes a confusion which is obvious from a special peculiarity of all European languages, and with regard to which one should be greatly on his [sic] guard since its frequent repetition shows how easily it can cause trouble. This is the linguistic custom of indicating by the same word both the general concept and the concrete thing which corresponds to that concept. (Ostwald 1907, 495)

8.1 INTRODUCTION: THE MORAL IMPERATIVE FOR EQUITY IN ENERGY

The attributes of energy are both physical and social. The value of energy goes beyond the kinetic forces abstracted into mathematical formulae or expressions of kWh or MW. This book provides a deeper discussion on power relations within our physical and social worlds. Energy cultures provide a unique avenue to understand the relational power of energy. These are not benign relations; rather, in the words of Ostwald, the 'European languages' demonstrate the deep historical power relations at play in Europe's energy system. The clash of energy cultures in Eastern Europe exposes diverging means to organize energy relations.

The general task of energy culture is to provide an efficient, sustainable, and affordable energy system to citizens of each country. The energy system is embedded with an ethical demand in the provision of energy services. Ostwald worked through this paradigm during the second industrial revolution at the turn of the twentieth century; 'energetics' reflected both the mathematical models and efforts of diplomats and engineers working on behalf of society rolling out a new energy system (Ostwald 1907, in Stewart 2014). In a similar call, Sovacool and other authors, "students, jurists, homeowners, business persons, investors and consumers" (Sovacool et al. 2016, 1), also have a responsibility to build an efficient energy system. There is a moral imperative within Ostwald's framing of culture – one that recognizes power relations. This is echoed by modern scholars' pursuit to expose inequalities and the unsustainable use of our natural resources underlining research into environmental injustices and climate change.

Politicians, as representatives of the state, hold the responsibility to deliver a just and equitable energy system (Bouzarovski and Simcock 2017, 645). The clash between a particular or universal framing of energy justice exposes the power relations both sustaining and challenging an energy culture. Within the energy system are embedded the physical and social energy systems – their representations are twofold: First, there is an explicit representation on the landscape and technologies and extends to how we cook and heat; second, there is an implicit energy culture, encompassing the values, norms, and regulations that sustain particular energy practices in social and state institutions. These structures organize around the point of combustion.

The release of the Earth's energy through a spark, or converted through technology from the sun or wind, express human action in the pursuit of well-being. This point of conversion is why there is a clash of culture because humanity brings to nature all the values, practices, and power relations to structure social relations around the point of combustion. Humans struggle over the site of combustion; they do this by constructing social and physical systems to regulate and control access and gain the benefits. The state intervenes to structure access and ensure the delivery of energy resources and services. The transference of sovereignty from the individual to the state requires the state to act in the interests of all citizens. This social contract requires the state to "secure order" (Vatn 2005, 26) as an articulation of human rights and values (Vatn 2005, 28). This jump to the Enlightenment viewpoint (Chapter 1), while cursory, enables the articulation of justice as an important state function within the modern energy system.

The role of the state is essential in the energy system. An equitable energy system requires a regulatory compact to organize businesses, society, and government. State intervention is fundamental to ensure the most efficient combustion of energy. The neoliberal model rejected by Hungary and Poland demonstrates the challenges of government intervention into free markets. Past practices, social expectations, and the built infrastructure influence the means by which a just energy system is delivered. There is a balance, between meeting universal expectations of affordability and access but delivered through a locally accepted manner. The implicit and explicit organization of the energy system reflects the complexities of an energy culture.

The creation of culture through struggle draws on Mitchell who identifies the role relationships provide in understanding why culture is produced and by whom (Mitchell 2000, xviii). By studying culture, power relations emerge; these appear as relations surrounding the site of combustion. In Poland, coal and gas serve as the foci for energy relations, even while an alternative culture in community energy clusters is emerging (Chapter 5). For Hungary, the value of energy culture is in delivering low-priced energy to homeowners; the conversion of heat from gas and the production of electricity from nuclear rely on relations with Russia (Chapter 4). The combustion of biomass in Lithuania creates its own technology and domestic value chain while also increasing energy security and political independence from Russia (Chapter 3). Culture provides a means to regulate relations, thereby producing power relations within the energy system.

And it is here, in the dominant energy culture, that the full weight of the political arena is brought to bear onto the construction of energy cultures. This authoritative power over culture emerges as a regulatory influence on the social and physical structure of the energy system. This builds on Geertz's observation that culture, "is not cults and customs, but the structures of meaning through which men (*sic*) give shape to their experience; and politics is not coups and constitutions, but one of the principal arenas in which such structures publicly unfold" (Geertz 1973, 312). This role of structure provides the scaffolding to perceive *energy culture as the social and physical interactions forming relations in the energy system, extending from resource extraction through technologies of conversion, combustion, and networks, providing for society's material and physical well-being.* The complex web of geopolitics in Eastern Europe, the formidable EU regulatory complex, and the assertion of the nation-state to determine the rate citizens are charged comes down to these structured relationships – and challenges to them – in the energy system.

The next section (8.2) focuses on the use of energy cultures as a contribution to better understand power relations within the energy system. Section 8.3 reviews the contribution of the three axioms to understand how energy culture reflects the functions of the energy system through a prism of social and political relations. Section 8.4 positions the energy cultures framework within a broader set of energy transitions literature, while highlighting the limitations within a cultural framing. And, finally, section 8.5 provides suggestions for how energy cultures can expose power relations within the EU's new initiative on a just energy transition. The ability to build a just transition rests on finding an equitable solution for society to express its culture; free from the power dynamics perpetuating current injustices within the EU's energy system.

8.2 CONTRIBUTION OF ENERGY CULTURE

The marginalization of culture from the energy transition literature relegates national interests into different framings that lack a strong social and historical context. The use of 'regimes' (Turnheim and Geels 2013) or national institutional complexes (Unruh 2000), or event alignment of social, economic, and political 'fits' (LaBelle and Goldthau 2013) provide a framing context emphasizing the structure that influences the choice of technologies. However, the relational struggles that make culture relevant for influencing the choice of energy technologies or impacting the environment are largely missing from engagement with the energy system. The 'circulation of energy', developed by Sheller (2014) on the aluminum industry, provides the context to understand social practices perpetuated within a specific energy loop, while the Energy Cultures Framework (Stephenson 2018) provides context to understand behavior shaped by and shaping the energy system, including the connection to policy framings and consumption habits. Each of these frameworks on culture is useful, but they provide a shallow to medium depth for understanding power relations fostering the energy culture that perpetuates particular social practices.

A more critical energy cultures approach contributes to the broader understanding of social practices by acknowledging culture is created by social interactions at all scales of the energy system. The implicit representation of energy cultures emerges as the point where power relations affect people's lives. Stories and narratives are powerful for their ability to convey the material lives of people. "The underground fires burnt the coal lying below my house," as told by a house owner in India, represents the poverty and health impact caused by fossil fuels (Pai and Carr-Wilson 2018, loc. 996). Identifying the 'cultural turn' (Smith et al. 2017, 287) in energy transition studies requires acknowledging and building a conceptual scaffold to understand power relations within the energy system. The re-emergence of justice studies and the shift from a focus on environmental justice to one on 'energy justice' demonstrates the energy system as a focus of study (Sovacool and Hess 2017; Jenkins 2018). Acknowledging the ways in which the system is broken down into explicit and implicit levels enables a multitude of disciplines to converge to understand how our modern society is built and grows on natural resources.

The cultural turn proposed here builds from a geographical understanding of power relations. It requires a turn to a radical critical critique of our energy system. To do this, it reproduces key questions to understand, "who produces culture and why" (Mitchell 2000), along with, "justice for whom" and "justice by whom" (Jenkins, McCauley, and Warren 2017, 837). The production of energy cultures is dependent on power relations in modern society, which are structured through state institutions and an international system of explicit and implicit geopolitical power relations. The state is the central organizing institution that regulates both society and relations with other states. But what is the state? To answer this question, I turned to the concept of our individual sovereignty and the transference of this to the collective actions of the state. In this transfer of sovereignty and what society gets back is where justice and injustice are delivered. The relational transference of sovereignty is passed between hands. Ultimately, politicians acting as representatives of society decide on the equity level within the energy system.

The simplicity in proclaiming politicians with the responsibility over our energy systems is acknowledged. Agency, as described above, rests with all of us. Nonetheless, it is important to not lose site of how a just energy system is built. The lens of energy justice provides a means to both label and critique actions where a clash of energy cultures emerges out of the tension between a universal and a particular interpretation of energy justice. The universal requires just procedures, distribution of the benefits of access to energy services, and acknowledgement of energy as necessary for fulfilling basic human rights (United Nations General Assembly 1948; Sovacool and Dworkin 2015; Sovacool, Sidortsov, and Jones 2013). Energy justice provides the tools to dissect culture; it provides the moral and value assessment Ostwald and others identify as important to deliver a just energy system. The state serves society – and politicians are required to serve the people. As Harvey acknowledges, there is no Eden of justice, but only the pursuit of justice (Harvey 1996, 333). The use of legal framings and philosophical grounding in the justice systems enable the relations-creating energy cultures to be assessed through a systematic review of interpretative framings of justice.

Power relations are not contained in the state. And as the 'soft-power with a hard-edge' demonstrates, culture holds political and economic power in international politics (Goldthau and Sitter 2015). The turn towards a 'geopolitics of culture' brings forth the cultural traditions of the state into the international sphere (Toal and Agnew 2002). There remain 'cardinal beliefs' within national cultures that affect international relations (Hadfield 2016, 781). Cooperation and disagreements are affected by domestic cultures and politics. Politically, citizens require their social contracts to be maintained between society and the state. The state takes international actions to fulfill this contract. The international orientation of the energy systems of Lithuania, Hungary, and Poland each indicates that the political values, as representative of their culture, influence the orientation of their energy systems. The soft power of the EU is contrasted with the interpreted hard power of Russia. Where Lithuania and Poland view Russia through a hard power lens, Hungary perceives relations with Russia through a lens of soft power of attraction. As Josef Nye describes, "Some aspects of human culture are universal, some are national … Culture is never static, and different cultures interact in different ways" (Nye 2011, 84). The different interpretation of geopolitical power by these three countries underscores both the evolving nature of culture and diversity of interactions. The interpretation of power relations between countries rests on interpreting cultural interactions, therefore there is a necessity to understand cultural relations within both the national and international energy systems.

8.3 THE SPACES AND SCALES OF ENERGY RELATIONS

Energy justice and geopolitical framing provide a mean of cultural expression in the value chain of the energy system. The 'social' and 'physical' energy systems denote different levels to perceiving the expression of culture and power. Each of these systems requires observation of both the physical artifacts on the landscape and in the social process influencing the politics of energy. It is the role of the researcher to utilize qualitative and quantitative techniques to observe and chronicle, and later categorize and assess, how the world – or in this case – systems, are organized. If the task of energy culture is to work from a personal agency and assist in changing the overall energy culture, then I as the researcher and author also hold a contribution based on my positionality and interpretation of Eastern Europe's energy culture (see Miller 2000).

Therefore, my interpretative and subjective understanding of the energy system is not without my cultural bias of an outsider (white American male with a geography PhD) looking in on the political and social systems of former Communist countries. My residence since 2006 has been Budapest and my field of research has extended from Lithuania down to North Macedonia. More informally, I have been coming to Budapest and traveling in Eastern Europe and even residing for shorter periods since 1998. Therefore, the social energy system holds a much more experiential viewpoint both as a resident, tourist, and as a researcher.

My awareness of the political-social dynamics in the region provides a subjective understanding of how the energy system reflects the perceived cultural attributes of each country. Here I take to heart Geertz's opening lines to the chapter on 'The Politics of Meaning,' "One of the things that everyone knows but no one can quite think how to demonstrate is that a country's politics reflect the design of its culture" (Geertz 1973, 311). This book attempts to explore and explain more than the politics on the surface. A reflecting pool only provides the images on the surface to those walking by. However, by looking closer, the ripples on the surface reflect the currents below. But even as a travel guidebook acknowledges, it can only share a few highlights and a few 'authentic' experiences of the country. Here, I have only been able to share a few snapshots of the highly-complex and contested arena of energy in three Eastern European countries.

My research and my 'gaze' on energy culture is organized in three ways. First, the lens of energy justice is developed to provide an objective view – even a normative position on energy cultures. This provides a means to assess the politics of energy. However, it excludes a more interpretative and subjective vantage point, which the second lens of a geopolitics of culture brings to reflect culture in the international arena. The third novel way the gaze is organized is by developing the three axioms to guide the deconstruction of energy culture. This provides a jumping point into the complexities of the variegated internal and external histories and relations of each country.

The three energy cultures axioms were developed from Heinberg's method for axiom creation: (1) tested using the methodology of science; (2) minimal definition (or descriptive in nature); (3) no glaring loopholes; (4) worded so that a layperson can understand (Heinberg 2010). Chapter 1 provides an accounting to comprehend the interlinkages between the ontological and epistemological framings supporting these axioms. This also includes their alignment with the spatial and scalar interactions taking place in the energy system. In this conclusion, it is important to summarize and apply the axioms both from an interpretivist framing of the author and researcher and acknowledging my own bias to the framing of energy cultures in the three countries. The first axiom emerges from the 'shallow' spaces to express the manifestation of culture in artifacts and practices through explicit representations:

1. Energy cultures are spatial expressions of the social milieu around energy systems and perceived through physical expressions of artifacts, imaginaries, and inequality of material and environmental differences.

The spatial expression of energy artifacts is essential to understand the outcome of the policy-making process. The high levels of energy poverty in all three countries provide a means to see how the built environment, from panel houses to village houses, reflects an energy culture of inefficiency and deep poverty. This neglected and aging infrastructure is contrasted with the new energy technologies that are the backbone of the centralized systems building a greater level of security into each system. During the field research stage, I was able to visit and tour both the *Independence* re-gasification ship (FSRU) in Klaipeda Harbor, and the Ignalina Nuclear Power Plant in Visaginas, Lithuania. The dismantling of Ignalina is actively underway and what preservation of the facility remains is an underfunded enterprise with the metal more valuable for its monetary value than its cultural value. In contrast, the *Independence* is paid for by each Lithuanian gas consumer. The preservation and projection of energy culture are handled in two opposing ways.

The NPP and the FSRU facilities are the embodiment of Lithuania's reorientation away from Russia and towards membership of the EU. The networks extending from these facilities express the new spatial relations. Whereas Ignalina once was an integral part of the USSR nuclear network (even depicted in the *Chernobyl* Netflix series), its decommissioning not only stopped the export of electricity, but it stopped the provision of heat to Visaginas. The *Independence* by contrast is now being interconnected into a Baltic gas pipeline ring, including Poland. The interconnected gas network extending from Poland to the Baltics reflects the roll-out of a new gas transmission network to diversify away from Russia and integrate into the EU, while Russia's Nord Stream 1 and 2 cross the Baltic Sea to Germany, avoiding both Lithuania and Poland. The Baltic region represents the confluence of international and national spatial networks of a new gas security era.

This new era builds on the 'imaginaries' which describe the extension of historical narratives or their reinterpretation to fit new political purposes. In Poland, it was the social resistance and support around shale gas where imaginaries and inequalities within society resulted in both active support and opposition to hydraulic fracturing technologies. Independence and security from Russia fueled the narrative to build a new gas industry with both domestic production and diversified imports producing a security and cultural narrative according to a repurposed cultural fit (LaBelle 2017a; Goldthau and LaBelle 2016). The argument for producing shale gas and retaining coal rests with the effort to ensure the "optimum use of Poland's own energy resources" (Polish Ministry of Energy 2018, 2). For Kuchler and Bridge, they see these efforts producing "powerful socio-technical imaginary that fuses the mining and burning of coal with national development" (Kuchler and Bridge 2018, 144). In Hungary, likewise, "the re-nationalisation of energy is part and parcel of a 're-imagining' of the state and its role in Hungarian political and economic life" (Isaacs and Molnar 2017, 112). The political use of reimagining of resources to sustain or shift cultural interpretations of the energy system highlights the centrality of power relations.

The second axiom addresses the role of power relations within and between scales leading to transformation within the social and economic systems:

2. Energy cultures play out at different *scales* and are both *socially and economically transformative* and reliant on *power relations* between the scales.

Inherent within this axiom is the exercise of political power to foster change within the other two spheres of society and economy. And it is here that extending the political exercise of reimagining of the state leads to social and economic transformation; the renationalization of the privately owned utilities "and [their] role in Hungarian political and economic life as well as a process of greater centralisation of political and economic power in Viktor Orbán and Fidesz" (Isaacs and Molnar 2017, 112). However, for Orbán, affording the renationalization was difficult without bringing Russia on board to provide political and economic support. It was necessary to secure Russian involvement by linking the gas and nuclear agreements to deliver lower-priced energy projects (Deak 2016). Power relations provide friction to create, alter, and sustain the constant social and economic changes. As Toal and Agnew stated in 2002, about the future research of culture in geopolitics,

> It is the slower structural tendencies tied to technoscientific modernity – relentless technoscientific change, turbulent capitalist globalization, unstable energy markets, failing states and systems, emerging diseases … that will continue to delimit the struggles over cultural geopolitics in the twenty-first century. (Toal and Agnew 2002, 461)

Instability in energy markets only highlights the slower structural changes but the relentless geopolitical power relations continue to change energy cultures. A constant readjustment occurs to policies and positions reliant on power relations to make the transitions from one orientation to the next. Whether this is EU membership or building a new gas pipeline, each physical alteration to the energy system is equivalent to economic or political changes. The third axiom captures this consistent change:

3. Energy cultures are *relationally transformative* in energy systems, including mechanical and thermal, social, political, and economic.

The spirit of Ostwald's energy culture was exemplified in the invention of a transformer that would provide benefit to the 'working class' greater than all the "welfare institutions in the world" (Ostwald 1907, in Stewart 2014, 344). Energetics for him, was a "science of the future," it was viewed as "the construction of human knowledge, both in direct and even more pertinently in indirect fashion" that could shape the future (Ostwald 1907, in Stewart 2014, 345). He spoke of the need to develop science to achieve this greater level of equity.

More than a century later, we do apply robust science and knowledge to our energy system. "Conflicts in the domain of energy and climate are not primarily due to lack of scientific facts or objectives truths." Rather, "a clash of priorities, interests, and normative assumptions" stands in the way of effective policy-making based on belief rather than science (Sovacool and Brown 2015, 36). But maybe the energy system *is* shaped by the clash of these normative assumptions in the energy system. Or more precisely, the clash of energy cultures is the social milieu (axiom 1) that gives energy meaning and value: energy cultures are the adhesive sustaining and unifying the different components of the energy system. A change to the energy system, based on scientific facts, also needs to be culturally acceptable from both a universal and a particular point of view. Energy cultures are reflecting the physical, social, and economic transformations around the site of combustion. Eliminating the subjective from the energy system would also eliminate culture – and the social, political, and economic voices and contestations that create culture.

Only artifacts like power plants would remain standing on the landscape but would exist without meaning or purpose. The social milieu gives the meaning to the artifacts. Significance is ascribed even to the inefficiencies of the energy system as cultural representations of social and political practices.

The energy system is composed of relations, whether mechanical, economic, or social, perceptible in both the social and physical energy systems. Striving to eliminate the subjective perspective negates the cultural relations that are the energy system. The geopolitics of culture reflect the domestic clash of power relations and who controls the expression of culture. For Mitchell, "culture explains action, behavior, resistance or social formations in a way that 'economics' or 'politics' cannot" (Mitchell 1995, 103). Therefore, as axiom 3 indicates, culture encapsulates more than just scientific facts of thermal dynamics, economics, or political science; rather it is 'relationally transformative' bringing together the subjective, the objective, and the physical and social sciences to produce the motive of action by people in a culture.

Culture turns out to be the social and physical structures surrounding the site of combustion – the spark – that represents the energy value chain, from resource extraction to technological conversion to delivery of an energy service, such as heat or light. The cultural geopolitics of a country represent the external expressive actions a country performs to ensure the delivery of resources or international conditions to secure the delivery of energy to citizens. To do this, the culture of a country experiences contestation and conflict over who controls or influences the production of an energy culture. This is why the narratives and imaginaries become essential to control and influence. The labeling of the '*Independence*' of the FSRU ship in Klaipeda, is reflective of a specific narrative. The use of the Polish government's fossil fuel slogan of 'Poland stands on coal' (Kuchler and Bridge 2018, 144) and the Hungarian government's 'Hungary Will Not Give In!' slogan expresses not scientific facts but cultural themes tied to deeper power relations. Hungary will not give into the EU, but it will let Russia in. The rationale of culture is the irrationality of politics for power.

These monikers which politicians pull out assist in shaping culture to ensure social support and demonstrate their actions align with an interpretivist framing of culture. They reflect norms and values within society (the very same that Sovacool and Brown (2015) argue against). They also resonate because they hold a cultural understanding of historical change and cultural difference, thereby demonstrating that "Meanings that have been produced do not go away but provide background material for the next round" (Geels and Verhees 2011, 912). The use of discourse and practices assist in developing agency – particularly by those in the position to control. "Culture thus becomes a 'toolkit': actors draw upon deep cognitive structures or 'repertoires' and actively use symbols and categories for sensemaking" (Geels and Verhees

2011, 912). It is these structures that both constrain society within a culture of regulation, but also emerge as points where culture can be contested to prompt change. There is an importance to engage with holders of power and challenge the projection of a national energy culture.

The invocation of a set of truisms in the form of axioms provides a guide to understanding the contestations and struggle over culture. They serve to provide clarity on what energy culture is, but without too much abstraction. As Geertz highlights, there is a need to provide a reality to concepts such as 'ideals' and 'judgments' but not in "some gauzy world of mental forms but in the concrete immediacy of partisan struggle" (Geertz 1973, 312). "The scholar who wishes to avoid this sort of perfected impressionism has thus to build this theoretical scaffold at the same time that he conducts his analysis" (Geertz 1973, 313). The development of the case studies in Chapters 3 to 5 provided the empirical backing to apply the axioms in the latter half of this book – fleshed out by using energy justice and cultural geopolitics. The 'gauzy mental forms' of concepts are perceived in the expressions of energy cultures. Despite this scaffold of concepts applied to the empirical world, there remains weakness and blind spots, as the next section describes.

8.4 ENERGY TRANSITION AND CULTURE

There is no shortage of conceptual framings to understand the energy transition. At the last count there were 96 theories and concepts covering 22 different disciplines (Sovacool and Hess 2017). However, there are limitations with a single theory attempting to explain the transition, with a consensus that a single theory cannot explain the multitude of factors influencing the energy transition (Cherp et al. 2018). Nonetheless, there is an acknowledgment that society does influence the energy system, which can provide a 'cultural legitimacy' (Geels and Verhees 2011) to any technologies. For example, this includes the reminder that technological innovation lies within specific scientific and engineering disciplines. While culture does play a role even in these fields (Stephenson 2018) there is a need to explain the processes without culture.

Rather, a nested approach with several theories assisting perspectives on the 'techno-economic,' 'socio-techno,' and 'political' perspectives – assisted by acknowledging the 'real-life' physical infrastructure – identify interaction points mediated by technology (Cherp et al. 2018, 179). This approach by Cherp and others emphasizes both the interdependence but also the independence of different plans comprising the energy system. By acknowledging both the static and active nature of the energy system, it assists the integration of other theories into a meta-theoretical framing.

Energy culture does incorporate other theories to explain what occurs in the social, political, and economic struggles. But culture – due to its illusiveness – is harder to apply when seeking out the explanation in areas involving vested interests ensuring regime formation influencing niche innovation. Financial and political motives can be ascribed to culture, but culture is also the "gauze" that inherently holds vagueness (Geertz 1973, 312). A more accurate picture could explain agency to individuals out of self-interest or group-interest, rather than the blurring concept of cultural dominance. Within the framing of Cherp and others, energy cultures are perceived to exist between the planes of the three framings, thereby lending support to the theories within the economic, social, and political planes, but not occupying the same conceptual framings. Culture is the mortar or the compound linking conceptual clarity given by other theories, such as energy justice or geopolitics of culture.

The broad perspective of culture neglects the sharpness elucidated from theories focused on actors, discourses, or the objective assessment of the justice. In this book, energy justice provides the objective viewpoint on a narrow field of norms and values, but broader perspectives using social justice theory or a greater analysis with discourse theory can deliver more nuanced accounts of injustices. Culture, as the axioms indicate, is abstract constructs that hold meaning only when attached through mediating theories, such as geopolitics or even the spatial and scale tools of geography. The earlier emphasis on the ontologies and epistemologies (Chapters 1 and 6) demonstrates the technical, conceptual framing necessary to identify what culture *is*. This hyper-focus on *what it is* distracts from empirical processes, which may express a culture, but blurs deeper processes, such as regime formation, or shallow processes such as coalition building.

Even within a cultural perspective, there are different views that transcend the subjective and objective interpretation. For example, the Interpretivist holds the ability to explain the physical energy system and how it operates from an objective point of view, while a different viewpoint, that of the radical Humanist, sees the energy system as a socio-political construct, able to understand power relations and subjugation. There are advantages and disadvantageous for holding one view over the other to explain an energy transition. Both Gioia and Pitre (1990) and Sovacool and Hess (2017) identify what each lens provides and does not provide. Notably, Sovacool and Hess outline 'goal's and assumptions' and other categories that the range of theoretical framing fit within (Sovacool and Hess 2017, 735). But there remains a third view: a 'mixed-transition' gray zone is acknowledged to reflect an overlapping of perspectives. And it is this gray zone, a 'topical focus', in which energy cultures come into focus. In the framing of this book, it is the overlap between energy justice and geopolitics of culture where culture is perceived in the relational struggles. Figure 8.1 demonstrates these divisions within the subjective paradigm between 'radical' and 'interpretivism', which look at culture through different lenses, including a mixed transition zone (Gioia and Pitre 1990, 598). Each category highlights a particular paradigm perspective, with the mixed-transition zone emphasizing the overlapping issues of power and the operational aspects of the energy system. While energy cultures cover the spectrum, it is in the reflecting pool of knowledge where we perceive the reflection but acknowledge the underlying currents as ripples on the water. A perception of culture is not the same as a definition of culture.

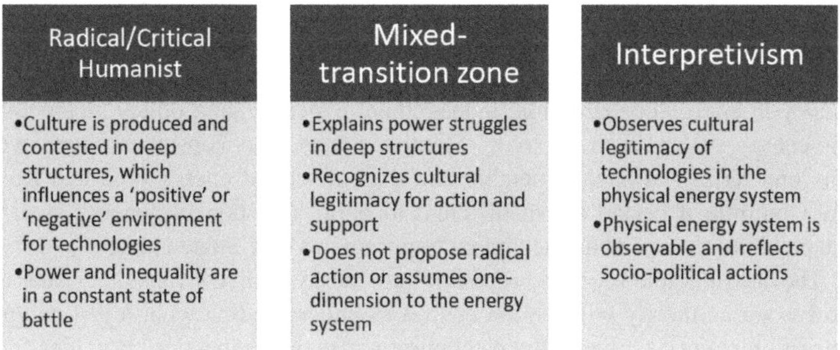

Source: Influenced by Geels and Verhees (2011); Gioia and Pitre (1990).

Figure 8.1 Description of subjective paradigm approaches

Chapter 1 provides a review of paradigms of knowledge through the different framings, and it was here that 'culture' was hidden from view through the four different paradigms of 'Functionalist-Institutionalist,' 'Interpretivist,' 'Critical Humanist,' and 'Conflict/Structuralist.' Culture was relegated as a 'topical focus' (Sovacool and Hess 2017, 735), stuck between 'goals' and 'methods' to explain the paradigms of how theories perceive the world. Culture does underlie and exists within each of the paradigms, but it remains elusive within the established energy transition theories. The strength of an energy cultures framework is in the illusiveness, the ability to explain without defining. Culture can play too much into jingoism and nationalism, thereby providing an 'us' vs. 'them' framing. Particular cultures may be perceived as trumping universal norms and rights. However, as many travelers will tell you, there is no 'right' culture or 'superior' culture; there are only different cultures. It is in these differences where there is the perception of culture and relations.

8.5 ENERGY CULTURES OF THE FUTURE

The intent of this book was to develop a conceptual framing that brought out the differences and similarities perceptible in Eastern Europe's energy landscape – the geopolitical tensions and the energy poverty experienced by many in the region. I felt that the plethora of theories and concepts already discussing and explaining the energy transition were ill-suited to explain the tensions within the EU's Eastern Member States. They failed to capture the historical relations and the economic pressures of conforming to a Western European perspective of what energy governance is. The massive privatization of the energy sector, or even just the threat of privatization, was sufficient for governments to erect foreign ownership barriers. Nonetheless, the high inefficiency in energy consumption, management expertise, and policy means that the energy system in many 'new' Member States costs consumers more over the long term. National ownership and the cultures of energy inherited from the Communist period are insufficient to build a sustainable energy system adaptable to the social and technical requirements of climate change.

The considerable scholarly research into energy justice means that issues of power and authority will remain central to understanding what a just energy transition means. Utilizing the catchphrase 'site of combustion' provides foci lacking in energy transitions studies. This book attempts to operationalize culture in both an ontological and metaphorical manner. The social and physical energy systems denote different processes that occur within what we call the energy system. But just as the benefit of using a diverse range of theories demonstrates, there is no single conceptualization of the energy system. These two notions of the physical and social attempt to provide a starting point to break up the massive construction of the modern energy system. There remains considerable work to understand power relations and how the use of culturally appropriate energy practices can provide a just energy transition.

During the years it took to write this book, terminology and understanding of justice within the energy system developed. The European Commission adopted the most recent iteration, the "Launching the Just Transition Mechanism – for a green transition based on solidarity and fairness" (European Commission 2020). The obvious question for this author to ask is 'solidarity and fairness for whom?' Because so far, as this book demonstrates, the energy transition debate in the EU has resulted in marginal improvements to the daily lives of citizens in Lithuania, Hungary, and Poland. The reliance on resources and technologies to supply homes still costs a larger slice of household income compared with Western Europe. The use of energy cultures demonstrates how politicians use a 'just transition' to fit their particular notion of an equitable energy system – whether that is retaining Polish coal or Hungary's reliance on

Russian resources and technologies to sustain a non-democratic and illiberal political system. Lithuania demonstrates the economic cost of developing an alternative energy system but again becoming overly reliant on imports for electricity and gas supplies. The determination of what a just energy transition is, and how to spend the money, should not be left to national or EU politicians. Since the 2004 EU expansion, it is hard to perceive how an equitable energy system was built; rather, resources built geopolitically secure energy systems. The 'wartime footing' marking Lithuania's actions also marks the gas diversification efforts of the EU since the 2009 Russia–Ukraine gas dispute. A just transition requires considerable recognition of deficiencies on the demand side of the energy system.

Energy cultures express power relations. Local initiatives, such as biomass in Lithuania, energy clusters in Poland, or the citizens' initiative to track hypothermia deaths in Hungary, all demonstrate reactions to failure at the national and EU levels. The transfer of sovereignty – the basis of the modern democratic state – from individuals to the state is failing in the EU's energy transition in Eastern Europe. The rise of populist governments in Poland and Hungary, delivering socially necessary low-cost and environmentally damaging energy, does not constitute an equitable energy transition. Energy geopolitics marked by relations with Russia – whether cheap coal (Poland) or nuclear technology (Hungary) – override citizens' initiatives to transition towards a more efficient energy housing stock with integrated renewable energy technologies. An equitable energy transition also requires a democratically functional state representing the interests of society. Political slogans tapping into cultural sentiments in the energy sector cover up injustices and inequity in the energy system. They take the perception of one injustice (high prices) to perpetuate other injustices, such as environmental damage or social exclusion.

Energy cultures expose power relations and underscore the importance of democratic norms in EU Member States. Building a just and equitable energy system in Eastern Europe requires recognizing the current injustices perpetuated by governments. Under the surface of the energy cultures in Lithuania, Poland, and Hungary are the social demands of an environmentally sustainable energy system. Inefficient homes are not just sites of energy poverty, but they represent a lack of recognition by the state for the plight of its citizens. A just energy transition in Europe requires citizens to participate to ensure the physical energy system serves their needs. The respect for democratic systems, with an independent judiciary able to protect citizens and firms against political injustice, is the only means to build a just transition.

References

3CSEP. 2012. "Employment Impacts of a Large-Scale Deep Building Energy Retrofit Programme in Poland: Executive Summary." European Climate Foundation. https://europeanclimate.org/documents/raport_eng.pdf.

Abaraviciene, Viktorija. n.d. "Visaginas Municipality: Your Next Investment Location."

Adamowicz, Krzysztof. 2019. "Mayor – Miedzyrzec Podlaski Commune Council, Poland." Panel discussion presented at the 5th European Congress of Local Governments, Krakow, Poland, April 9.

AFP. 2014. "Hungary's Orban Calls for EU-Russia Reset." *Space Daily*. January 31, 2014. http://www.spacedaily.com/reports/Hungarys_Orban_calls_for_EU-Russia_reset_999.html.

AFP. 2018. "Poland, Denmark Agree Baltic Sea Gas Pipeline – The Local." December 3, 2018. https://www.thelocal.dk/20181203/poland-denmark-agree-baltic-sea-gas-pipeline.

Alexander's Gas and Oil Connections. 2015. "Hungary State-Owned MVM Buys 50% Stake in Gas Trader Panrusgáz from E.ON —." March 28, 2015. http://www.gasandoil.com/news/2015/02/hungary-state-owned-mvm-buys-50-stake-in-gas-trader-panrusgaz-from-e.on.

Andersen, Svein S., Andreas Goldthau, and Nick Sitter, eds. 2017. *Energy Union Europe's New Liberal Mercantilism?* London: Palgrave Macmillan. https://doi.org/10.1057/978-1-137-59104-3.

Atlatszo. 2014. "Akár 600 Milliárd Forint Veszteséget Okozhat Az Eon Földgáz-Nagykereskedő Megvásárlása." August 13, 2014. http://atlatszo.hu/2014/08/13/akar-600-milliard-forint-veszteseget-okozhat-az-eon-foldgaz-nagykereskedo-megvasarlasa/.

Bassin, Mark. 1987. "Imperialism and the Nation State in Friedrich Ratzel's Political Geography." *Progress in Human Geography* 11 (4): 473–95. https://doi.org/10.1177/030913258701100401.

BBC. 2019. "Trump Signs off Sanctions on Russia Gas Pipeline." BBC News, December 21, 2019, sec. Europe. https://www.bbc.com/news/world-europe-50875935.

Berend, Ivan T., and Tamas Csato. 2001. *Evolution of the Hungarian Economy 1848–1989*. Vol. 1. *One-and-a-Half Centuries of Semi-Successful Modernization 1848–1989*. New York: Columbia University Press.

Bernat, Tivadar, ed. 1989. *An Economic Geography of Hungary*. 2nd ed. Budapest: Akadémiai Kiadó.

Bogel, Gyorgy, Vincent Edwards, Marian Wax, and Tibor Benko. 1997. *Hungary since Communism*. Basingstoke: Macmillan Business.

Bouzarovski, Stefan. 2009. "East-Central Europe's Changing Energy Landscapes: A Place for Geography." *Area* 41 (4): 452–63. https://doi.org/10.1111/j.1475-4762.2009.00885.x.

Bouzarovski, Stefan, and Neil Simcock. 2017. "Spatializing Energy Justice." *Energy Policy* 107 (August): 640–48. https://doi.org/10.1016/j.enpol.2017.03.064.

Bouzarovski, Stefan, Michael Bradshaw, and Alexander Wochnik. 2015. "Making Territory through Infrastructure: The Governance of Natural Gas Transit in Europe." *Geoforum* 64 (August): 217–28. https://doi.org/10.1016/j.geoforum.2015.06.022.

Bouzarovski, Stefan, Sergio Tirado Herrero, Saska Petrova, and Diana Ürge-Vorsatz. 2015. "Unpacking the Spaces and Politics of Energy Poverty: Path-Dependencies, Deprivation and Fuel Switching in Post-Communist Hungary." *Local Environment* 64: 1–20. https://doi.org/10.1080/13549839.2015.1075480.

Buckley, Neil. 2012. "Resources: Shale Gas Will Have Its Day in Europe – But Not Just Yet." *Financial Times*, November 8, 2012. http://www.ft.com/intl/cms/s/0/3b56d8b2-1c42-11e2-a63b-00144feabdc0.html#axzz2C1Rl9yNW.

Burrell, Gibson, and Gareth Morgan. 1979. *Sociological Paradigms and Organisational Analysis: Elements of the Sociology of Corporate Life*. 1st ed. Portsmouth, NH: Heinemann Educational Books.

CBC News. 2012. "Canada and Poland Set to Expand Energy Relationship – World." May 14, 2012. http://www.cbc.ca/news/world/story/2012/05/14/pol-cp-poland-visit-tusk-harper.html.

Cherp, Aleh, Vadim Vinichenko, Jessica Jewell, Elina Brutschin, and Benjamin Sovacool. 2018. "Integrating Techno-Economic, Socio-Technical and Political Perspectives on National Energy Transitions: A Meta-Theoretical Framework." *Energy Research & Social Science* 37 (March): 175–90. https://doi.org/10.1016/j.erss.2017.09.015.

Cloke, Jonathan, Alison Mohr, and Ed Brown. 2017. "Imagining Renewable Energy: Towards a Social Energy Systems Approach to Community Renewable Energy Projects in the Global South." *Energy Research & Social Science* 31 (September): 263–72. https://doi.org/10.1016/j.erss.2017.06.023.

Dalby, Simon. 2018. "Firepower: Geopolitical Cultures in the Anthropocene." *Geopolitics* 23 (3): 718–42. https://doi.org/10.1080/14650045.2017.1344835.

DBDH. 2015. "The Czech Republic: District Energy Potential for a Low Carbon Economy." https://dbdh.dk/2015/02/16/the-czech-republic-district-energy-potential-for-a-low-carbon-economy/.

Deak, András. 2016. "Captured by Power: The Expansion of the Paks Nuclear Power Plant." In *Twenty-Five Sides of a Post-Communist Mafia State*, edited by Bálint Magyar, Júlia Vásárhelyi, Balázs Trencsényi, and András Bozóki, 323–44. Budapest; New York: CEU Press, in association with Noran Libro, 2016.

Dew, Nicholas, Kathryn Aten, and Geraldo Ferrer. 2017. "How Many Admirals Does It Take to Change a Light Bulb? Organizational Innovation, Energy Efficiency, and the United States Navy's Battle over LED Lighting." *Energy Research & Social Science* 27 (May): 57–67. https://doi.org/10.1016/j.erss.2017.02.009.

Directorate-General for Energy. 2017. "EU Energy in Figures: Statistical Pocketbook 2017." https://publications.europa.eu/en/publication-detail/-/publication/2e046bd0-b542-11e7-837e-01aa75ed71a1/language-en/format-PDF.

Eberlein, Burkhard. 2008. "The Making of the European Energy Market: The Interplay of Governance and Government." *Journal of Public Policy* 28 (1): 73–92. https://doi.org/10.1017/S0143814X08000780.

Edwardes-Evans, Henry. 2020. "Polish Utilities Suspend Funding for Ostroleka Coal Project | S&P Global Platts." SPGlobal. February 14, 2020. https://www.spglobal.com/platts/en/market-insights/latest-news/coal/021420-polish-utilities-suspend-funding-for-ostroleka-coal-project.

Energiaklub. 2015. "A Magyarországi Lakossági Villamosenergiaárak Növekedésének Okai Az Elmúlt Két Évtizedben. (Reasons behind the Rise of Residential Electric

Energy Rates in the Past Two Decades in Hungary).” Energiaklub. https://www.energiaklub.hu/files/study/energiaar_tanulmany_web.pdf.

EU Energy Poverty Observatory. 2019a. *Inability to Keep Houses Warm: Selected Countries*. https://www.energypoverty.eu.

EU Energy Poverty Observatory. 2019b. *Arrears on Utility Bills – Hungary – 2004 – 2016, by Income Deciles*. https://www.energypoverty.eu/indicator?primaryId=1462&type=line&from=2004&to=2016&countries=HU&disaggregation=income.

EU Energy Poverty Observatory. 2020. “High Share of Energy Expenditure in Income (2M).” https://www.energypoverty.eu/indicator?primaryId=1460&type=bar&from=2010&to=2010&countries=BG,CZ,EE,HU,HR,LT,LV,PL,RO,SI,SK&disaggregation=none.

EurActiv.com. 2014. “Poland Calls for EU Action to End Russia’s Energy Stranglehold.” April 22, 2014. https://www.euractiv.com/section/energy/news/poland-calls-for-eu-action-to-end-russia-s-energy-stranglehold/844915/.

European Commission. 2015a. “2014 EU Energy Benchmarking Report: Lithuania Country Study, Analysis and Recommendations.” Directorate General for Energy, European Commission. https://ec.europa.eu/energy/sites/ener/files/documents/2014_countryreports_lithuania.pdf.

European Commission. 2015b. “Energy Union Package: A Framework Strategy for a Resilient Energy Union with a Forward-Looking Climate Change Policy.” European Commission.

European Commission. 2016a. “Towards a Smart, Efficient and Sustainable Heating and Cooling Sector.” February 16, 2016. http://europa.eu/rapid/press-release_MEMO-16-311_en.htm.

European Commission. 2016b. “Towards Energy Union: The Commission Presents Sustainable Energy Security Package.” New Europe. February 16, 2016. http://neurope.eu/wires/towards-energy-union-the-commission-presents-sustainable-energy-security-package/.

European Commission. 2020. “Launching the Just Transition Mechanism – for a Green Transition Based on Solidarity and Fairness.” January 15, 2020. https://ec.europa.eu/info/news/launching-just-transition-mechanism-green-transition-based-solidarity-and-fairness-2020-jan-15_en.

European Commission Joint Research Centre. 2018. “EU Coal Regions: Opportunities and Challenges Ahead.” European Commission. https://ec.europa.eu/jrc/en/publication/eur-scientific-and-technical-research-reports/eu-coal-regions-opportunities-and-challenges-ahead.

European Environment Agency. 2018. “Poland – Industrial Pollution Profile 2018.” December 3, 2018. https://www.eea.europa.eu/themes/industry/industrial-pollution/industrial-pollution-country-profiles-2018/poland-industrial-pollution-profile-2018.

European Environment Agency. 2019. “Air Quality Index.” http://airindex.eea.europa.eu/.

Eurostat. 2018a. “Energy Import Dependency by Products.” https://ec.europa.eu/eurostat/tgm/table.do?tab=table&init=1&language=en&pcode=sdg_07_50&plugin=1.

Eurostat. 2018b. “Share of Renewable Energy in Gross Final Energy Consumption.” https://ec.europa.eu/eurostat/tgm/table.do?tab=table&init=1&language=en&pcode=t2020_31&plugin=1.

Eurostat. 2019. “EU Imports of Energy Products – Recent Developments.” European Commission. https://ec.europa.eu/eurostat/statistics-explained/pdfscache/46126.pdf.

Eurostat. 2020a. "Arrears on Utility Bills – EU-SILC Survey." https://bit.ly/3dqskWz.
Eurostat. 2020b. "Electricity Prices for Household Consumers – Bi-Annual Data (from 2007 Onwards)." https://bit.ly/2Wxo54r.
Eurostat. 2020c. "Inability to Keep Home Adequately Warm – EU-SILC Survey." https://bit.ly/2YD5tCU.
Eurostat. 2020d. "Mean Monthly Earnings by Sex, Age and Occupation." https://appsso.eurostat.ec.europa.eu/nui/show.do?dataset=earn_ses14_21&lang=en.
Eurostat. 2020e. "Population by Sex, Age Group and Country of Citizenship." https://appsso.eurostat.ec.europa.eu/nui/show.do?dataset=cens_01nsctz&lang=en.
Eurostat. 2020f. "Real GDP per Capita." https://ec.europa.eu/eurostat/tgm/table.do?tab=table&init=1&language=en&pcode=sdg_08_10&plugin=1.
Eurostat. 2020g. "Structure of Consumption Expenditure by Income Quintile and COICOP Consumption Purpose." https://bit.ly/3dnG0Sa.
Eurostat, European Commission. 2009. "Panorama of Energy: Energy Statistics to Support EU Policies and Solutions." Eurostat. http://ec.europa.eu/eurostat/documents/3217494/5713267/KS-GH-09-001-EN.PDF/6e94b4de-2c3c-4cf6-91ab-f72a2b97c430.
Eurostat, European Commission. 2018. "Electricity Price Statistics." https://ec.europa.eu/eurostat/statistics-explained/index.php/Electricity_price_statistics.
Felsmann, Balazs. 2014. *Winners and Losers on the Liberalized Energy Sector in Hungary: A Co-Evolutionary Approach*. Budapest: Corvinus University of Budapest.
Felsmann, Balázs. 2018. *Firm Performance Under Institutional Constraints: Strategic Adaptation and Corporate Co-Evolution in the Hungarian Energy Retail Sector*. Budapest: Corvinus University of Budapest.
Forum Energii. 2017. "Energy Transition in Poland 2017." http://forum-energii.eu/public/upload/articles/files/Energy%20transition%20in%20Poland%202017%20final.pdf.
Fuller, Sara, and Darren McCauley. 2016. "Framing Energy Justice: Perspectives from Activism and Advocacy." *Energy Research & Social Science* 11 (January): 1–8. https://doi.org/10.1016/j.erss.2015.08.004.
Geels, Frank W. 2002. "Technological Transitions as Evolutionary Reconfiguration Processes: A Multi-Level Perspective and a Case-Study." *Research Policy* 31 (8–9): 1257–74. https://doi.org/10.1016/S0048-7333(02)00062-8.
Geels, Frank W. 2010. "Ontologies, Socio-Technical Transitions (to Sustainability), and the Multi-Level Perspective." *Research Policy*, Special Section on Innovation and Sustainability Transitions, 39 (4): 495–510. https://doi.org/10.1016/j.respol.2010.01.022.
Geels, Frank W., and Johan Schot. 2007. "Typology of Sociotechnical Transition Pathways." *Research Policy* 36 (3): 399–417. https://doi.org/10.1016/j.respol.2007.01.003.
Geels, Frank W., and B. Verhees. 2011. "Cultural Legitimacy and Framing Struggles in Innovation Journeys: A Cultural-Performative Perspective and a Case Study of Dutch Nuclear Energy (1945–1986)." *Technological Forecasting and Social Change* 78 (6): 910–30. https://doi.org/10.1016/j.techfore.2010.12.004.
Geertz, Clifford. 1973. *The Interpretation of Cultures. [Electronic Resource]: Selected Essays*. New York: Basic Books. http://eds.a.ebscohost.com/eds/detail/detail?vid=0&sid=0b66d14a-d4fa-4e89-9a20-3f76f824c118%40sdc-v-sessmgr02&bdata=JnNpdGU9ZWRzLWxpdmU%3d#AN=ceul.b1155500&db=cat00823a.
Georgi. 2015. "Duda Slams Russia's Second Baltic Gas Pipeline to Germany." Text. EurActiv | EU News & Policy Debates, across Languages. September 9, 2015. http://

www.euractiv.com/sections/energy/polish-president-slams-russias-second-baltic-gas-pipeline-germany-317457.

Gibson-Graham, J. K. 1996. *The End of Capitalism (As We Knew It): A Feminist Critique of Political Economy*. Cambridge, MA: Blackwell Publishers.

Giddens, Anthony. 1982. *Profiles and Critiques in Social Theory*. London: Macmillan Education UK. https://doi.org/10.1007/978-1-349-86056-2.

Gioia, D. A., and E. Pitre. 1990. "Multiparadigm Perspectives on Theory Building." *Academy of Management Review* 15 (4): 584–602.

Global Studies Initiative. 2018. "The Transformation of the Polish Coal Sector." Global Studies Initiative. https://www.iisd.org/sites/default/files/publications/transformation-polish-coal-sector.pdf.

Goldthau, Andreas, and Michael LaBelle. 2012. "Regulating a Nascent Sector: Explaining Diverging Shale Gas Policies in Bulgaria and Poland." European Consortium for Political Research.

Goldthau, Andreas, and Michael LaBelle. 2016. "The Power of Policy Regimes: Explaining Shale Gas Policy Divergence in Bulgaria and Poland: The Power of Policy Regimes." *Review of Policy Research* 33 (6): 603–22. https://doi.org/10.1111/ropr.12204.

Goldthau, Andreas, and Nick Sitter. 2015. "Soft Power with a Hard Edge: EU Policy Tools and Energy Security." *Review of International Political Economy* 0 (0): 1–25. https://doi.org/10.1080/09692290.2015.1008547.

Goldthau, Andreas, and Benjamin K. Sovacool. 2012. "The Uniqueness of the Energy Security, Justice, and Governance Problem." *Energy Policy, Modeling Transport (Energy) Demand and Policies*, 41 (February): 232–40. https://doi.org/10.1016/j.enpol.2011.10.042.

Grigas, Agnia. 2017. *The New Geopolitics of Natural Gas*. Cambridge, MA: Harvard University Press. http://www.hup.harvard.edu/catalog.php?isbn=9780674971837.

Gustafson, Thane. 1989. *Crisis amid Plenty: The Politics of Soviet Energy under Brezhnev and Gorbachev*. A Rand Corporation Research Study. Princeton, NJ: Princeton University Press.

Hadfield, Amelia. 2016. "EU-Russia Strategic Energy Culture: Progressive Convergence or Regressive Dilemma?" *Geopolitics* 21 (4): 779–98. https://doi.org/10.1080/14650045.2016.1219342.

Harvey, David. 1996. *Justice, Nature and the Geography of Difference*. Oxford: Wiley. http://eu.wiley.com/WileyCDA/WileyTitle/productCd-1557866813.html.

Heffron, Raphael J., and Darren McCauley. 2014. "Achieving Sustainable Supply Chains through Energy Justice." *Applied Energy* 123: 435–37. https://doi.org/10.1016/j.apenergy.2013.12.034.

Heffron, Raphael J., and Darren McCauley. 2017. "The Concept of Energy Justice across the Disciplines." *Energy Policy* 105 (June): 658–67. https://doi.org/10.1016/j.enpol.2017.03.018.

Heffron, Raphael J., Darren McCauley, and Benjamin K. Sovacool. 2015. "Resolving Society's Energy Trilemma through the Energy Justice Metric." *Energy Policy* 87 (December): 168–76. https://doi.org/10.1016/j.enpol.2015.08.033.

Heinberg, Richard. 2010. "What Is Sustainability?" In *The Post Carbon Reader: Managing the 21st Century's Sustainabilty Crises*, edited by Richard Heinberg and Daniel Lerch, 13–24. Healdsburg, CA: Watershed Media.

Hinchey, Nathalie and Anna Mikulska. 2017. "LNG Versus Russian Gas in Central And Eastern Europe: Playing Poker On A Continental Scale." August 17, 2017. https://

www.forbes.com/sites/thebakersinstitute/2017/08/24/lng-versus-russian-gas-in-central-and-eastern-europe-playing-poker-on-a-continental-scale/#5fe7d9532c3a.

Hirsch, Daniel. 2015. "More Power to Government's Elbow." Newsportal. *The Budapest Times*, March 15, 2015. http://budapesttimes.hu/2015/03/08/more-power-to-governments-elbow/.

Hirsh, R. 1999. *Power Loss: The Origins of Deregulation and Restructuring in the American Electric Utility System*. Cambridge, MA and London: The MIT Press.

Hiteva, Ralitsa, and Benjamin Sovacool. 2017. "Harnessing Social Innovation for Energy Justice: A Business Model Perspective." *Energy Policy* 107 (August): 631–9. https://doi.org/10.1016/j.enpol.2017.03.056.

Högselius, Per. 2013. *Red Gas: Russia and the Origins of European Energy Dependence*. 1st ed. Palgrave Macmillan Transnational History Series. New York: Palgrave Macmillan.

Horvath Kadar, Agnes. 2012. "Barriers to a Real Competitive Business Environment on the Liberalised Energy Market." *Club of Economics in Miskolc* 8 (2): 37–43.

Hungary Around the Clock. 2013. "Parliament Places Energy Price Rules beyond the Reach of Courts." March 18, 2013. https://hatc.hu/index.php.

Hungary Around the Clock. 2019a. "Eurstat Warns on Gas Storage Data." April 24, 2019. https://hatc.hu/index.php.

Hungary Around the Clock. 2019b. "Magyar Posta Completes Delivery of Utility Vouchers." October 1, 2019. https://hatc.hu/index.php.

IAEA. 2004. "Energy Supply Options for Lithuania: A Detailed Multi-Sector Integrated Energy Demand, Supply and Environmental Analysis." International Atomic Energy Agency.

IEA. 2017. "Energy Policies of IEA Countries: Hungary 2017 Review." International Energy Agency.

IEA. 2018. "Electricity Generation by Fuel Hungary 1990–2016." International Energy Agency. https://www.iea.org/statistics/?country=HUNGARY&year=2016&category=Electricity&indicator=ElecGenByFuel&mode=chart&dataTable=ELECTRICITYANDHEAT.

Instytut Badan Strukturalnych. 2015. "It's Cold Inside – Energy Poverty in Poland."

International Consulting Firm. 2013. "Current Status of the Hungarian Energy Industry." Presented at the Presentation for Clients, September 13.

Isaacs, Rico, and Adam Molnar. 2017. "Island in the Neoliberal Stream: Energy Security and Soft Re-Nationalisation in Hungary." *Journal of Contemporary European Studies* 25 (1): 107–26. https://doi.org/10.1080/14782804.2016.1198688.

Jando, Zoltan. 2018. "A Kormány a Rezsidémon Mellé Állt | G7 – Gazdasági Sztorik Érthetően." G7. February 19, 2018. https://g7.hu/kozelet/20180219/a-kormany-a-rezsidemon-melle-allt/.

Janeliunas, Tomas. 2018. Professor, TSPMI / International Relations Insitute at Vilnius University.

Jenkins, Kirsten. 2018. "Setting Energy Justice Apart from the Crowd: Lessons from Environmental and Climate Justice." *Energy Research & Social Science* 39 (May): 117–21. https://doi.org/10.1016/j.erss.2017.11.015.

Jenkins, Kirsten, Darren McCauley, and Charles R. Warren. 2017. "Attributing Responsibility for Energy Justice: A Case Study of the Hinkley Point Nuclear Complex." *Energy Policy* 108 (September): 836–43. https://doi.org/10.1016/j.enpol.2017.05.049.

Jenkins, Kirsten, Benjamin K. Sovacool, and Darren McCauley. 2018. "Humanizing Sociotechnical Transitions through Energy Justice: An Ethical Framework for

Global Transformative Change." *Energy Policy* 117 (June): 66–74. https://doi.org/10.1016/j.enpol.2018.02.036.

Jenkins, Kirsten, Darren McCauley, Raphael Heffron, Hannes Stephan, and Robert Rehner. 2016. "Energy Justice: A Conceptual Review." *Energy Research & Social Science* 11: 174–82. https://doi.org/10.1016/j.erss.2015.10.004.

Kaderjak, Peter, Andras Kiss, Csaba Kovacs, Michael LaBelle, and Palma Szolnoki. 2007. *INNOGATE Training Handbook: Regulating Our Energy Supply*. Edited by Michael LaBelle. Kiev: INOGATE Technical Secretariat.

Kasztelewicz, Zbigniew. 2018. Professor, Head of Surface Mining Department, AGH University of Science and Technology in Cracow, Poland. Personal interview with the author, Krakow, Poland, November 14.

Kasztelewicz, Zbigniew. 2019. "Professor, Head of Surface Mining Department, AGH University of Science and Technology in Cracow, Poland." Presentation at the 5th European Congress of Local Governments; Coal Mining Regions in Transformation, Good Practices, Krakow, Poland, April 9.

Kivimaa, Paula, and Florian Kern. 2016. "Creative Destruction or Mere Niche Support? Innovation Policy Mixes for Sustainability Transitions." *Research Policy* 45 (1): 205–17. https://doi.org/10.1016/j.respol.2015.09.008.

Knutsen, Torbjørn L. 1992. *A History of International Relations Theory*. 1st ed. Manchester: Manchester University Press.

Kohler, Jonathan, Frank W. Geels, Florian Kern, Jochen Markard, Elsie Onsongo, Anna Wieczorek, Floortje Alkemade, et al. 2019. "An Agenda for Sustainability Transitions Research: State of the Art and Future Directions." *Environmental Innovation and Societal Transitions* 31 (June): 1–32. https://doi.org/10.1016/j.eist.2019.01.004.

Kopec, Slawomir. 2019. "Head of the Centre of Advanced Technologies for Future City, AGH University of Science and Technology in Cracow, Poland." Interview presented at the 5th European Congress of Local Governments, Krakow, Poland, April 8.

KPMG Global Energy Institute. 2012. "Central and Eastern European Shale Gas Outlook." KPMG.

Kuchler, Magdalena, and Gavin Bridge. 2018. "Down the Black Hole: Sustaining National Socio-Technical Imaginaries of Coal in Poland." *Energy Research & Social Science* 41 (July): 136–47. https://doi.org/10.1016/j.erss.2018.04.014.

Kumiega, Jaroslaw. 2019. Energy Planning Department, Office of the Marshal of the Pomorskie Voivodeship. Personal interview with the author, Gdansk, Poland, November 7.

Kureth, Andrew. 2015. "Why Poland Still Clings to Coal – POLITICO." POLITICO. October 17, 2015. https://www.politico.eu/article/why-poland-still-clings-to-coal-energy-union-security-eu-commission/.

LaBelle, M. 2006. "Finding the Barriers Preventing Increased Cooperation and Coordination in Central and Eastern Europe." Regional Centre for Energy Policy Research Working Paper. http://rekk.uni-corvinus.hu./index-en.html.

LaBelle, Michael. 2009. "Expanding Opportunities: Strategic Buying of Utilities in New EU Member States." *Energy Policy* 37 (11): 4672–78. https://doi.org/doi: DOI: 10.1016/j.enpol.2009.06.022.

LaBelle, Michael. 2011. *Celebrating 10 Years: Assessing a Decade of Regulatory Cooperation*. Budapest: Energy Regulators Regional Association. http://energyscee.com/wp-content/uploads/2009/10/10-Years-brochure-11_04_12.pdf.

LaBelle, Michael. 2012a. "Constructing Post-Carbon Institutions: Assessing EU Carbon Reduction Efforts through an Institutional Risk Governance Approach." *Energy Policy* 40 (January): 390–403. https://doi.org/10.1016/j.enpol.2011.10.024.

LaBelle, Michael. 2012b. "Citizens' Petitions on Shale Gas Extraction in Bulgaria and Poland." Committee on Petitions, European Parliament, Directorate General For Internal Policies Policy Department C: Citizens' Rights and Constitutional Affairs. http://www.europarl.europa.eu/committees/en/peti/studiesdownload.html?languageDocument=EN&file=77871.

LaBelle, Michael. 2012c. "Part 1: Fracking to Reduce Risks: Bulgaria and Poland Redefine Their Gas Dependency." *Natural Gas Europe*, November 19, 2012. http://www.naturalgaseurope.com/fracking-risks-bulgaria-poland.

LaBelle, Michael. 2012d. "Part 2: Fracking to Reduce Risks: Bulgaria and Poland Redefine Their Gas Dependency." *Natural Gas Europe*, December 3, 2012. http://www.naturalgaseurope.com/bulgaria-poland-fracking-for-reducing-risk.

LaBelle, Michael. 2015. "The Day Hungary Cleaved from Europe: The True Cost of Russian Gas | EnergySCEE." February 23, 2015. http://energyscee.com/2015/02/23/the-day-hungary-cleaved-from-europe-the-true-cost-of-russian-gas/.

LaBelle, Michael. 2017a. "A State of Fracking: Building Poland's National Innovation Capacity for Shale Gas." *Energy Research & Social Science* 23 (January): 26–35. https://doi.org/10.1016/j.erss.2016.11.003.

LaBelle, Michael. 2017b. "Failure to Frack: Pitfalls of Governance and Risk in Polish Shale Gas." In *Risks Rewards and Regulation of Unconventional Gas: A Global Perspective*, edited by R. Quentin Grafton, Ian Cronshaw, and Michael Moore, 267–85. Cambridge: Cambridge University Press. http://www.cambridge.org/hu/academic/subjects/earth-and-environmental-science/environmental-policy-economics-and-law/risks-rewards-and-regulation-unconventional-gas-global-perspective.

LaBelle, Michael. 2017c. "In Pursuit of Energy Justice." *Energy Policy* 107 (August): 615–20. https://doi.org/10.1016/j.enpol.2017.03.054.

LaBelle, Michael. 2018. "Pitfalls of Shale Gas Exploration in Poland." In *Risks, Rewards and Regulation of Unconventional Natural Gas*, edited by R. Quentin Grafton, Ian Cronshaw, and Michael Moore. UNESCO.

LaBelle, Michael, and Andras Deak. 2015. "2014 EU Energy Benchmarking Report: Hungary Country Study, Analysis and Recommendations." Directorate General for Energy, European Commission. https://ec.europa.eu/energy/en/topics/markets-and-consumers/single-market-progress-report.

LaBelle, Michael, and Atanas Georgiev. 2015. "The Socio-Political Capture of Utilities: The Expense of Low Energy Prices in Bulgaria and Hungary." In *Energy Law and Energy Infrastructure Development for a Low-Carbon World*. Cambridge: Cambridge University Press.

LaBelle, Michael, and Andreas Goldthau. 2013. "Escaping the Valley of Death? Comparing Shale Gas Technology Policy Prospects to Nuclear and Solar in Europe." *The Journal of World Energy Law & Business* 7 (2): 93–111. jwt020. https://doi.org/10.1093/jwelb/jwt020.

LaBelle, Michael, and Peter Kaderják, eds. 2008. *Impact of the 2004 Enlargement on the EU Energy Sector*. Budapest: Regional Centre for Energy Policy Research, Corvinus University of Budapest.

Lapinskas, Remigijus. 2018. President, World Biomass Association.

Larner, Wendy, and Nina Laurie. 2010. "Travelling Technocrats, Embodied Knowledges: Globalising Privatisation in Telecoms and Water." *Geoforum* 41 (2): 218–26. https://doi.org/10.1016/j.geoforum.2009.11.005.

Lipinska, Karolina. 2018. Office of Entrepreneurship and Innovation Development. Personal interview with the author, Gdansk, Poland, November 7.

Lithuanian Energy Ministry Official A. 2018. Energy Ministry of Lithuania.

Macdonald, Graeme. 2017. "Containing Oil: The Pipeline in Petroculture." In *Petrocultures: Oil, Politics, Culture*, edited by Sheena Wilson, Adam Carlson, and Imre Szeman, 36–77. Kingston, ON: MQUP.

Mackinder, H. J. 2004. "The Geographical Pivot of History (1904)." *Geographical Journal* 170 (4): 298–321. https://doi.org/10.1111/j.0016-7398.2004.00132.x.

Massey, Doreen. 1973. "Towards a Critique of Industrial Location Theory." *Antipode* 5 (3): 33–9.

Mateusz, Richert. 2018. Provincial Inspector, Pomeranian Regional Planning Office. Personal interview with the author, Gdansk, Poland, November 7.

Mathieu, Gilbert. 1970. "'The History of the ECSC: Good Times and Bad' from Le Monde." *Le Monde*, May 9, 1970.

McCauley, Darren, and Raphael Heffron. 2018. "Just Transition: Integrating Climate, Energy and Environmental Justice." *Energy Policy* 119 (August): 1–7. https://doi.org/10.1016/j.enpol.2018.04.014.

Miller, R. 2000. *Research Life Stories and Family Histories*. London: Sage Publications.

Ministry of Energy of the Republic of Lithuania. 2017. "Renewable energy sources." July 17, 2017. http://enmin.lrv.lt/en/sectoral-policy/renewable-energy-sources.

Ministry of Energy of the Republic of Lithuania. 2018. "Seimas Approves Progressive and Innovative Lithuanian Energy Strategy." June 22, 2018. https://enmin.lrv.lt/en/news/seimas-approves-progressive-and-innovative-lithuanian-energy-strategy.

Mitchell, Donald. 1995. "There's No Such Thing as Culture: Towards a Reconceptualization of the Idea of Culture in Geography." *Transactions of the Institute of British Geographers* 20 (1): 102–16. https://doi.org/10.2307/622727.

Mitchell, Donald. 2000. *Cultural Geography: A Critical Introduction*. 1st ed. Malden, MA: Blackwell Publishing Limited.

Moezzi, Mithra, Kathryn B. Janda, and Sea Rotmann. 2017. "Using Stories, Narratives, and Storytelling in Energy and Climate Change Research." *Energy Research & Social Science, Narratives and Storytelling in Energy and Climate Change Research*, 31 (September): 1–10. https://doi.org/10.1016/j.erss.2017.06.034.

Molin, Anna. 2014. "Finland, Estonia Move to Reduce Reliance on Russian Gas." *The Wall Street Journal*, 2014. https://www.wsj.com/articles/finland-estonia-move-to-reduce-reliance-on-russian-gas-1416314204.

Molis, Arunas. 2018. Adviser to the President of Lithuania.

MTI. 2011. "Orbán Says Hungary Pursuing New Kind of Economic Policy." Realdeal.Hu. January 6, 2011. http://www.realdeal.hu/20110601/orban-says-hungary-pursuing-new-kind-of-economic-policy/.

Nagevičius, Martynas. 2018. President of the Lithuanian Confederation of Renewable Energy.

Nagy, Gabor. 2014. Personal communication.

Nye, Joseph S. 2011. *The Future of Power*. 1st ed. New York: PublicAffairs.

Nye Jr., Joseph S. 2004. *Soft Power: The Means to Success in World Politics*. New York: PublicAffairs.

Nyga-Łukaszewska, Honorata. 2015. "Poland's Energy Security Strategy." November 27, 2015. http://www.ensec.org/index.php?option=com_content&view=article&id

=279:assessing-polands-energy-security-strategy&catid=114:content0211&Itemid =374.Net4Gas. 2018. "The Czech and the Austrian Gas Markets Are Connected by a New Service 'Trading Region Upgrade' (TRU)." https://www.net4gas.cz/en/media/press-releases/news-list/the-czech-austrian-gas-markets-are-connected-new-service-trading-region-upgrade-tru.html.

O Tuathail, Gearoid, and John Agnew. 1992. "Geopolitics and Discourse." *Political Geography* 11 (2): 190–204. https://doi.org/10.1016/0962-6298(92)90048-X.

Office for Democratic Institutions and Human Rights. 2018. "Hungary: Parliamentary Elections 8 April 2018, ODIHR Limited Election Observation Mission Final Report." Organization for Security and Cooperation in Europe. https://www.osce.org/odihr/elections/hungary.

Olszewski, Michal. 2018. "Polish Electricity Prices on the Rise." Energy Transition. November 18, 2018. https://energytransition.org/2018/11/polish-electricity-prices-on-the-rise/.

Orban, Anita. 2008. *Power, Energy, and the New Russian Imperialism*. PSI Reports. Westport, CT: Praeger Security International.

Ostwald, Wilhelm. 1907. "The Modern Theory of Energetics." *The Monist* 17 (October): 481–515.

Pai, Sandeep, and Savannah Carr-Wilson. 2018. *Total Transition: The Human Side of the Renewable Energy Revolution*. Victoria, BC: Rocky Mountain Books.

Pakalkaite, Vija. 2012. "Gazprom and the Natural Gas Markets of the East Baltic States." Regional Centre for Energy Policy Research – Budapesti Corvinus Egyetem. https://rekk.hu/downloads/projects/wp2012-1.pdf.

Pakalkaite, Vija. 2016. "Lithuania's Strategic Use of EU Energy Policy Toóls: A Transformation of Gas Dynamics." Oxford Institute for Energy Studies. https://www.oxfordenergy.org/wpcms/wp-content/uploads/2016/09/Lithuanias-Strategic-Use-of-EU-Energy-Policy-Tools-A-transformation-of-Gas-Market-Dynamics-NG-111.pdf.

PHYS.ORG. 2013. "Poland Anchors Energy Strategy in Coal, Shale Gas: PM." September 10. http://phys.org/news/2013-09-poland-anchors-energy-strategy-coal.html.

Pirani, Simon, Jonathan Stern, and Katja Yafimava. 2009. "The Russo-Ukrainian Gas Dispute of January 2009: A Comprehensive Assessment." Oxford Institute for Energy Studies. http://www.oxfordenergy.org/pdfs/NG27.pdf.

Pitchford, Ruth. 2016. "UPDATE 2-Court Orders Bulgaria to Pay Russia over Cancelled Nuclear Project: Officials." *Reuters*, 2016. https://www.reuters.com/article/bulgaria-russia-arbitration/update-2-court-orders-bulgaria-to-pay-russia-over-cancelled-nuclear-project-officials-idUSL8N1981YO.

PKN ORLEN. 2018a. "A New Gas Deposit of ORLEN and PGNiG." August 9, 2018. https://www.orlen.pl/EN/PressOffice/Pages/A-new-gas-deposit-of-ORLEN-and-PGNiG.aspx.

PKN ORLEN. 2018b. "PKN ORLEN's Exploration Success in Rzeszów Province." October 17, 2018. https://www.orlen.pl/EN/PressOffice/Pages/PKN-ORLEN%E2%80%99s-exploration-success-in-Rzesz%C3%B3w-province.aspx.

Polish Geological Institute-National Research Institute/Państwowy Instytut Geologiczny-Państwowy Instytut Badawczy. 2012. "Assessment of Shale Gas and Shale Oil Resources of the Lower Paleozoic Baltic-Podlasie-Lublin Basin in Poland." Warsaw. https://www.pgi.gov.pl/docman-dokumenty-pig-pib/docman/aktualnosci-2012/zasoby-gazu/769-raport-en/file.html.

Polish Ministry of Energy. 2018. "Polish Energy Policy to 2040 – English Translation – Extract from Draft." https://www.gov.pl/documents/33372/436746/EN_Extract_EPP2040.pdf/ca2760d6-f9ab-9a87-c3a9-61063abe3681.

Polska Agencja Prasowa SA. 2018. "Poland's Parliament Passes Electricity Price Bill." Polish Press Agency. December 28, 2018. https://www.pap.pl/en/news/news%2C380299%2Cpolands-lower-house-passes-electricity-price-law.html.

Portfolio.hu. 2014. "Hungary's Orban May Want to 'Nationalise' These Energy Companies." Portfolio.Hu, January 20, 2014. http://www.portfolio.hu/en/users/reg.php?redir=/en/economy/hungarys_orban_may_want_to_nationalise_these_energy_companies.27238.html.

Portfollio.hu. 2016. "European Commission to Present Radical Energy Supply Plan." Portfolio.Hu EN. February 4, 2016. http://www.portfolio.hu/en/economy/european_commission_to_present_radical_energy_supply_plan.30851.html.

Power Technology. n.d. "Mochovce Nuclear Power Plant, Nitra, Slovakia." https://www.power-technology.com/projects/mochovce-nuclear-power-plant-nitra-slovakia/.

Pujiastuti, Isna. 2020. "COMECON and the European Union." Map.

Radio Poland. 2018. "Poland's Air Pollution Worst in Europe: Auditors." December 8, 2018. http://www.thenews.pl/1/9/Artykul/396103,Poland%E2%80%99s-air-pollution-worst-in-Europe-auditors-.

Ramanauskas, Virginijus. 2018. CEO and Chairman, Enerstena.

Rosicki, Remigiusz. 2015. "Poland's Gas Security." *Przeglad Politologiczny* 1: 159–72. https://doi.org/10.14746/pp.2015.20.1.11.

Rosicki, Remigiusz. 2017. "Energy Security Cultures in the European Union." *Przegląd Politologiczny* 4 (December): 45. https://doi.org/10.14746/pp.2017.22.4.4.

Ruotsalainen, Juho, Joni Karjalainen, Michael Child, and Sirkka Heinonen. 2017. "Culture, Values, Lifestyles, and Power in Energy Futures: A Critical Peer-to-Peer Vision for Renewable Energy." *Energy Research & Social Science* 34 (December): 231–9. https://doi.org/10.1016/j.erss.2017.08.001.

S.A, Telewizja Polska. 2018. "Polish Industry Concerned about Rise in Electricity Prices." August 27, 2018. https://polandin.com/38674629/polish-industry-concerned-about-rise-in-electricity-prices.

Sabaitiene, Lina. 2018. Vice Minister of Energy, Energy Ministry of Lithuania.

Safian, Fanni. 2015. "The World Without Paks II: Energy Vision of Energiaklub by 2030 Using EnergyPLAN Software." Energiaklub. http://www.energiaklub.hu/sites/default/files/the_world_without_paks2.pdf.

Schlosberg, David. 2004. "Reconceiving Environmental Justice: Global Movements and Political Theories." *Environmental Politics* 13 (3): 517–40. https://doi.org/10.1080/0964401042000229025.

Schonherr Legal Insights. 2013. "Hungary: New Taxes on Utility and Energy Sector – No Exemption for Transmission Operators." http://www.schoenherr.eu/uploads/tx_news/schoenherr_new_taxes_on_utility_and_energy_sector.pdf.

Sebestyén Szép, Tekla. 2016. "Energy Convergence of the European Union toward 2020." *Deturope* 8 (3): 88–106.

Sebestyén Szép, Tekla. 2017. "The Effects of Utility Cost Reduction on Residential Energy Consumption in Hungary – A Decomposition Analysis." *International Journal of Sustainable Energy Planning and Management* 13 (September). https://doi.org/10.5278/ijsepm.2017.13.5.

Sebestyén Szép, Tekla, and Csaba Weiner. 2020. "The Hungarian Utility Cost Reduction Programme – An Impact Assessment." Centre for Economic and Regional

Studies, Institute of World Economics. http://vki.hu/news/news_1491.html?fbclid=IwAR1MW-o5cx_jn47mCexKDO3-Sir2X4-Z0cBDnH3pI5xu1hbFxi3BLQ31z3I.

Seyfang, Gill, and Adrian Smith. 2007. "Grassroots Innovations for Sustainable Development: Towards a New Research and Policy Agenda." *Environmental Politics* 16 (4): 584–603. https://doi.org/10.1080/09644010701419121.

Sheller, Mimi. 2014. "Global Energy Cultures of Speed and Lightness: Materials, Mobilities and Transnational Power." Edited by David Tyfield and John Urry. *Theory, Culture & Society* 31 (5): 127–54. https://doi.org/10.1177/0263276414537909.

Simo, Endre. 2018. "Hypothermia Deaths in Hungary." June 13, 2018. https://mszfszk.hu/.

Sitarski, Krzysztof. 2019. "Member of Polish Parliament (Sejm)." Panel discussion presented at the 5th European Congress of Local Governments, Transformation of Coal Mining Territories, Krakow, Poland, April 9.

Smith, Joe, Robert Butler, Rosie J. Day, Axel H. Goodbody, David H. Llewellyn, Mel Rohse, Bradon T. Smith, Renata A. Tyszczuk, Julia Udall, and Nicola M. Whyte. 2017. "Gathering around Stories: Interdisciplinary Experiments in Support of Energy System Transitions." *Energy Research & Social Science* 31 (September): 284–94. https://doi.org/10.1016/j.erss.2017.06.026.

Smolen, Pawel. 2018. Country Manager, Poland, Kiwa Inspecta. Personal interview with the author, Krakow, Poland, November 13.

Soja, Rafal. 2019. "President of the Board, Tauron." Panel discussion presented at the 5th European Congress of Local Governments, Krakow, Poland, April 9.

Sovacool, Benjamin K. 2009. "The Cultural Barriers to Renewable Energy and Energy Efficiency in the United States." *Technology in Society* 31 (4): 365–73. https://doi.org/10.1016/j.techsoc.2009.10.009.

Sovacool, Benjamin K. 2016. "Differing Cultures of Energy Security: An International Comparison of Public Perceptions." *Renewable and Sustainable Energy Reviews* 55 (March): 811–22. https://doi.org/10.1016/j.rser.2015.10.144.

Sovacool, Benjamin K., and Marilyn A. Brown. 2015. "Deconstructing Facts and Frames in Energy Research: Maxims for Evaluating Contentious Problems." *Energy Policy* 86 (November): 36–42. https://doi.org/10.1016/j.enpol.2015.06.020.

Sovacool, Benjamin K., and Michael H. Dworkin. 2014. *Global Energy Justice*. Cambridge: Cambridge University Press.

Sovacool, Benjamin K., and Michael H. Dworkin. 2015. "Energy Justice: Conceptual Insights and Practical Applications." *Applied Energy* 142 (March): 435–44. https://doi.org/10.1016/j.apenergy.2015.01.002.

Sovacool, Benjamin K., and David J. Hess. 2017. "Ordering Theories: Typologies and Conceptual Frameworks for Sociotechnical Change." *Social Studies of Science* 47 (5): 703–50. https://doi.org/10.1177/0306312717709363.

Sovacool, Benjamin K., Roman V. Sidortsov, and Benjamin R. Jones. 2013. *Energy Security, Equality and Justice*. New York and London: Routledge.

Sovacool, Benjamin K., Raphael J. Heffron, Darren McCauley, and Andreas Goldthau. 2016. "Energy Decisions Reframed as Justice and Ethical Concerns." *Nature Energy* 1 (5): 16024. https://doi.org/10.1038/nenergy.2016.24.

Sovacool, Benjamin K., Johannes Kester, Lance Noel, and Gerardo Zarazua de Rubens. 2019. "Energy Injustice and Nordic Electric Mobility: Inequality, Elitism, and Externalities in the Electrification of Vehicle-to-Grid (V2G) Transport." *Ecological Economics* 157 (March): 205–17. https://doi.org/10.1016/j.ecolecon.2018.11.013.

Sovacool, Benjamin K., Matthew Burke, Lucy Baker, Chaitanya Kumar Kotikalapudi, and Holle Wlokas. 2017. "New Frontiers and Conceptual Frameworks for Energy

Justice." *Energy Policy* 105 (June): 677–91. https://doi.org/10.1016/j.enpol.2017.03.005.

Stephenson, Janet. 2018. "Sustainability Cultures and Energy Research: An Actor-Centred Interpretation of Cultural Theory." *Energy Research & Social Science* 44 (October): 242–9. https://doi.org/10.1016/j.erss.2018.05.034.

Stephenson, Janet, Barry Barton, Gerry Carrington, Daniel Gnoth, Rob Lawson, and Paul Thorsnes. 2010. "Energy Cultures: A Framework for Understanding Energy Behaviours." *Energy Policy* 38 (10): 6120–9. https://doi.org/10.1016/j.enpol.2010.05.069.

Stewart, Janet. 2014. "Sociology, Culture and Energy: The Case of Wilhelm Ostwald's 'Sociological Energetics' – A Translation and Exposition of a Classic Text." *Cultural Sociology* 8 (3): 333–50. https://doi.org/10.1177/1749975514523937.

Straupaite, Dalia. 2018. Mayor of Visaginas.

Tauron. 2015. "Fuel Mix." About Tauron – Fuel Mix. 2015. https://en.tauron.pl/tauron/about-tauron/Pages/fuel-mix.aspx.

Tchorzewski, Krzysztof. 2016. "Keynote Address at the Energy 21, Energy Futures Week." Speech presented at Energy Futures Week, Poznan, Poland, May 10.

The European Parliament and the Council of the European Union. 2017a. *2017/684 Establishing an Information Exchange Mechanism with Regard to Intergovernmental Agreements and Non-Binding Instruments between Member States and Third Countries in the Field of Energy, and Repealing Decision No 994/2012/EU*. https://eur-lex.europa.eu/legal-content/EN/TXT/PDF/?uri=CELEX:32017D0684&from=EN.

The European Parliament and the Council of the European Union. 2017b. *Regulation (EU) 2017/1938 of The European Parliament and of The Council of 25 October 2017 Concerning Measures to Safeguard the Security of Gas Supply and Repealing Regulation (EU) No 994/2010*. https://eur-lex.europa.eu/legal-content/EN/TXT/PDF/?uri=CELEX:32017R1938&from=EN.

The Orange Files. 2016. "Government Public Utility Fee Cuts." *The Orange Files* (blog). June 11, 2016. http://theorangefiles.hu/2013-government-utility-fee-cuts/.

The Oxford Institute for Energy Studies. 2014. "Reducing European Dependence on Russian Gas: Distinguishing Natural Gas Security from Geopolitics." The Oxford Institute for Energy Studies. http://www.oxfordenergy.org/wpcms/wp-content/uploads/2014/10/NG-92.pdf.

The Republic of Lithuania Seimas. 2018. "National Energy Independence Strategy." https://enmin.lrv.lt/uploads/enmin/documents/files/National_energy_independence_strategy_2018.pdf.

The World Bank. 1999. *Privatization of the Power and Natural Gas Industries in Hungary and Kazakhstan*. World Bank Technical Papers. The World Bank. https://elibrary.worldbank.org/doi/abs/10.1596/0-8213-4483-8.

Toal, Gerard, and John Agnew. 2002. "Introduction: Political Geographies, Geopolitics and Culture." In *Handbook of Cultural Geography*, edited by Kay Anderson, Mona Domosh, Steve Pile, and Nigel Thrift, 455–61. London: Sage Publications.

Tobolewicz, Joanna. 2018. Energy Planning Director, City of Gdansk, Office of the Mayor. Personal interview with the author, Gdansk, Poland, November 8.

Turnheim, Bruno, and Frank W. Geels. 2013. "The Destabilisation of Existing Regimes: Confronting a Multi-Dimensional Framework with a Case Study of the British Coal Industry (1913–1967)." *Research Policy, Economics, Innovation and History: Perspectives in Honour of Nick von Tunzelmann* 42 (10): 1749–67. https://doi.org/10.1016/j.respol.2013.04.009.

United Nations General Assembly. 1948. "Universal Declaration of Human Rights." United Nations. http://www.un.org/en/universal-declaration-human-rights/.
United States Congress. 1975. *Energy Policy and Conservation Act. Public Law.* https://www.govinfo.gov/content/pkg/STATUTE-89/pdf/STATUTE-89-Pg871.pdf.
Unruh, Gregory C. 2000. "Understanding Carbon Lock-In." *Energy Policy* 28 (12): 817–30. https://doi.org/doi: DOI: 10.1016/S0301-4215(00)00070-7.
Unruh, Gregory C. 2002. "Escaping Carbon Lock-In." *Energy Policy* 30 (4): 317–25. https://doi.org/doi: DOI: 10.1016/S0301-4215(01)00098-2.
US Department of State. 2013. "Hungary." Report. Department of State. The Office of Website Management, Bureau of Public Affairs. Hungary. http://www.state.gov/e/eb/rls/othr/ics/2013/204657.htm.
US Energy Information Administration. 2011. "World Shale Gas Resources: An Initial Assessment of 14 Regions Outside the United States." US Department of Energy. http://www.eia.gov/analysis/studies/worldshalegas/pdf/fullreport.pdf.
US Energy Information Administration. 2016. "Poland." US Energy Information Administration, November. https://www.eia.gov/international/analysis/country/POL.
Varga, Judit. 2020. "Time for a Christian Conservative Green Policy." POLITICO. January 7, 2020. https://www.politico.eu/article/christian-conservative-green-policy/?utm_source=POLITICO.EU&utm_campaign=8b63f2acfd-EMAIL_CAMPAIGN_2020_01_27_05_32&utm_medium=email&utm_term=0_10959edeb5-8b63f2acfd-189695893.
Vatn, Arild. 2005. *Institutions and the Environment.* Cheltenham, UK and Northampton, MA, USA: Edgar Elgar.
Vinichenko, Vadim. 2018. "Mechanisms of Energy Transitions: National Cases and the Worldwide Uptake of Wind and Solar Power." PhD dissertation, Budapest, Hungary: Central European University.
Vita, Alvaro de. 2007. "Inequality and Poverty in Global Perspective." In *Freedom from Poverty as a Human Right*, edited by Thomas Pogge, 103–32. Oxford: Oxford University Press, 2007.
Walker, Gordon, and Rosie Day. 2012. "Fuel Poverty as Injustice: Integrating Distribution, Recognition and Procedure in the Struggle for Affordable Warmth." *Energy Policy*, Special Section: Fuel Poverty Comes of Age: Commemorating 21 Years of Research and Policy, 49 (October): 69–75. https://doi.org/10.1016/j.enpol.2012.01.044.
Warsaw Institute. 2017a. *The North Gate.* https://warsawinstitute.org/wp-content/uploads/2017/03/North_Gate_infogr.jpg.
Warsaw Institute. 2017b. "Will Poland Liberate East-Central Europe from Gazprom's Dictates?" March 13. https://warsawinstitute.org/will-poland-liberate-east-central-europe-from-gazproms-dictates/.
Weber, Max, Jon Mark Mikkelsen, and Charles Schwartz. 1984. "'Energetic' Theories of Culture." *Mid-American Review of Sociology* 9 (2): 33–58.
Wilson, Sheena, Adam Carlson, and Imre Szeman, eds. 2017. *Petrocultures: Oil, Politics, Culture.* Kingston, ON: MQUP.
WISE. 2015. "Whither Are You Headed Polish Coal? Development Prospects of the Polish Hard Coal Mining Sector." Warsaw Institute for Economic Studies. http://wise-europa.eu/wp-content/uploads/2016/03/Whither-are-you-headed-Polish-coal.pdf.
World Energy Council. 2016. "Poland." https://www.worldenergy.org/data/resources/country/poland/coal/.

World Nuclear Association. 2017. "Nuclear Power in Lithuania | Lithuanian Nuclear Energy." May 2017. http://www.world-nuclear.org/information-library/country-profiles/countries-g-n/lithuania.aspx.

Young, Iris Marion. 1990. *Justice and the Politics of Difference*. Princeton, NJ: Princeton University Press.

Index